11836

Religion and the Social Sciences

ALSO BY JEFF LEVIN

UPON THESE THREE THINGS:
Jewish Perspectives on Loving God

JUDAISM AND HEALTH:
A Handbook of Practical, Professional, and Scholarly Resources
(Edited with M. F. Prince)

HEALING TO ALL THEIR FLESH:
Jewish and Christian Perspectives on Spirituality, Theology, and Health
(Edited with K. G. Meador)

DIVINE LOVE:
Perspectives from the World's Religious Traditions
(Edited with S. G. Post)

FAITH, MEDICINE, AND SCIENCE:
A Festschrift in Honor of Dr. David B. Larson
(Edited with H. G. Koenig)

RELIGION IN THE LIVES OF AFRICAN AMERICANS:
Social, Psychological, and Health Perspectives
(with R. J. Taylor and L. M. Chatters)

GOD, FAITH, AND HEALTH:
Exploring the Spirituality-Healing Connection

ESSENTIALS OF COMPLEMENTARY AND ALTERNATIVE MEDICINE:
(Edited with W. B. Jonas)

RELIGION IN AGING AND HEALTH:
Theoretical Foundations and Methodological Frontiers
(Edited)

Religion and the Social Sciences

Basic and Applied Research Perspectives

Edited by

Jeff Levin

TEMPLETON PRESS

Templeton Press
300 Conshohocken State Road, Suite 500
West Conshohocken, PA 19428
www.templetonpress.org

Set in Sabon LT Std by S4Carlisle Puplishing

Library of Congress Control Number: 2018943025
ISBN: 978-1-59947-471-7 (cloth: alk. paper)

This paper meets the requirements of ANSI/NISO Z39.48-1992 (Permanence of Paper).

A catalogue record for this book is available from the Library of Congress.

18 19 20 21 22   10 9 8 7 6 5 4 3 2 1

Printed in the United States of America.

For C. Eric Lincoln, my first academic mentor,
who introduced me to
the social scientific study of religion

CONTENTS

FOREWORD

———◆◆———

When I began graduate school, the social scientific study of religion barely existed, and nearly all of my professors and fellow students thought it was a dead-end because religion was sure to disappear within our lifetimes. On the other hand, it was widely agreed that the "founding fathers" of social science had paid considerable attention to religion. However, as I proceeded through a course on the history of social thought, taken during my first semester, I realized that claim about the "founders" was not so.

Durkheim, for example, did not even believe that religion was a phenomenon in itself, but only a mask for social integration, the object of all worship being nothing but society itself. Because he believed that religion was universal, and because he mistakenly believed that Buddhism was a "godless" religion, Durkheim incorrectly excluded belief in the gods from his definition of religion. Accordingly, his famous *The Elementary Forms of the Religious Life* has very little in it that is germane to the role of religion in the modern world, while leading anthropologists have claimed it bears little relationship to religion in "primitive" societies either. As for Marx, religion was but the enemy of human progress, a source of false consciousness, and certainly nothing anyone would care to study per se. Weber paid a bit more attention to religion, but, unlike my fellow students, I quickly recognized that his classic work on the Protestant ethic was silly because, as many historians had pointed out, fully developed capitalism existed many centuries before the Reformation.

So I concluded that religion had always been pretty much ignored in the social sciences, not that it mattered that much to me since it had not occurred to me to make religion one of my specialties. That I did was a happy accident.

Very few in my entering cohort at Berkeley had received financial support. During my first semester, I worked nights as a reporter for the *Oakland Tribune*. Then, when the first semester grading put me at the top of the class, I was offered a research assistantship at the newly formed Survey Research Center. There, I went to work for the center's director, Charles Y. Glock, who was one of the very few sociologists of religion at that time. He assigned me to a newly funded, very large study of anti-Semitism, and soon I was in charge of designing both a regional and a national survey to explore the link between Christian beliefs and hatred of Jews. I recognized almost at once that, in addition to doing the primary study, this was a priceless opportunity to collect a huge trove of survey data on religiousness in its many aspects. And in pursuing this opportunity, I became a sociologist of religion—officially so when Glock and I published *Religion and Society in Tension* in 1965.

Now, fifty years and forty books later, I find Jeff Levin referring to me in his introduction to Part One of this volume as "a father of the social scientific of religion." Whatever role I may have played, this well-written volume makes it clear that the social scientific study of religion is no longer a tiny collection of scholars at third-rate colleges and universities. Anyone who is serious about any of the social sciences must take religious effects into account. As will be revealed in the following chapters, religion has potent effects on crime; on mental and physical health; and on economics, politics, history, and family life. And very often these effects are not those assumed by secularists. For example, religious Americans have sex more often than do the irreligious and are more likely to attend concerts and plays. They also live longer, even when the effects of "clean living" are taken into account. I have had enormous fun pursuing all these matters. I also have the pleasure of knowing the distinguished authors of the chapters in this book.

Rodney Stark, PhD
Distinguished Professor of the Social Sciences
Baylor University
Waco, Texas

ACKNOWLEDGMENTS

---◆◆◆---

At first glance, it may seem odd that a book providing state-of-the-field overviews of social science research on religion would be edited by an epidemiologist, of all things. Yet by training and throughout my academic career, I have functioned at the intersection of my discipline and the social sciences. While my graduate work was undertaken in schools of public health and biomedical sciences and while my first two academic appointments were in medical schools, it has been my good fortune to be mentored exclusively, at every stage, by sociologists: C. Eric Lincoln, Preston Schiller, Berton Kaplan, Kyriakos Markides, and Jersey Liang. And among my colleagues in the religion and health field over the past three decades have been a cadre of sociologists, including Christopher Ellison, Robert Taylor, Ellen Idler, David Williams, Linda George, Neal Krause, and Kenneth Ferraro. Finally, I am privileged to serve on the faculty at Baylor University, at a research institute founded and co-directed by sociologists Rodney Stark and Byron Johnson.

While I make no formal claim to be a social scientist (my lone credential being a second major in sociology completed as an undergraduate at Duke), I have been blessed with mentors and colleagues who have helped me to refine my sociological imagination and skill set. All epidemiologists have a secondary or cognate field, corresponding to their substantive or methodological expertise. This is typically microbiology or parasitology or a clinical medical specialty (e.g., cardiology, oncology, psychiatry), or perhaps a basic biomedical science discipline (e.g., biochemistry, genetics), or a newer interdisciplinary field (e.g., environmental science, neurotoxicology). For social epidemiologists, it may also be a social or behavioral science discipline (e.g., sociology, psychology, anthropology) or another public health field (e.g., health behavior). By dint of my hybrid background and interests, it is my distinction to be the only credentialed epidemiologist I have ever heard of who can truthfully say that his cognate field is the sociology of religion! I have never been quite certain if this is something to be proud of or amused by, but this I can say with certainty: Without great mentors and colleagues from whom I have learned to function as a social scientist, and who have shared my intellectual curiosity about religion and its impact on human well-being, I would probably be working in a lab somewhere or in a public health department or in the medical care field and would not have been privileged to devote my career as a biomedical scientist to something as mysterious and wonderful as the study of faith and spirituality.

There have been distinct challenges but also distinct rewards on this path. For one, I have gotten to know so many people in so many social science disciplines and fields who share my fascination with religion and who have sought to elevate the study of religion within their respective domains. I have learned that, just like me within epidemiology, there are folks laboring in so many unexpected places, each with their own story of overcoming perceptions of marginality and dealing with barriers, all because of an interest in religion. We share an appreciation for religion and a recognition of its salience as a driving force in the affairs of human beings, for better or worse, yet we recognize its continuing status as a taboo in our respective academic worlds. I often make light of my marginality as a religious scholar among epidemiologists, but is this really any more unlikely than those of my colleagues found in other strange places like political science, criminology, economics, or education? One thing that I learned early is that, to be successful at this kind of work, one must have thick skin and a healthy sense of stick-to-itiveness.

It is a privilege to be affiliated with the Institute for Studies of Religion at Baylor University, a research shop that serves as a very model of collaborative and interdisciplinary scholarship across social science disciplines and fields. We have among us distinguished faculty and affiliated scholars trained in most of the social sciences and beyond—even epidemiology—all of whom share a focus on research and scholarship on the broad topic of religion. These scholars include Rod and Byron, as well as Philip Jenkins, David Jeffrey, Gordon Melton, and Thomas Kidd. I learn something from these distinguished colleagues every day, and I am in awe of their productivity and the depth of their learning beyond their home disciplines. This is the only place that I have ever worked where being a biomedical scientist who utilizes the methods of social science research to investigate subject matter most typically engaged within the humanities does not seem the least bit odd. For this I am continually thankful.

I am also grateful to our wonderful staff: Frances Malone, Leone Moore, and Meg Thompson; former staff member Cameron Andrews; and our work-study students. They have supported my efforts in more ways than I can enumerate here, and I would be unable to function without them. As with my previous two books for Templeton Press, I am especially thankful to Susan Arellano and her wonderful staff, who are all so professional, courteous, and patient. It is such a pleasure to work with such fine people.

Finally, thanks go out to my beloved wife, Lea, and to the Creator of the universe, who together are the source of all the good in my life, who inspire and sustain me, and who support me in completing the tasks that I have been assigned.

Religion and the Social Sciences

1

Introduction

————◆————

Jeff Levin

In 2008, Templeton Press launched a book series on the theme of science and religion.[1] This was a signal event for scholars whose research and writing falls at the intersection of these two great institutional domains. Religion and science evolved as a formal field of study many decades ago, and journals such as *Zygon* provide a scholarly home for the best work in this field, as do edited works such as *The Oxford Handbook of Religion and Science*.[2] But the Templeton Religion and Science Series was instrumental in providing, for the first time, detailed state-of-the-science summaries for work on religion within numerous respective scientific disciplines and fields, including contributions from medicine, neuroscience, technology, cosmology, paleontology, mathematics, genetics, environmental science, and cognitive science. The book series is also notable for providing guidance for prospective investigators—both bibliographies of key works in each field as well as a blueprint for the future of scientific investigation on each respective subject.

As I began working my way through these fascinating monographs, it struck me that a project such as this might be usefully replicated for the social sciences. If not an entire series of books, then certainly a single volume covering the state of the science for many of the most prominent and promising social science disciplines and fields. The Templeton series made clear that there is lots of existing religious scholarship taking place outside the traditional religious studies fields such as theology, biblical studies, comparative religion, pastoral studies, church history, and so on. Scientists from across the intellectual spectrum have focused their research on religion and have contributed important works on the intersection of their particular domain of science with faith, spirituality, and religious experience. The same can be said for the social sciences.

RELIGION IN THE SOCIAL SCIENCES

Of all the social sciences, sociology has given the greatest attention, by far, to religious phenomena, including the impact of religion on human lives and social institutions, and the impact of human life and social institutions on religion. Each of the classical theorists whose work led to the evolution of the most significant grand-theoretical perspectives for sociology—Karl Marx,[3] Émile Durkheim,[4] and Max Weber[5]—wrote significant early-career works on religion, which continue to be read and to influence scholarship a century after their publication. These individuals, and specifically their prominent writing on religion, were influential in the development, respectively, of conflict structuralism, functionalism, and symbolic interactionism.[6] More than any other profession of social scientists, whether from established disciplines or newer applied fields, sociologists have been attuned to researching, theorizing about, and commenting on the impact and salience of religion, for better or worse, on phenomena of interest.

Following the classical theorists, significant work on religion continued to appear in sociology throughout the subsequent decades. This includes important early to mid-century contributions by Ernst Troeltsch, H. Richard Niebuhr, Joachim Wach, and Pitirim Sorokin. Troeltsch, a German theologian, posited his famous church-sect typology in *The Social Teaching of the Christian Churches*,[7] the grandfather of all subsequent such typologies and schemata by sociologists. Niebuhr, a Yale theological scholar, in his *Social Sources of Denominationalism*, offered a trenchant and extended commentary on the "ethical failure of the divided church" and on the thesis that the "history of schism has been a history of Christianity's defeat,"[8] a perspective that still resonates among many sociologists. In *Sociology of Religion*, Wach, a University of Chicago historian of religions, defined the thematic foundations for much of what followed, including germinal discussions of the functions of religion, religion and natural groups, religion and social stratification, and types of religious authority.[9] Sorokin, a Russian expatriate who founded Harvard's Department of Social Relations, wrote in his later career a series of expansive works on the religious and spiritual roots and correlates of altruistic love,[10] a subject experiencing a renaissance among contemporary researchers.[11] Works such as these influenced the generation that followed, whose research on religion began to engage modern methodological innovations such as use of large-scale community or national probability-sample survey data, as well as to integrate theoretical and conceptual contributions from other disciplines, including psychology, economics, and political science.

In the 1950s and 1960s, a cohort of sociologists emerged who began the social construction of what today is recognizable as the sociology of religion, an established specialty within sociology. Pioneering works in this vein include Will Herberg's *Protestant-Catholic-Jew*;[12] J. Milton Yinger's *Religion, Society, and the Individual*;[13] Gerhard Lenski's *The Religious Factor*;[14] C. Eric Lincoln's *The Black Muslims in America*;[15] Charles Y. Glock and Rodney Stark's *Religion and Society in Tension*;[16] Peter Berger's *The Sacred Canopy*;[17] Bryan Wilson's *Religion in Secular Society*;[18] and important books and articles by Andrew M. Greeley, Robert Wuthnow, Robert N. Bellah, Jeffrey K. Hadden, Wade Clark Roof, Phillip E. Hammond, William Martin, William Sims Bainbridge, and others.[19] Bellah's essay, "Civil Religion in America," was especially influential,[20] and a good source of his collected writings is available.[21] Also significant were the earliest efforts at multidimensional religious assessment, which evolved in equal parts from Glock's five-dimensional model of religiosity[22] and Stark's taxonomy of religious commitment,[23] and which represent ground zero for all subsequent social measurement of religion by sociologists.[24] Greeley and his colleague, William C. McCready, also contributed by ensuring that religion was a major focus from the beginning of the annual General Social Surveys conducted by the National Opinion Research Center at the University of Chicago.[25]

Today, the sociology of religion is a vibrant field of research comprising, in large part, sophisticated empirical research programs that use national and global population data. Multiple professional societies of long standing publish associated peer-reviewed journals,[26] and important academic handbooks have been published for the field.[27] Most large university departments of sociology have experts who conduct research on religion and teach undergraduate and/or graduate courses in the sociology of religion.[28]

Significant figures in sociology continue to explore religion, whether as an "independent" or a "dependent" variable. That is, studies have examined religion as a meta-construct whose impact contributes to and shapes experiences and phenomena in numerous sectors of life, including politics; crime; family dynamics; fertility; sexuality; social stratification; occupational mobility; nationalism; mental health; and myriad other beliefs, attitudes, behaviors, and statuses.[29] Other studies have investigated dimensions of religiousness as constructs that are in turn shaped by these experiences and phenomena, and are conditioned in part by sociodemographic characteristics such as age, gender, race, ethnicity, and social class.[30] Sociological research, from population-based survey investigations to the results of qualitative and social-historical studies, points to the ubiquity of religion's influence on the lives of human beings, both individually and collectively. Sociologists continue, as well, to contribute insightful theoretical syntheses that seek to make sense of the how and why of religion's place in society.[31]

So, to summarize, within sociology the study of religion has long been an established and flourishing area of investigation. But this is less the case—or is not the case at all—in other social sciences. Either the history of scholarship does not go back as far, or contemporary efforts are less voluminous, less sophisticated, or of more recent vintage.

An exception is the psychology of religion. Notable work in this field goes back at least as far as William James's *The Varieties of Religious Experience*,[32] first published in 1902, and important research and writing have appeared in the century since that time. The field's trajectory, however, has been somewhat of a broken line. Benjamin Beit-Hallahmi has described the "rapid decline and final demise" of the psychology of religion as an academic field after about 1930.[33] Only since Gordon W. Allport's *The Nature of Prejudice*,[34] published in 1954, and the subsequent psychometric development of intrinsic/extrinsic (I/E) religiosity as an empirical construct,[35] in the 1960s, has study of the psychology of religion begun to evolve into a large and influential area of empirical research. Within psychology today, as within sociology, are multiple established peer-reviewed journals and major edited volumes focusing on religion, as well as, significantly, a formal division within the American Psychological Association with thousands of members.[36] A very important milestone has been publication of the two-volume *APA Handbook of Psychology, Religion, and Spirituality*, whose editor-in-chief, Kenneth I. Pargament, is lead author of the psychology of religion chapter in this book.[37]

Aside from sociology and more recently psychology, religion has been much less a focus of scholarly work in the other basic social science disciplines and applied social research fields. Fortunately, this is beginning to change. Evidence suggests that, in some disciplines and fields, this evolution is happening quite rapidly. For example: specialists in religion have become the largest topical subgroup of the American Historical Association; the Association for the Study of Religion, Economics, and Culture just sponsored its seventeenth annual conference; and the Religion, Spirituality, and Aging interest group is among the most flourishing specialty groups within the Gerontological Society of America.

All of these developments suggest that the time is right for this book. The intention in this volume has been to solicit state-of-the-science reviews from among the leading and most senior religious scholars within respective social science disciplines and fields. The sociology of religion has garnered the largest share of attention up to now, as noted, but in all of the other disciplines and fields covered in this book there is a story to tell about the emergence of programmatic religious research. There is a need for a single resource that focuses in depth on the subject of religion as investigated by social scientists whose work draws on theoretical, methodological, and professional traditions outside sociology. As noted, religion is becoming a mainstream and nearly ubiquitous topic of research within sociology, and one can find summaries of this work in many places. But the "story" of religion within other areas of social science is still about a collective work in progress.

For those who nonetheless would have wished to see this book include yet another field summary on sociological research on religion, two of the chapters in this book—on criminology and on aging—are authored by prominent sociologists. The author of the chapter on epidemiology (and the editor of this book) has a degree in sociology, and others among the chapter authors are regular collaborators with sociologists or publish in sociology journals. Finally, the author of this book's foreword, who has given this book his imprimatur, is the dean of all sociologists of religion. So sociology is well represented here, but, as just noted, there is an especially pressing need for a single book that brings together the best of what the *other* social sciences have to offer on the subject of religion. It is my hope that *Religion and the Social Sciences* will spark a renaissance of social science research on religion, especially from outside the province of academic sociology where it appears to be well established.

RELIGION AND THE SOCIAL SCIENCES

The Templeton Science and Religion Series provides "brief tours," summary statements for general audiences interested in the relation between science and religion and theology. This book, by contrast, offers detailed and comprehensive statements on religion from the perspective of nine academic social science disciplines or fields. Each of the chapters is written in language that will be accessible to knowledgeable general audiences with interests in religion and in the social sciences, but the purpose is more explicitly to provide guidance for prospective academic investigators. Each chapter includes an overview and history of religion as investigated within a respective social science, a thorough summary of existing findings and theories, a roadmap for future research, and an annotated bibliography of seminal works. Each chapter is also thoroughly referenced. The authors were given a simple instruction: to write their "ultimate" statement on religion from within their respective social science, and they were given carte blanche to be as comprehensive, scholarly, and provocative as they wished. The end product, I hope, is a series of prolegomena and detailed field overviews for the social scientific study of religion that will serve to introduce this subject to both new and established investigators and to offer resources to jumpstart their own work on religion.

Each of the following four chapters in *Religion and the Social Sciences* provides a state-of-the-field summary overview of research and scholarship on religion for a respective basic social science discipline. These disciplines include psychology, political science, economics, and history. Each chapter author is widely recognized as a leading expert on the study of religion within his or her home discipline.

In their chapter on the *psychology of religion* (Chapter 2) Pargament and Exline outline the substantive contributions made by psychology to our understanding of religion. These contributions include research and writing on religious motivations, on the mechanisms of religious development over the life span (including discovery, conservation, struggles, transformation), and on the different ways of being religious.

In his discussion of *religion and political science* (Chapter 3), Gill begins by providing a helpful conceptual roadmap for engaging the place of religion and the church in politics and the state. He then follows with a lucid theoretical discussion that goes into considerable depth on two schools of thought, which he terms the ideational and economic perspectives.

The chapter on the *economics of religion* (Chapter 4), by North, begins by proposing a model of individual religious choice, including the role of religious capital. Also included are a detailed summary of research on the behavior of religious organizations, a lucid discussion of religious markets and regulation, and an introduction to research on religion and economic growth.

In his sweeping summary of the *historical study of religion* (Chapter 5), Hankins traces the evolution of the field from the work of church historians to the emergence of the history of religion as an academic discipline. Focusing primarily on twentieth-century American religion, he offers a comprehensive summary of trends in contemporary scholarship, including the new social history, studies of evangelicalism and fundamentalism, mainline Protestant and Roman Catholic history, and the rise of global Christianity.

Throughout these four chapters, and within each of these disciplines, major points of narrative keep repeating.

First, until recently (and perhaps still), the study of religion has been taboo or at least marginalized. As a result, there has been a price to pay for a career focus on the impact of faith, spirituality, and religious beliefs and practices.

Second, despite this perceived status, scholarly writing on religious themes dates to the earliest days of the discipline as an organized intellectual endeavor. Writing on religious themes can be identified among the work of the discipline's founding fathers.

Third, contrary to a general sense within the discipline that not much work on religion has been done or that existing work is inconclusive, large amounts of research and scholarship have been published. Further, where empirical studies are the norm, the weight of evidence is statistically and substantively significant and is mostly positive (that is, religion on the whole is a force for good).

Fourth, there is much in the way of conceptual development and theory—however each discipline may choose to define *theory*. This has enabled sophisticated interpretation of historical and contemporary phenomena and, where pertinent, findings drawn from analyses of data.

Fifth, notwithstanding these observations, and until recently, the cohort of self-identified religious scholars within most of these disciplines has been a beleaguered lot. Thus, religious investigators often make common cause with scholars from other disciplines or fields who share an interest in religion.

This latter phenomenon can be observed, for example, within the emerging field of study that has grown up around investigation of religion's impact on physical and mental health. The authors of this book's chapters on psychology, gerontology, and epidemiology each have made major contributions to this area of research, including in collaboration with each other and with sociologists, and the authors of the criminology and family studies chapters have made significant contributions here as well. This observation, taken from one discrete area of research, underscores how often religious scholars, at least those who do empirical studies, tend to know one another and even work together across disciplines and fields. This lends an esprit de corps that takes the edge off the marginality that can surround identification as a religious scholar in one's home discipline or field.

Each of the next five chapters in this book provides a state-of-the-field summary overview of research and scholarship on religion for each of five respective applied social research fields. These fields include family studies, criminology, gerontology, education, and epidemiology. Again, each chapter author is considered a leading expert on the study of religion within his or her field. Whereas the first group of chapters explores religion from the vantage point of major social science disciplines, this next group of chapters looks at religion from the perspective of applied fields of social research that are, by their nature, interdisciplinary. The authors of the chapters on criminology and gerontology are sociologists by training, but other types of social scientists have weighed in on religion within these fields. The author of the family studies chapter is a psychologist, but sociologists, especially, as well as social workers and others, have been prominent within that field. For the education and epidemiology chapters, the respective authors are trained within education and epidemiology, but, as their chapters show, contributions to religious research in these fields have come from throughout the social sciences, both basic and applied.

In her chapter on *religion and family studies* (Chapter 6), Mahoney provides a comprehensive summary of a century of research on the intersections of faith and family life. She applies her Relational Spirituality Framework to describe how our relationships with God and our respective faith communities, as well as the spiritual values that exist within families, serve to structure, maintain, and transform family relationships.

In his chapter on *religion and criminology* (Chapter 7), Johnson summarizes evidence for religious commitment as a protective factor against delinquent behavior, among both youth and adults. Program evaluations and evaluative research demonstrate that exposure to faith-based prosocial behaviors and attitudes can reduce the risk of subsequent criminal activities.

In the chapter on *religious gerontology* (Chapter 8), George reviews over sixty years of empirical research on religion and aging, including studies of religion's impact on categories of health outcomes (e.g., mental and physical health, cognitive functioning, disability, biomarkers, mortality) and on measures of subjective well-being. She also details results of aging, period, and cohort analyses of religious participation over the life course and identifies potential mediating factors that help to explain a salutary impact of religion.

The chapter on *religion and education* (Chapter 9), by Jeynes, narrates the history of faith-based schooling, emphasizing research on the effects of attendance on subsequent academic outcomes. He also surveys the evidence that religious commitment exhibits a positive impact more generally on educational experiences and offers explanations for these positive effects.

Finally, in his chapter on the *epidemiology of religion* (Chapter 10), Levin, the editor of this volume, outlines the century-plus history of population health research on religion. He then reviews study findings suggestive of a positive impact of religion on various outcomes (e.g., heart disease, hypertension, cancer, mortality, health status, psychiatric diagnoses), and discusses theoretical work that has proposed models and mechanisms of explanation for these results.

The common themes among these "applied" chapters are fewer than among the first group of chapters, perhaps because these latter chapters are a disparate collection of newer interdisciplinary fields that do not maintain, to the same extent, longstanding structures of social control and ideological boundary maintenance that constrain what are or are not acceptable topics for investigation. This is not to say that such barriers do not exist. For four of these chapters—the ones on family studies, criminology, education, and epidemiology—the story of how religion came to be (modestly) accepted within these fields reads like the same script repeating itself: an intrepid investigator who, to his or her surprise, identified important but underpublicized findings and then, in the face of formidable resistance, wrote field-defining reviews and conducted original observational or evaluative research that helped to define, give shape to, and legitimize the study of religion within that field.

The story for gerontology is a bit different. Religion has been a topic for research and programming since the earliest days of the field, following World War II. Some of the most prominent social gerontologists have published on this topic, a trend that continues today. But no one, least of all anybody doing this work, would claim that religion is a mainstream and universally accepted subject for academic gerontologists, even if it does come the closest to that status of any of the applied fields described in this book.

A final point of commonality is the presence of a single seminal figure referenced in over half the chapters in this book. The work of sociologist Rodney Stark, a founder of the modern social scientific study of religion, is an important part of the narratives of religious research in political science and economics, and he is referenced in the criminology, education, and epidemiology chapters as well. Outside these chapters, Stark's sociological research and writing is also liberally cited throughout the contemporary literature in the psychology of religion and religious gerontology, he has received some attention within family studies, and his recent writing on Christianity has been cited by historians.

For those keeping track, the breadth of Stark's impact thus encompasses the entirety of the content of this book. If there is a common thread among most of the chapters in *Religion and the Social Sciences*, it is this: The pioneers of these subdisciplines and subfields of religious research that have risen up over the past few decades are, directly or indirectly, heirs to Rodney Stark and his resuscitation of intellectual attention to religion among the social sciences beginning over fifty years ago at Berkeley. It is fitting, then, that his foreword introduces this collection.

A final note: The chapters in this book do not exhaust the possible fields, disciplines, and subjects that might merit detailed reviews of religious research. Similar to the natural sciences, the social sciences are a big tent. Throughout the basic and applied social sciences, broadly defined, are substantial literatures on religion within cultural anthropology, mass communication, public administration, and legal studies. Entire volumes also could be assembled, respectively, for summaries of religious scholarship across humanities disciplines and across public policy domains. I hope that this book will inspire future efforts to summarize the history and scope of religious scholarship in all of these other fields, as well.

NOTES

1. See J. Wentzel van Huyssteen and Khalil Chamsteen, eds., *The Templeton Science and Religion Reader* (West Conshohocken, PA: Templeton Press, 2012).
2. Philip Clayton and Zachary Simpson, eds., *The Oxford Handbook of Religion and Science* (Oxford, U.K: Oxford University Press, 2006).
3. See, for example, Karl Marx and Friedrich Engels, *On Religion* [1957] (Mineola, NY: Dover Publications, 2008).
4. See, for example, Émile Durkheim, *The Elementary Forms of the Religious Life* [1915], translated by Joseph Ward Swain (New York: The Free Press, 1965).
5. See, for example, Max Weber, *The Sociology of Religion* [1922] (Boston: Beacon Press, 1991).
6. Research and writing on religion have made seminal contributions to these theoretical perspectives throughout the history of the field of sociology. This can be seen in various places throughout the chapters of Talcott Parsons, Edward Shils, Kaspar D. Naegele, and Jesse R. Pitts, eds., *Theories of Society: Foundations of Modern Sociological Theory* (New York: The Free Press of Glencoe, 1961); and Walter L. Wallace, ed., *Sociological Theory: An Introduction* (New York: Aldine Publishing Company, 1969).
7. Ernst Troeltsch, *The Social Teaching of the Christian Churches* [1912], translated by Olive Won (Louisville, KY: Westminster/John Knox Press, 1992).

8. H. Richard Niebuhr, *Social Sources of Denominationalism* [1929] (Gloucester, MA: Peter Smith, 1987), quotations on p. 3 and p. 264.

9. Joachim Wach, *Sociology of Religion* (Chicago: University of Chicago Press, 1944).

10. For example, Pitirim A. Sorokin, *The Ways and Power of Love: Types, Factors, and Techniques of Moral Transformation* [1954] (Philadelphia: Templeton Foundation Press, 2002).

11. For example, Jeff Levin and Berton H. Kaplan, "The Sorokin Multidimensional Inventory of Love Experience (Smile): Development, Validation, and Religious Determinants," *Review of Religious Research* 51 (2010): 380–401.

12. Will Herberg, *Protestant-Catholic-Jew: An Essay in American Religious Sociology* (Chicago: University of Chicago Press, 1955).

13. J. Milton Yinger, *Religion, Society, and the Individual: An Introduction to the Sociology of Religion* (New York: The Macmillan Company, 1957).

14. Gerhard Lenski, *The Religious Factor: A Sociological Study of Religion's Impact on Politics, Economics, and Family Life*, revised edition (Garden City, NY: Anchor Books, 1963).

15. C. Eric Lincoln, *The Black Muslims in America* (Boston: Beacon Press, 1961).

16. Charles Y. Glock and Rodney Stark, *Religion and Society in Tension* (Chicago: Rand McNally & Company, 1965).

17. Peter L. Berger, *The Sacred Canopy: Elements of a Sociological Theory of Religion* (Garden City, NY: Anchor Books, 1967).

18. Bryan Wilson, *Religion in Secular Society: A Sociological Comment* (Hammondsworth, UK: Penguin Books, 1966).

19. Significant collections of sociological writing on religion that appeared during this time period include Irving I. Zaretsky and Mark P. Leone, eds., *Religious Movements in Contemporary America* (Princeton, NJ: Princeton University Press, 1974); Robert Wuthnow, ed., *The Religious Dimension: New Directions in Quantitative Research* (New York: Academic Press, 1979); and Phillip E. Hammond, ed., *The Sacred in a Secular Age: Toward Revision in the Scientific Study of Religion* (Berkeley: University of California Press, 1985).

20. Robert N. Bellah, "Civil Religion in America," *Daedalus* 96, no. 1 (1967): 1–21.

21. For a collection of Bellah's writings from over the course of his career, see his *Beyond Belief: Essays on Religion in a Post-Traditionalist World* (Berkeley: University of California Press, 1970).

22. Charles Y. Glock, "On the Study of Religious Commitment," *Religious Education* 57, suppl. 4 (1962): 98–110.

23. Rodney Stark, "A Taxonomy of Religious Commitment," *Journal for the Scientific Study of Religion* 5 (1965): 97–116.

24. This line of research had its radix in Joseph E. Faulkner and Gordon F. De Jong, "Religiosity in 5-D: An Empirical Analysis," *Social Forces* 45 (1966): 246–54. Today, well over a hundred substantive measurement instruments of dimensions and domains of religiousness, broadly defined, have been validated for use by social scientists. See Peter C. Hill and Ralph W. Hood, Jr., eds., *Measures of Religiosity* (Birmingham, AL: Religious Education Press, 1999).

25. A representative collection of this research can be found in Andrew M. Greeley, *Unsecular Man: The Persistence of Religion* [1972] (New York: Schocken Books, 1985).

26. Most prominently in the United States: the Society for the Scientific Study of Religion, which publishes *Journal for the Scientific Study of Religion*; the Association for the Sociology of Religion, which publishes *Sociology of Religion* (formerly *Sociological Analysis*); and the Religious Research Association, which publishes *Review of Religious Research*.

27. Most notably, Peter B. Clarke, ed., *The Oxford Handbook of the Sociology of Religion* (Oxford, UK: Oxford University Press, 2009); Michele Dillon, ed., *Handbook of the Sociology of Religion* (New York: Cambridge University Press, 2003); and James A. Beckford and N. J. Demerath III, eds., *The SAGE Handbook of the Sociology of Religion* (London: Sage Publications, 2007).

28. Perhaps most prominently at Baylor University, which has the largest cadre of sociologists of religion affiliated with an academic department of sociology.

29. See, for example, the chapters in Clarke, *The Oxford Handbook of the Sociology of Religion*; Dillon, *Handbook of the Sociology of Religion*; and Beckford and Demerath, *The SAGE Handbook of the Sociology of Religion*.

30. For an early take on this, using national probability-survey data, see Greeley, *Unsecular Man*.

31. See, for example, Rodney Stark's recent *Why God?: Explaining Religious Phenomena* (West Conshohocken, PA: Templeton Press, 2017), a substantial updating of the classic work by Stark and William Sims Bainbridge, *A Theory of Religion* (New Brunswick, NJ: Rutgers University Press, 1987).

32. William James, *The Varieties of Religious Experience* [1902] (New York: Mentor Books, 1958).

33. Benjamin Beit-Hallahmi, *Prolegomena to the Psychological Study of Religion* (Lewisburg, PA: Bucknell University Press, 1989), quotation on p. 24.

34. Gordon W. Allport, *The Nature of Prejudice* [1954] (New York: Basic Books, 1979).

35. For an insightful conceptual history of the I/E construct, see Lee A. Kirkpatrick and Ralph W. Hood, Jr., "Intrinsic-Extrinsic Religious Orientation: The Boon or Bane of Contemporary Psychology of Religion?," *Journal for the Scientific Study of Religion* 29 (1990): 442–62.

36. In 1976, the American Psychological Association established its Division 36 as Psychologists Interested in Religious Issues. Known today as the Society for the Psychology of Religion and Spirituality, it hosts an annual professional conference; sponsors multiple scholarly awards; and publishes a peer-reviewed journal, *Psychology of Religion and Spirituality*.

37. Kenneth I. Pargament, editor-in-chief, *APA Handbook of Psychology, Religion, and Spirituality* (Washington, DC: American Psychological Association, 2013).

2

The Psychology of Religion
The State of an Evolving Field

◆◆◆◆

Kenneth I. Pargament and Julie J. Exline

Religion was a vital topic of concern for the founding figures of psychology. Nineteenth-century leaders such as William James, G. Stanley Hall, and Edwin Starbuck believed that religious experiences such as conversion and mysticism were central phenomena of interest for psychological study. In the twentieth century, however, the picture changed as psychology distanced itself from religion in an effort to establish itself as a scientifically respectable discipline. When religion was considered, it was treated harshly, even disparagingly, by eminent figures in the field, such as Sigmund Freud, B. F. Skinner, and Albert Ellis. While there were important exceptions to this rule (e.g., Gordon Allport, James Fowler, Viktor Frankl, Erich Fromm, Carl Jung, and Paul Pruyser), religion was often described as defensive, irrational, delusional, or a source of pathology.

The latter part of the twentieth century witnessed renewed interest in the psychology of religion for a number of reasons. First, the zeitgeist of the discipline began to shift from a focus on pathology to a focus on human strength, resilience, and potential. Religion, with its emphasis on the virtues, has been difficult to ignore in this movement toward a more positive psychology, as illustrated by its inclusion in Peterson and Seligman's pioneering handbook on character strengths and virtues.[1]

Second, influenced by the growth of Asian religious and philosophical thought and practice in the United States, many theorists and researchers began to differentiate spirituality as a personal, subjective, inner-directed experience from institutional religious affiliation, beliefs, and practices. Although this led to an unfortunate polarization in the meanings of the terms *spirituality* and *religion*, it also stimulated a great deal of interest in the psychological study of spiritual phenomena.

Third, empirical studies emerged that made it clear that, contrary to earlier prognostications, religion was far from dead in the United States. Studies such as the U.S. Religious Landscape Survey indicated that a majority of people report belief in God; pray at least once or more a day; believe in heaven, the devil, angels, and miracles; and feel "God's presence in all of life."[2] Perhaps even more important, empirical investigations also demonstrated significant links between various dimensions of religiousness and health and well-being.[3] Sparked by these forces, the number of published articles on spirituality in psychological and behavioral journals increased eightfold from 1965 to 2000.[4]

Interest in the psychology of religion remains strong today, with an active section of researchers and practitioners in the American Psychological Association (i.e., Division 36: Psychology of Religion and Spirituality), several journals devoted to the topic (e.g., *Psychology of Religion and Spirituality, International Journal for the Psychology of Religion, Spirituality in Clinical Practice*, and *Archive for the Psychology of Religion*), and texts and handbooks covering the field (e.g., by Hood, Hill, and Spilka;[5] Pargament, Mahoney, Exline, Jones, and Shafranske;[6] and Paloutzian and Park[7]). In addition, contributions from the psychology of religion can be found in the journals, textbooks, and handbooks of other subdisciplines of psychology, including social, personality, clinical, community, developmental, cross-cultural, neuropsychological, and positive psychology.

In this chapter, we will provide an overview of the current state of knowledge in the psychology of religion. Given the rapid growth, breadth, and depth of the field, it is beyond the scope of this chapter to offer comprehensive coverage. Instead, we will highlight some of the most substantive contributions the psychology of religion has made to an understanding of religious life. We will conclude by discussing several important directions for research and practice that may advance the state of knowledge in the field.

SUBSTANTIVE CONTRIBUTIONS FROM THE PSYCHOLOGY OF RELIGION

Psychological studies are yielding a portrait of religion as a rich, multidimensional domain of functioning that evolves and changes dynamically over the course of the life span. Whether religion serves as a constructive or destructive force in human functioning depends on the specific way that religion is experienced and expressed. We will highlight these points in this section.

The Variety of Religious Motivations

Why are people religious? This question has garnered perhaps the most attention and debate by psychological theorists and researchers. A number of answers have been offered. Freud maintained that religion is motivated first and foremost by the child's need to ward off his or her sense of utter helplessness in a harsh world that cannot be made hospitable even by parents.[8] Religious beliefs and practices, he believed, provide a source of emotional comfort and solace in the face of human frailty and finitude. Empirical studies have offered some support for this perspective. Religious involvement has been consistently associated with lower levels of death anxiety.[9] Other experimental studies have shown that reminders of personal mortality lead to significant increases in religious beliefs and beliefs in an afterlife more specifically.[10]

Freud went on to articulate a second important function of religion: the need to control human impulses that pose a threat to oneself, others, and civilization.[11] In support of this idea, numerous studies have linked higher levels of religious involvement to lower levels of alcohol and drug abuse, criminality, extramarital sexual activity, suicidality, and other markers of impulsiveness.[12] Experimental studies have also revealed that people exposed to religious primes respond more slowly to temptation-related words, such as those that refer to premarital sex and substance use.[13]

Émile Durkheim took a different tack, asserting that religion is rooted in social rather than psychological needs.[14] He wrote, "If religion has given birth to all that is essential in society, it is because the idea of society is the soul of religion."[15] The hundreds of thousands of religious institutions testify to the human need to seek intimacy, belonging, and identity within communities of faith. Empirical studies have also demonstrated how religion can facilitate social attachment and the binding of people into moral communities.[16]

Other theorists have emphasized how religion responds to the human need for meaning. Crystal Park and her colleagues describe how religious systems are designed in part to answer basic questions of meaning and purpose: Why am I here? What is the purpose of my life? What will happen to me when I die?[17] Religious systems of belief can also lend greater coherence and order to the potentially overwhelming array of choices, possibilities, and situations that people confront in today's world. And in times of stress, suffering, and injustice, many people turn to their religious beliefs to make sense of what may seem to be incomprehensible; religious appraisals such as "God has a reason" offer the reassurance that there is an ultimate meaning even though it may defy human understanding.

To the religiously minded, efforts to identify the psychological or social motivations of religiousness miss a critical point. As psychologist Paul Johnson stated, "It is the ultimate thou the religious person seeks most of all."[18] Similarly, Pargament suggests that people are motivated to seek out something sacred in life; this yearning for the sacred lies at the root of spirituality.[19] In support of this notion, empirical studies have shown that many people organize their lives around religious and spiritual strivings, investing their resources and deriving support, strength, and satisfaction from whatever they may hold sacred.

How do we reconcile these different perspectives and findings on religious motivation? Perhaps there is no need to do so. The findings as a whole may simply reflect the reality that people are motivated toward religion for many reasons. In fact, part of the staying power of the world's religions may lie in their capacity to meet the diverse needs of their diverse adherents.

The Mechanisms of Religious Development over the Life Span

Psychologists of religion generally agree that religion is not a fixed set of beliefs and practices. Rather it evolves over the life span in different ways. Theorists and researchers have focused on four processes that shape the religious journey: discovery, conservation, struggles, and transformation.

Discovery. In his book, *The Spiritual Life of Children*, Robert Coles provides numerous examples of children seeking out and discovering something transcendent. As one child put it, "I guess I'm trying to get from me, from us, to Him with my ideas when I'm looking up at the sky!"[20] Theorists have provided several explanations for this propensity to search for the sacred. Some, such as Newberg and Waldman,[21] suggest that children are "hard-wired" through genetics for spirituality. Others maintain that the child's intrapsychic capacity to symbolize and fantasize divine beings is an essential part of human character.[22] Still others assert that the religious discovery process grows out of the confrontation with life events that illustrate human frailty and limitations.[23] Social scientists emphasize the pivotal role of families, institutions, and the larger social context in understandings of the sacred.[24] Finally, it must be added that many people experience the discovery of the sacred not as the result of an active personal quest or socialization, but as a revelation—God has come to them.

The discovery of the sacred is not limited to childhood. Many adults report that they have had some type of religious awakening or encounter at some point in their lives. For instance, Yamane and Polzer examined several national surveys of adults who responded to the question, "Have you ever felt as though you were close to a powerful spiritual force that seemed to lift you out of yourself?"[25] Thirty-one to 40 percent of the samples responded affirmatively. Experiences in later life can also foster the discovery of new forms of sacredness. Lambert and Dollahite describe how religious weddings imbue the marriage with sacred qualities and the sense that God is actively present in the marriage.[26]

Similarly, experiences in nature can instill a sense of sacredness in the outdoors. For example, a Swedish woman, an atheist coping with cancer, describes the way she perceives nature as sacred:

> Whatever happens in the world for me or others, nature is still there, it keeps going. That is a feeling of security when everything else is chaos. The leaves fall off, new ones appear, somewhere there is a pulse that keeps going. . . . It is a spiritual feeling if we can use that word without connecting it to God, this is what I feel in nature.[27]

Thus, the discovery of the sacred is not restricted to traditional concepts of God.

Empirical studies suggest that the discovery of the sacred has several consequences: (1) the sacred becomes an organizing force for peoples' lives; (2) people invest more of their resources into what they hold sacred; and (3) people derive particular satisfaction, support, strength, and powerful spiritual emotions from the sacred.[28] For example, in one study of college students, those who perceived their bodies as a manifestation of God or the sacred in nature engaged in more health-protective behaviors (e.g., less drug and alcohol use, more exercise, better eating habits) and reported greater satisfaction with their bodies.[29]

Conservation. Once discovered, the developmental task shifts to conservation—that is, efforts to sustain and foster a relationship with whatever the individual holds sacred. Toward this end, the religions of the world provide their adherents with a variety of pathways. These pathways include systems of religious belief; traditional religious practices such as prayer, reading of sacred texts, and rites of passage; involvement in religious institutions; and religious methods of coping. People can also take nontraditional pathways to maintain and foster a relationship with their sacred values. Music, art, yoga, social action, 12-step programs, and newer spiritual movements (e.g., feminist, goddess, ecological) are just a few of the ways that people can conserve relationships with the sacred apart from traditional religious institutions.

These pathways of belief, practice, coping, and group involvement can serve a number of psychological and social functions (e.g., physical health, community, meaning, emotional comfort, identity, self-regulation), not just spiritual ones. In fact, hundreds of studies have linked these religious and spiritual pathways to a variety of indicators of psychological, social, and physical well-being, such as higher levels of happiness, life satisfaction, hope, and intimacy, and lower levels of depression, suicide, anxiety, alcohol and drug use, and criminality.[30] These pathways are also by and large quite successful in helping people sustain a relationship with their sacred values. Empirical studies, such as by Pargament,[31] have shown that people generally maintain or even strengthen their levels of religious faith, belief, and practice following major life traumas. It is difficult to imagine an event more horrific than the Holocaust, but, according to one retrospective survey of 709 survivors, 61 percent showed no change in their religious practices from before the Holocaust to after the Holocaust, to today. Only 29 percent indicated that their level of belief in God had changed during or immediately following the Holocaust.[32]

Struggles. Although spiritual resilience appears to be the norm rather than the exception to the rule, many people do experience periods of religious and spiritual struggle over the course of their lives when they encounter tension, strain, and conflicts about sacred matters with the supernatural (e.g., divine, demonic), within themselves (e.g., moral struggles, religious doubts, questions of ultimate meaning), and with others.[33] For example, Johnson and Hayes sampled over 5,000 university students and found that 25 percent reported considerable distress related to religious or spiritual issues.[34] In a study of oncology, diabetic, and congestive heart failure patients, Fitchett and colleagues found that about 20 percent indicated moderate to high levels of religious struggle.[35] According to another study of patients hospitalized for a sudden cardiac event, 58 percent reported some level of religious struggle.[36]

Religious and spiritual struggles may grow out of personal forces such as negative images of God; a history of insecure attachment to others; and personality vulnerability including narcissism, entitlement, and neuroticism.[37] They may also emerge from developmental transitions and major stressors that pose a challenge to the individual's orienting system of religious beliefs and practices.[38] In any case, a growing body of empirical research, including from Exline[39] and Pargament and associates,[40] has shown robust ties between religious and spiritual struggles, poorer mental health, poorer physical health, and even greater risk of dying. A few studies have also tied struggles to signs of personal growth.[41] Researchers are currently pursuing the question of what determines the trajectory of religious and spiritual struggles. One recent study revealed that growth following the experience of religious and spiritual struggles was predicted by indicators of a stronger religious orientation to life, including religious support, positive religious coping, the ability to make meaning of the struggle, and greater personal integration of religious beliefs.[42]

Transformation. Over the course of the life span, people encounter major life events and developmental transitions (e.g., birth, coming of age, marriage, retirement, illness, death) that propel them into new phases of life and require a transformation of significant goals and values, including sacred ones. Transformation can also grow out of dissatisfaction with unfulfilling life pursuits, such as workaholism, materialism, and addictions.

The religions of the world provide people with methods for facilitating life transformations. Researchers have studied several of these transformational mechanisms, including rites of passage (e.g., baptism, bar/bat mitzvah, wedding, funeral) that help people face the reality of fundamental change while they are reassured about their continued religious identity and connection,[43] and conversion experiences that involve sudden or gradual changes in the place or character of the sacred in an individual's life.[44]

In their review of the literature on religious conversion, Paloutzian, Richardson, and Rambo found little evidence to indicate that conversion leads to personality change.[45] However, conversion does appear more strongly linked to shifts in goals, values, strivings, motivations, and feelings, and to changes in the way people construct the narrative accounts of their lives. For example, according to Miller and Baca, men and women who experienced dramatic, surprising, "quantum change" indicated value shifts that ran counter to gender-stereotyped roles.[46] For men, the top five values changed from "wealth, adventure, achievement, pleasure, and be respected" to "spirituality, personal peace, family, God's will, and honesty"; for women, the top values shifted from "family, independence, career, fitting in, and attractiveness" to "growth, self-esteem, spirituality, happiness, and generosity."[47] McAdams found that the narratives of highly generative adults often contained a strong theme of redemption; that is, a fundamental realignment toward an orientation of caring for others as the result of some trauma or crisis.[48] These shifts were not necessarily rooted in a traditional religious context, but they resonated with spiritual meaning and change.

It is also important to note the growing body of work on religious apostasy and atheism, which might be defined as fundamental transformations away from religious belief, identity, and involvement. Initial findings from Streib and Klein point to several factors that may lead to apostasy, agnosticism, and atheism, including

(1) the unbelievability of religious doctrine; (2) disappointment with organized religious institutions; (3) failed or unanswered prayer; and (4) spiritual struggles including anger at, feeling punished by, and feeling abandoned by God.[49]

Pargament has noted that, once a religious transformation has occurred, the religious task once again returns to the process of conserving the individual's new set of goals and values.[50] Thus, the four mechanisms—discovery, conservation, struggle, and transformation—may express themselves repeatedly as religiousness evolves over the life span.

Different Ways of Being Religious

A considerable body of theory and research in the psychology of religion rests on the assumption that it matters less *whether* someone is religious than *how* someone is religious. In this vein, Allport and Ross distinguished between intrinsically oriented individuals (i.e., those who live their religion as their central organizing force) and extrinsically oriented people (i.e., those who use their religion for nonspiritual purposes).[51] While this distinction generated a significant amount of research, the distinction between "living" and "using" one's faith has been criticized as overly simplistic on empirical and conceptual grounds; for example, many people both live their faith and use their faith to respond to human needs.[52] More recently, theorists and researchers have turned their attention to other ways of being religious that are grounded in established psychological bodies of work.

In one important area of study, psychologists have examined the linkages between the psychology of religion and Bowlby's attachment theory, asserting that God can be fruitfully understood as an attachment figure.[53] Like the secure attachment to a parent, God can serve as a safe haven for comfort when distressed and a secure base for exploration. However, as is the case with parents, not all relationships with God are necessarily secure. Individuals can also manifest anxious, ambivalent, and avoidant attachments to God. A number of studies suggest that the character of the individual's attachments to parents influences the type of relationship they form with God.[54] While these attachments often correspond to each other, there is also evidence to suggest that people may develop a close attachment to God to compensate for insecure relationships with parents, often as a response to stressful situations.[55] Additional research has shown that secure relationships with God are associated with indicators of psychological adjustment, while insecure attachments to God are tied to signs of greater psychological distress. Once again, these findings parallel and extend those that have emerged from the literature on secure–insecure parental attachments.[56]

Another significant area of research has grown out of Lazarus and Folkman's theory of stress and coping.[57] In an extension of this theory to the religious realm, Pargament illustrated how religion can be part of each aspect of the coping process, including the character of life stressors, appraisals of these stressors, specific ways of coping, and the outcomes of the coping process.[58] Empirical studies indicate that people often look to their faith for support and assistance in their most difficult times, from major illness, injury, and the loss of loved ones to natural disasters, divorce, and unemployment.[59] Factor-analytic studies have identified a variety of specific ways that people draw on their religion to cope with major life stressors, such as through benevolent religious reappraisals, collaborative religious coping, active spiritual surrender, seeking spiritual support and connection, and religious confession.[60] Positive religious coping methods such as these have generally been associated with better mental health outcomes.[61]

For example, in one study of patients and loved ones dealing with kidney transplant surgery, those who made more use of positive religious coping reported better adjustment concurrently and at three and twelve months postsurgery.[62] Notably, these effects remained statistically significant after controlling for other general coping variables, including internal locus of control, social support, and cognitive restructuring. Others have reported similar results, which suggests that religious resources add a distinctive dimension to the coping process.

With the rise of "positive psychology," research on religious virtues such as gratitude, forgiveness, and altruism has sharply increased in the last fifteen years. In some sense, these virtues can be conceptualized as "psychospiritual" constructs; they are deeply grounded in the world's religious traditions, yet they can also be understood in purely secular terms. Empirical studies have found links between measures of religiousness and these virtues. For example, Lambert and colleagues had participants pray on a daily basis for four weeks, while a comparison group of people involved themselves in nonreligious daily activities.[63] Those who prayed daily manifested significantly higher levels of a grateful personality disposition than those in the nonreligious activities group, even after controlling for initial religiousness and frequency of prayer.

Similar findings have emerged from studies of prayer's effects on forgiveness toward others.[64] Research has also linked religiousness and higher levels of altruistic behavior under limited conditions: when the targets are in-group members and known individuals, when others do not threaten the values of the religious group, and when the costs of altruism are not too high.[65] However, higher levels of prosociality may be facilitated by broadening religious conceptions of the in-group and triggering values of self-transcendence. A number of studies have shown that these virtues are positively associated with a variety of indicators of adjustment and well-being, yet questions remain about whether the virtues have added health benefits when they are understood and experienced from a religious perspective.[66]

FUTURE DIRECTIONS FOR THE PSYCHOLOGY OF RELIGION

Given the rapid growth of research, which continues in the field, it is difficult to envision the psychology of religion of the future. However, three important trends can be discerned.

First, the field is likely to move beyond its current emphasis on studies of largely Christian samples in Western contexts. Already, a number of researchers, such as Piedmont and Leach,[67] have examined the generalizability of established concepts and measures of religiousness to other traditions, such as Islam, Hinduism, Judaism, and Buddhism. The findings, such as by Abu-Raiya and Pargament,[68] point to areas of commonality and distinctiveness among members of diverse religions located in diverse sociocultural contexts.

Investigators are also considering how religious beliefs and practices develop and decline among atheists, agnostics, and apostates, and the implications of these religious developmental patterns for health and well-being.[69] Drawing on this literature as well as on cross-cultural studies, Streib and Klein suggest that the relationships between religiousness and mental health may in fact be U-shaped, with the most religious and least religious groups manifesting greater well-being than the moderately religious.[70] Positive correlations between religion and mental health, they assert, may grow largely out of studies in the United States in which participants tend to be more religious. In Europe, where people tend to be less religious, nonsignificant or even negative correlations might emerge between religiousness and mental health. Their work underscores the need for cross-cultural studies among samples that represent the full range of religious belief and nonbelief.

Second, the psychology of religion is becoming more biologically oriented, as is the field of psychology more generally. Building on recent advances in brain-imagery techniques and the measurement of neurotransmitters and biomarkers, researchers are turning their attention to the biological correlates of various religious expressions, such as prayer, meditation, and mystical experiences. The findings are rich and complex, defying easy summary. In this vein, Maselko concluded from her review of the literature that different parts of the brain may be implicated with different aspects of religiousness.[71] Mystical experiences, for instance, may be tied to engagement of the limbic system and the temporal lobes, while more regular religious practices such as prayer may be accompanied by changes in the parts of the brain responsible for sociality and cognition.

One double-blind experimental study deserves special mention. Griffiths, Richards, McCann, and Jesse evaluated the effects of a high dose of a hallucinogen, psilocybin, on spiritual experience in a sample of community volunteers involved in spiritual or religious activities.[72] In comparison to a group that received an active non-hallucinatory drug (methylpenidate), those who were administered psilocybin reported significantly higher levels of spiritual and mystical experience, and deep and persistent impacts. For instance, 33 percent rated the experience with the hallucinogen as "the single most significant spiritual experience of his or her life"; another 38 percent rated it among the top five spiritually meaningful experiences.[73] Provocative as they are, these findings highlight the value in pursuing studies that integrate the biological dimension more fully into the psychology of religion.

Finally, the psychology of religion appears to be moving from a field devoted to basic research to one that puts this knowledge into practice with individuals, families, institutions, and communities.[74] Researchers and practitioners have designed and evaluated spiritually integrated treatments with some encouraging results. These interventions involve spiritual meditation, spiritually integrated cognitive behavioral therapy, spiritually integrated eclectic treatments, and virtues such as forgiveness and gratitude.[75] For instance, one study compared the effects of spiritual and secular mantra-based meditation in a sample of chronic vascular headache sufferers.[76] Four groups were compared: those taught to meditate to a spiritual phrase (e.g., "God is joy"), to an internal secular phrase (e.g., "I am joyful"), to an external secular phrase (e.g., "Grass is green"), and a group trained in progressive muscle relaxation. Over the one-month course of the study, participants in the spiritual meditation group experienced sharper declines in their frequency of headaches, negative affect, and anxiety and greater increases in pain tolerance, self-efficacy, and existential well-being.

Work in the applied arena is not limited to psychotherapy research; it is now incorporating religiously integrated programming in prevention, assessment, education, and community change. For example, in one program in the medical domain, oncologists were trained to include a brief assessment of religion in the initial diagnostic interview. The religious assessment added only six minutes to the interview, the large majority of oncologists were "very" comfortable with the program, and their patients indicated less depression, higher quality of life, and a more caring relationship with their physicians over a three-week period than a comparison group of patients.[77] Another study highlights the promise of preventive programming that makes use of the resources of religious institutions. This program evaluated the effects of a spiritually based prostate cancer education program in African American churches.[78] In comparison to those who received a non-spiritually-oriented educational program, men in the spiritual program read more of their materials and demonstrated greater knowledge about prostate cancer. We expect to see further studies evaluating whether more religiously sensitive and integrated psychological programs provide added benefits over and above those of secular programs.

Although we cannot see into the future, we do expect the psychology of religion to continue to evolve in exciting ways as both a basic and applied field of study. It seems clear that religion represents a vital dimension of life. Findings from the field as a whole underscore the need to attend to religion in psychological study and practice.

A psychology that neglects the religious side of human functioning will be incomplete.

NOTES

1. Christopher Peterson and Martin E. P. Seligman, eds., *Character Strengths and Virtues: A Handbook and Classification* (Washington, DC: APA/ Oxford University Press, 2004), 599–622.
2. Pew Forum on Religion and Public Life, *U.S. Religious Landscape Survey* (Washington: Pew Research Center, 2008).
3. Harold G. Koenig, Dana E. King, and Verna Benner Carson, *Handbook of Religion and Health*, 2nd ed. (New York: Oxford University Press, 2012).
4. Andrew J. Weaver, Kenneth I. Pargament, Kevin J. Flannelly, and Julia E. Oppenheimer, "Trends in the Scientific Study of Religion, Spirituality, and Health: 1965–2000," *Journal of Religion and Health* 45 (2006): 208–14.
5. Ralph W. Hood, Jr., Peter C. Hill, and Bernard Spilka, *The Psychology of Religion: An Empirical Approach*, 4th ed. (New York: Guilford Press, 2009).
6. Kenneth I. Pargament, ed.-in-chief, Julie J. Exline, James Jones, Annette Mahoney, and Edward Shafranske, assoc. eds., *APA Handbook of Psychology, Religion, and Spirituality, Vols. 1 and 2* (Washington, DC: APA Press, 2013).
7. Raymond F. Paloutzian and Crystal Park, eds., *Handbook of the Psychology of Religion and Spirituality*, 2nd ed. (New York: Guilford, 2013).
8. Sigmund Freud, *The Future of an Illusion* [1927] (New York: Norton, 1961).
9. Melissa Soenke, Mark J. Landau, and Jeff Greenberg, "Sacred Armor: Religion's Role as a Buffer against the Anxieties of Life and the Fear of Death," in Pargament et al., eds., *APA Handbook of Psychology, Religion, and Spirituality, Vol. 1*, 105–22.
10. Kenneth E. Vail, Zachary K. Rothschild, Dave R. Weise, Sheldon Solomon, Tom Pyszczynski, and Jeff Greenberg, "A Terror Management Analysis of the Psychological Functions of Religion," *Personality and Social Psychology Review* 14 (2010): 84–94.
11. Freud, *The Future of an Illusion*.
12. Michael E. McCullough and Evan. C. Carter, "Religion, Self-Control, and Self-Regulation: How and Why Are They Related?," in Pargament et al., eds., *APA Handbook of Psychology, Religion, and Spirituality, Vol. 1*, 123–38.
13. Ayelet Fishbach, Ronald S. Friedman, and Arie W. Kruglanski, "Leading Us Not unto Temptation: Momentary Allurements Elicit Overriding Goal Activation," *Journal of Personality and Social Psychology* 84 (2003): 296–309.

14. Émile Durkheim, *The Elementary Forms of Religious Life* [1912] (New York: Free Press, 1995).

15. Ibid., 432–33.

16. Jesse Graham and Jonathan Haidt, "Beyond Beliefs: Religions Bind Individuals into Moral Communities," *Personality and Social Psychology Review* 14 (2010): 140–50.

17. Crystal L. Park, Donald Edmondson, and Amy Hale-Smith, "Why Religion? Meaning as Motivation," in Pargament et al., eds., *APA Handbook of Psychology, Religion, and Spirituality, Vol. 1*, 157–71.

18. Paul E. Johnson, *Psychology of Religion* (Nashville, TN: Abingdon Press, 1959), 70.

19. Kenneth I. Pargament, "Searching for the Sacred: Toward a Non-reductionistic Theory of Spirituality," in Pargament et al., eds., *APA Handbook of Psychology, Religion, and Spirituality, Vol. 1*, 257–74.

20. Robert Coles, *The Spiritual Life of Children* (Boston: Houghton Mifflin, 1990), 142.

21. Andrew B. Newberg and Mark Robert Waldman, *Born to Believe: God, Science, and the Origin of Ordinary and Extraordinary Beliefs* (New York: Free Press, 2007).

22. Ana Rizzuto, *The Birth of the Living God: A Psychoanalytic Study* (Chicago: University of Chicago Press, 1979).

23. Johnson, *Psychology of Religion*.

24. Doug Oman, "Spiritual Modeling and the Social Learning of Spirituality and Religion," in Pargament et al., eds., *APA Handbook of Psychology, Religion, and Spirituality, Vol. 1*, 187–204.

25. David Yamane and Megan Polzer, "Ways of Seeing Ecstasy in Modern Society: Experimental-Expressive and Cultural-linguistic Views," *Sociology of Religion* 55 (1994): 1–25.

26. Nathaniel M. Lambert and David C. Dollahite, "The Threefold Cord: Marital Commitment in Religious Couples," *Journal of Family Issues* 29 (2008): 592–614.

27. Fereshteh Ahmadi, *Culture, Religion, and Spirituality in Coping: The Example of Cancer Patients in Sweden* (Uppsala, Sweden: Uppsala University, 2006), 134.

28. Annette Mahoney, Kenneth I. Pargament, and Krystal M. Hernandez, "Heaven on Earth: Beneficial Effects of Sanctification for Individual and Interpersonal Well-Being," in *The Oxford Handbook of Happiness*, ed. Susan A. David, Ilona Boniwell, and Alana Conley Ayers (New York: Oxford University Press, 2013), 397–410.

29. Annette Mahoney, Robert A. Carels, Kenneth I. Pargament, Amy B. Wachholtz, Edwards Laura Edwards Leeper, Mary Kaplar, and Robin Frutchey, "The Sanctification of the Body and Behavioral Health

Patterns of College Students," *International Journal for the Psychology of Religion* 15 (2005): 221–38.

30. Koenig, King, and Carson, *Handbook of Religion and Health*.

31. Kenneth I. Pargament, *The Psychology of Religion and Coping: Theory, Research, Practice* (New York: Guilford Press, 1997).

32. Reeve Robert Brenner, *The Faith and Doubt of Holocaust Survivors* (New York: Free Press, 1980).

33. Julie J. Exline, Kenneth I. Pargament, Joshua B. Grubbs, and Anne Marie Yali, "The Religious and Spiritual Struggles Scale: Development and Initial Validation," *Psychology of Religion and Spirituality* 6 (2014): 208–22.

34. Chad V. Johnson and Jeffrey A. Hayes, "Troubled Spirits: Prevalence and Predictors of Religious and Spiritual Concerns among University Students and Counseling Center Clients," *Journal of Counseling Psychology* 50 (2003): 409–19.

35. George Fitchett, Patricia E. Murphy, Jo Kim, James L. Gibbons, Jacqueline R. Cameron, and Judy A. Davis, "Religious Struggle: Prevalence, Correlates and Mental Health Risks in Diabetic, Congestive Heart Failure, and Oncology Patients," *International Journal of Psychiatry in Medicine* 34 (2004): 179–96.

36. Gina Magyar-Russell, Iain Tucker Brown, Inna R. Edara, Michael T. Smith, Joseph E. Marine, and Roy C. Ziegelstein, "In Search of Serenity: Religious Struggle among Patients Hospitalized for Suspected Acute Coronary Syndrome," *Journal of Religion and Health* 53 (2014): 562–78.

37. Julie J. Exline, "Religious and Spiritual Struggles," in Pargament et al., eds., *APA Handbook of Psychology, Religion, and Spirituality, Vol. 1*, 459–75.

38. Kenneth I. Pargament, *Spiritually Integrated Psychotherapy: Understanding and Addressing the Sacred* (New York: Guilford Press, 2007).

39. Exline, "Religious and Spiritual Struggles."

40. Kenneth I. Pargament, Nichole Murray-Swank, Gina Magyar, and Gene Ano, "Spiritual Struggle: A Phenomenon of Interest to Psychology and Religion," in *Judeo-Christian Perspectives on Psychology: Human Nature, Motivation, and Change*, ed. William R. Miller and Harold D. Delaney (Washington, DC: APA Press, 2005), 245–68.

41. Kenneth I. Pargament, Kavita M. Desai, and Kelly M. McConnell, "Spirituality: A Pathway to Posttraumatic Growth or Decline?" in *Handbook of Posttraumatic Growth: Research and Practice*, ed. Lawrence G. Calhoun and Richard G. Tedeschi (Mahwah, NJ: Lawrence Erlbaum, 2006), 121–37.

42. Kavita M. Desai and Kenneth I. Pargament, "Predictors of Growth and Decline Following Spiritual Struggle," *International Journal for the Psychology of Religion* 25 (2015): 42–56.
43. Ellen Idler, "Rituals and Practices," in Pargament et al., eds., *APA Handbook of Psychology, Religion, and Spirituality, Vol. 1*, 329–48.
44. Brian J. Zinnbauer and Kenneth I. Pargament, "Spiritual Conversion: A Study of Religious Change among College Students," *Journal for the Scientific Study of Religion* 37 (1998): 161–80.
45. Raymond F. Paloutzian, James T. Richardson, and Lewis R. Rambo, "Religious Conversion and Personality Change," *Journal of Personality* 67 (1999): 1047–79.
46. William R. Miller and Janet Baca, *Quantum Change: When Epiphanies and Sudden Insights Transform Ordinary Lives* (New York: Guilford Press, 2001).
47. Ibid., 131.
48. Daniel P. McAdams, *The Redemptive Self* (New York: Oxford University Press, 2006).
49. Heinz Streib and Constantin Klein, "Atheists, Agnostics, and Apostates," in Pargament et al., eds., *APA Handbook of Psychology, Religion, and Spirituality, Vol. 1*, 713–28.
50. Pargament, *Spiritually Integrated Psychotherapy*.
51. Gordon W. Allport and J. Michael Ross, "Personal Religious Orientation and Prejudice," *Journal of Personality and Social Psychology* 5 (1967): 432–43.
52. Kenneth I. Pargament, "Of Means and Ends: Religion and the Search for Significance," *International Journal for the Psychology of Religion* 2 (1992): 201–29.
53. Lee A. Kirkpatrick, *Attachment, Evolution, and the Psychology of Religion* (New York: Guilford Press, 2005).
54. Pehr Granqvist and Lee A. Kirkpatrick, "Religion, Spirituality, and Attachment," in Pargament et al., eds., *APA Handbook of Psychology, Religion, and Spirituality, Vol. 1*, 139–55.
55. Pehr Granqvist and Lee A. Kirkpatrick, "Religious Conversion and Perceived Childhood Attachment: A Meta-Analysis," *International Journal for the Psychology of Religion* 14 (2004): 223–50.
56. Granqvist and Kirkpatrick, "Religion, Spirituality, and Attachment."
57. Richard S. Lazarus and Susan Folkman, *Stress, Appraisal, and Coping* (New York: Springer, 1984).
58. Pargament, *Spiritually Integrated Psychotherapy*.
59. Terry L. Gall, and Manal Guirguis-Younger, "Religious and Spiritual Coping: Current Theory and Research," in Pargament et al., eds., *APA Handbook of Psychology, Religion, and Spirituality, Vol. 1*, 349–64.

60. Kenneth I. Pargament, David S. Ensing, Kathryn Falgout, Hannah Olsen, Barbara Reilly, Kimberly Haitsma, and Richard Warren, "God Help Me: I. Religious Coping Efforts as Predictors of the Outcomes to Significant Negative Life Events," *American Journal of Community Psychology* 18 (1990): 793–824.

61. Gene G. Ano and Erin B. Vasconcelles, "Religious Coping and Psychological Adjustment to Stress," *Journal of Clinical Psychology* 61 (2005): 461–80.

62. Andrew P. Tix and Patricia A. Frazier, "The Use of Religious Coping during Stressful Life Events: Main Effects, Moderation, and Mediation," *Journal of Consulting and Clinical Psychology* 66 (1998): 411–22.

63. Nathaniel M. Lambert, Frank D. Fincham, Scott R. Braithwaite, Steven M. Graham, and Steven R. H. Beach, "Can Prayer Increase Gratitude?," *Psychology of Religion and Spirituality* 1 (2009): 139–49.

64. Nathaniel M. Lambert, Frank D. Fincham, Tyler F. Stillman, Steven M. Graham, and Steven R. H. Beach, "Motivating Change in Relationships: Can Prayer Increase Forgiveness?," *Psychological Science* 21 (2010): 126–32.

65. Vassilis Saroglou, "Religion, Spirituality, and Altruism," in Pargament et al., eds., *APA Handbook of Psychology, Religion, and Spirituality, Vol. 1*, 349–64.

66. Robert D. Carlisle and Jo-Ann Tsang, "The Virtues: Gratitude and Forgiveness," Pargament et al., eds., *APA Handbook of Psychology, Religion, and Spirituality, Vol. 1*, 423–37.

67. Ralph L. Piedmont and Mark M. Leach, "Cross-Cultural Generalizability of the Spiritual Transcendence Scale in India: Spirituality as a Universal Aspect of Human Experience," *American Behavioral Scientist* 45 (2002): 1888–901.

68. Hisham Abu-Raiya and Kenneth I. Pargament, "Religious Coping Among Diverse Religions: Commonalities and Divergences," *Psychology of Religion and Spirituality* (2014): online publication.

69. Streib and Klein, "Atheists, Agnostics, and Apostates."

70. Ibid.

71. Joanna Maselko, "The Neurophysiology of Religious Experience," in Pargament et al., eds., *APA Handbook of Psychology, Religion, and Spirituality, Vol. 1*, 205–20.

72. Roland R. Griffiths, W. A. Richards, U. McCann, and R. Jesse, "Psilocybin Can Occasion Mystical-Type Experiences Having Substantial and Sustained Personal Meaning and Spiritual Significance," *Psychopharmacology* 187 (2006): 268–83.

73. Ibid., 277.

74. Kenneth I. Pargament, Annette Mahoney, Edward P. Shafranske, Julie J. Exline, and James W. Jones, "From Research to Practice: Towards

an Applied Psychology of Religion and Spirituality," in Pargament et al., eds., *APA Handbook of Psychology, Religion, and Spirituality,* Vol. 2, 3–22.

75. Everett L. Worthington, Jr., Joshua N. Hook, Don E. Davis, and Michael A. McDaniel, "Religion and Spirituality," in *Psychotherapy Relationships That Work: Evidence-Based Responsiveness,* 2nd ed., ed. John C. Norcross (New York: Oxford University Press, 2011), 402–20.

76. Amy B. Wachholtz and Kenneth I. Pargament, "Migraines and Meditation: Does Spirituality Matter?," *Journal of Behavioral Medicine* 31 (2008): 351–66.

77. Jean L. Kristeller, Mark Rhodes, Larry D. Cripe, and Virgil Sheets, "Oncologist Assisted Spiritual Intervention Study (Oasis): Patient Acceptability and Initial Evidence of Effects," *International Journal of Psychiatry in Medicine* 35 (2005): 329–47.

78. Cheryl L. Holt, Theresa Ann Wynn, Mark S. Litaker, Penny Southward, Sanford E. Jeames, and Emily K. Schulz, "A Comparison of a Spiritually Based and Non-Spiritually Based Educational Intervention for Informed Decision Making for Prostate Cancer Screening among Church-Attending African-American Men," *Urologic Nursing* 29 (2009): 249–58.

SUGGESTED READINGS

Allport, Gordon W. *The Individual and His Religion: A Psychological Interpretation.* New York: Macmillan, 1950. Allport highlighted different ways of being religious, distinguishing between mature and immature forms of the religious sentiment. His book set the stage for a considerable body of research on religious orientations and their implications for prejudice and mental health.

Barrett, Justin L. *Why Would Anyone Believe in God?* Walnut Creek, CA: AltMira Press, 2004. Barrett draws on exciting findings emerging from cognitive science and religion to provide a cogent explanation for the prevalence of religious belief. Beliefs in God, he maintains, are an "inevitable" outcome of the way our minds, conscious and unconscious, are designed.

Carlisle, Robert D., and Jo-Ann Tsang. "The Virtues: Gratitude and Forgiveness." In Pargament et al., eds., *APA Handbook of Psychology, Religion, and Spirituality: Vol. 1,* 423–38. Washington, DC: APA. This chapter reviews the burgeoning conceptual and empirical literature on forgiveness and gratitude, the two most frequently studied virtues.

Exline, Julie J. "Religious and Spiritual Struggles." In Pargament et al., eds., *APA Handbook of Psychology, Religion, and Spirituality: Vol 1,* 459–76. This chapter offers an overview of the growing literature on one potentially problematic form of religiousness: religious and spiritual struggles. These struggles have been consistently tied to declines in mental health, physical health, and well-being.

Fowler, James. *Stages of Faith: The Psychology of Human Development and the Quest for Meaning*. New York: Harper and Row, 1981. Paralleling the work of other developmental theorists such as Piaget, Erikson, and Kohlberg, Fowler articulated seven stages of faith that reflect differences in the ways the individual understands and relates to the world. His work remains influential among many theorists and counselors.

Frankl, Viktor. *Man's Search for Meaning* [1959]. New York: Washington Square Press, 1984. From his experiences in the concentration camps of Nazi Germany, Frankl observed that people needed a "why to live" to survive their ordeal. His work was a foundation for the development of existential psychotherapy and current emphases in the field on meaning making.

Freud, Sigmund. *The Future of an Illusion* [1927]. New York: Norton, 1961. In perhaps the most provocative of all books in the field, Freud asserted that religion is rooted in the child's search for a response to his or her sense of utter helplessness. Better to be "educated to reality," he said, then seek comfort in "illusory" beings.

James, William. *The Varieties of Religious Experience: A Study in Human Nature* [1907]. New York: Modern Library, 1975. James argues persuasively that religious experience is an essential aspect of what it means to be human. His pluralistic approach to religion continues to guide much of the work in the field today.

Kirkpatrick, Lee A. *Attachment, Evolution, and the Psychology of Religion*. New York: Guilford Press, 2005. Kirkpatrick asserts that God can be understood as an attachment figure who operates similarly to parental attachment figures in providing people with a safe haven and a secure base for exploration. His theory is sparking considerable interest and empirical study.

Koenig, Harold G., Dana E. King, and Verna Benner Carson. *Handbook of Religion and Health*, 2nd ed. New York: Oxford University Press, 2012. This handbook contains a comprehensive review of the empirical literature on the links between multiple dimensions of religiousness and multiple dimensions of physical and mental health. This is an essential resource for researchers interested in religion and health.

Pargament, Kenneth I. *The Psychology of Religion and Coping: Theory, Research, Practice*. New York: Guilford Press, 1997. Drawing on research, theory, and practice, Pargament's book describes how religion adds a vital dimension to the process of coping with the major problems of living. Religious coping represents one of the major topics of study in the psychology of religion today.

Pargament, Kenneth I., ed.-in-chief, Julie J. Exline, James Jones, Annette Mahoney, and Edward Shafranske, associate eds. *APA Handbook of Psychology, Religion, and Spirituality, Vols. 1 and 2.* Washington, DC: APA Press, 2013. This seventy-five-chapter, two-volume handbook provides the most comprehensive and current coverage of the state of the field. The first volume focuses on theoretical and empirical contributions; the second volume focuses on advances in the applied psychology of religion.

Worthington, Everett L., Jr., Joshua N. Hook, Don E. Davis, and Michael A. McDaniel. "Religion and Spirituality." In John C. Norcross, ed., *Psychotherapy Relationships That Work: Evidence-Based Responsiveness,* 2nd ed. New York: Oxford University Press, 2011, 402–20. This chapter reports on the results of the most recent meta-analysis of studies on the efficacy of religiously integrated approaches to psychotherapy. The findings indicate that religiously integrated treatments are at least as effective as their secular counterparts.

3

Religion and Political Science

The Dimensions of a Social Scientific Great Awakening

Anthony Gill

RELIGION AND POLITICS: SCHOLARLY BLIND SPOTS AND A GREAT AWAKENING

Since the dawn of civilization, human beings have been mixing religion and politics. Despite various attempts to "separate church and state" or "secularize" society by confining matters of spiritual belief to the private sphere, the realms of religion and politics have remained intertwined and will, in all likelihood, continue to be. Indeed, speaking of "separate realms" may be misleading given that people with religious convictions take their beliefs and values into the political arena on a daily basis as a way of informing their choices and behavior. These people include both citizens and leaders. Political authorities, regardless of their own faith or lack thereof, must factor in the existence of people with religious beliefs. Even self-proclaimed atheistic rulers such as Vladimir Lenin and Josef Stalin[1] had to devise policies for dealing with the remnants of the Orthodox Church that they could not extinguish. And today in North Korea, history's most recent paragon of secular totalitarianism, President Kim Jong-Un must repeatedly enforce restrictions on Christians who refuse to vanish. Religion and politics will continue to mix, and it behooves social scientists to understand why and how.

Academically speaking, the study of religion and politics has been, at best, a minor subfield in the discipline of political science. At worst, it has been utterly ignored. While most political science departments at top research universities, particularly nonreligious institutions,[2] would have multiple professors studying Congress, ethnic conflict, or social revolutions, you would be hard pressed (until recently) to find anyone who devoted her or his professional career to understanding the influence of religion on politics, and vice versa. Those that did study this topic were usually confined to religious institutions (e.g., Notre Dame, Baylor). And among the faculty at secular schools who did note the presence of religion in politics, the reference often would be to note it as some outlying curiosity that probably did not have much importance. The profession's flagship journal—the *American Political Science Review*—did not even publish a single article devoted to the topic between 1993 and 2000, and other top-shelf journals did not fare much better.[3] Prior to that dry spell, articles on religion that did appear tended toward normative political philosophy rather than empirical social science. Voting behavior studies that contained a single "religion" variable within a larger regression were the primary exceptions, and then again religion was but one of many factors being examined.

The general neglect of religion within political science is an intriguing topic. Religious movements, historically, have played an important role in shaping power relations in every corner of society. In the United States, efforts to abolish slavery, prohibit alcohol, grant women voting rights, promote civil liberties for racial minorities, ban nuclear weapons, and limit the availability of abortion all have had strong religious influence guiding them.[4] The rise of religious opposition to military dictatorships in Latin America during the 1970s and the 1979 Islamic Revolution in Iran foreshadowed the power of religious ideas and organizations in regions of the world that many thought were on the path to secular modernization. Researchers who studied these topics gave only cursory attention to the role of religious mobilization. This is curious considering that confessional groups have been organizing successful collective action for millennia.

Scholars examining the rise of "new social movements"—i.e., protest movements, nongovernmental organizations, and other civil society organizations—have paid little heed to "old social movements."[5] Think about this for a moment. Whereas political scientists are fascinated by the rise and endurance of various hierarchical organizations—from political parties to nation-states—few have stopped to consider the staying power and influence of one of history's most enduring formal hierarchies—the Roman Catholic Church, an entity that has outlasted every secular government and monarchical dynasty and that today claims the adherence of roughly one billion people worldwide.[6] No other single, identifiable entity can claim such an achievement.[7] If we relax the requirement of having a formal hierarchy with clearly designated lines of authority, you can add Hinduism, Judaism, Buddhism, Shintoism, and Islam to the list of "collective social movements" that have exercised influence over large numbers of people for several millennia. The historical record is unambiguously clear: Religion matters, a fact that political scientists only now appear to be recognizing in any significant form.[8]

With all this being fairly obvious, why has there been such neglect of the study of religion and politics over the past century? This academic blind spot can be laid at the feet of scholars in the nineteenth century who were foundational to the rise of modern social science, with its championing of the "theory of secularization" implicitly embedded in a wide array of other theoretical paradigms that set agendas for questions to be studied. If religious belief was about to wither under the weight of modernization, why bother devoting much attention to studying all those spiritual folks and their increasingly anachronistic rituals? Perhaps it is a bit unfair to make such an accusation against the likes of Friedrich Nietzsche, Sigmund Freud, Karl Marx, Émile Durkheim, and Max Weber. After all, they wrote at a time when the natural sciences and industrial technology were transforming our world and giving us greater understanding and mastery of our surroundings. The supernatural explanations for phenomena in the past were falling to theories of plate tectonics and genetic mutation. And we no longer needed to rely upon prayer to cure a sick child but could reach for medicines instead. In the context of the late nineteenth and early twentieth centuries, it was reasonable to think that religion was a thing of the past.

Contemporary theorists carry much more of the blame for relegating the study of religion to a mere oddity. At least Weber and Durkheim took the topic seriously enough to write entire books on the topic. Their twentieth-century progeny quite simply refused to examine it much at all, despite daily indications that religiosity was not on the decline outside the European continent. But history rarely stays silent, and the Iranian revolution in January 1979, sent scholars a reminder that religion was still politically potent. In the United States, evangelical Christians became a significant factor in electoral politics in the last decades of the century, with the creation of groups such as the Moral Majority and Focus on the Family. In Latin America, Catholic clergy were mobilizing opposition to military dictators, and Pope John Paul II became a key player in the decline of communism. Pentecostalism was sweeping across the developing nations of the world, often in some of the most unlikely places, such as communist China, remapping political preferences and setting an agenda for greater religious freedom.

By the 1990s, several individuals began noticing these international trends and urging greater consideration for religion as a significant factor in political behavior.[9] But if these clarion calls were not enough, the terrorist attacks of September 11, 2001, finally (and dramatically) demonstrated that theological concerns continue to provide salient motivations for individual behavior. At this point, established researchers and graduate students suddenly came to the realization that more people should be studying religion's role in politics.[10] Not surprisingly, the dangling string of increased funding for studying the link between religion and political violence also served to attract a horde of scholarly kittens. Political science had finally experienced its great awakening to religion.

This chapter lays out where the study of religion and politics has been and is today, and what fields of research may prove fertile in the future (recognizing that the foresight of social scientists is cloudy at best). We begin with a brief conceptual framework defining key elements within the study of religion and politics that will help provide a roadmap for where we have been and where we have to go. The good news is that "rediscovery" of the influential role of religion in public life has led to an explosion of empirical avenues down which many creative scholars have been traveling. Graduate students looking for dissertation topics would do well to consider these pathways. Unfortunately, the space allotted is too small to do comprehensive justice to all the work being done. I have chosen to emphasize a set of scholars who tend to encapsulate larger trends in the field, either because they were the first to plow new intellectual territory or because their work has affected the thought of others. Just as social scientists in the past have had their blind spots to religion in general, I also plead guilty to being a bit myopic and neglecting a number of important research agendas that have escaped my attention. Those who have feel passed over are welcomed to contact me shaking their fist in indignant anger and I will endeavor to make them whole in future writings. With that caveat and invitation in mind, let us now explore the intersecting worlds of religion and politics.

RELIGION, POLITICS, CHURCH, AND STATE:
A CONCEPTUAL ROADMAP

Understanding the interplay of religion and politics first requires a definition of these terms, as the scope of a definition plays an important role in defining how we understand such a relationship. With respect to religion, there is a tendency to go back to classical sociologists of the early twentieth century, particularly Durkheim, who defined religion as "a unified system of beliefs and practices relative to sacred things . . . [, and that] unite into one single moral community called a Church, all those who adhere to them."[11] While calling attention to the ideational and ritualistic aspect of religion, this definition may be too broad to be useful when studying politics. Durkheim's definition is vague as to what can be considered "sacred," leading to the inclusion of all sorts of ideologies such as Marxism, fascism, liberalism, Robert Bellah's concept of "civil religion,"[12] or rabid support for the Oakland Raiders. Each of these ideologies possesses some notion of "the sacred"—e.g., the working class, the nation, individual liberties, John Madden—and can easily involve ritualistic behavior such as parades, pledges of allegiance, or black and silver face paint. Not surprisingly, such an expansive definition has been a mainstay of secularization theorists because it disregards the unique differences between what we commonly think of as religion and political ideologies. If religion is defined merely as a "set of beliefs about the sacred," and "sacred" remains ill-defined, then simply substituting "state" or "Madden's coaching" for "god" leads to a modern world less reliant on superstitions—i.e., a more secular world. The mistaken notion among Soviet apparatchiks that they could erase belief in God among the citizenry by replacing divine icons with other idols (e.g., the Stakhanovite worker) was the natural outgrowth of such a conceptualization of religion.[13] If humans only need some random referent point to create a community, it matters not if it is some metaphysical being or a flag with stars, stripes, and sickles. Replaceable religion was no religion at all and need not be studied. Multiply each side of the equation by zero and the problem goes away.

But history has demonstrated that secular ideologies have not had the staying power of what are commonly recognized as the world's great religions. Marxism-communism lasted less than a century and a half, and fascism and the Raiders fared even worse. This indicates that "religion" must contain something more than what Durkheim was willing to credit it. Common sense tells us that religion is different than Marxism-Leninism or any other secular set of beliefs. Moreover, the general failure of history's strongest secular ideologies by the end of the twentieth century may help explain why many scholars are abandoning the secularization paradigm. What we all thought would replace religion failed miserably in doing so.

Rodney Stark, an early critic of the secularization thesis,[14] provides a more useful definition that corresponds more closely with what the average person on the street would consider to be religion. For Stark, "*Religion* consists of *explanations of existence* based on *supernatural assumptions* and including statements about the *nature* of the *supernatural* and about *ultimate meaning*." Stark further asserts, "*Supernatural* refers to *forces or entities* (conscious or not) that are *beyond or outside nature* and which can suspend, alter, or ignore physical forces," with "*Gods*" being "*conscious supernatural beings*."[15] In other words, religion does not just deal with "sacred things" but is related explicitly to supernatural things beyond human control and can exert control over human beings.

This definition, rooted in the supernatural, is not trivial for the study of religion and politics. If religion is a social phenomenon based only on "sacred things," as Durkheim would have us accept, then government can create or expropriate these "sacred things" and fuse religious authority with political authority. Humans can control the sacred. Kim Il-Sung's deification and ubiquitous iconography in North Korea epitomize a Durkheim-based conceptualization of religion. On the other hand, if we follow Stark and define religion as dealing with supernatural entities and meaning beyond the control of man, then an alternative source of authority in contradistinction to the state exists.[16] Tension between these two sources of authority may lead to conflict, including use of violence to eliminate one source or the other. History is replete with such battles. Alternatively, the control by clergy over access to supernatural entities and ideas could lead political rulers to seek means of co-opting such sources of authority in an attempt to bolster their own power yet still be frustrated by the inability to completely expropriate godly power. Again, history lays before us numerous examples. Few people ever thought divine right kings were a substitute for the actual divine, and many a monarch lost his or her head assuming such.

A critical extension of the definition of religion is the concept of a confessional organization. Ideas do not exist of their own accord but instead are codified and passed on from individual to individual and generation to generation. The mechanism for doing this constitutes the organizational aspect of religion, or "church," an admittedly Christian-centric term that also encompasses the organizational structure of other faiths such as synagogue, mosque, and temple.[17] A church is defined as the authoritative relationships within a group of people that help to determine how ideas (theologies) are interpreted and propagated. Such institutions can range from very hierarchical entities, such as the Roman Catholic Church, to more decentralized forms of organization such as Sunni Islam, a loose-knit connection of independent imams and mosques.[18] Such institutions require resources to exist and grow: Priests must eat, temples must be built and maintained, and missionaries must be sent to faraway lands. The need to compete for resources in a world of scarcity means that churches must enter the competitive economic landscape and cannot avoid political entanglement. Despite claims that "church and state" have been (or should be) separated, there is no escaping the link between religion and politics in that religious organizations control alternative sources of authority (relative to secular rulers and laws) and must compete for scarce resources that other organizations also seek to claim.

This brings us to definitions of *politics* and *state*. Politics represents the activities associated with attempting to use power to divert social resources to one use or another, with power being further defined as an ability to make others do what they ordinarily would not do on their own. In short, politics is the application of coercion to get what one wants. While "politics" normally conjures up images of elections,[19] parliamentary debates, law making, and palace coups, it also occurs within more mundane places of human life including "office politics." Even churches experience politics when different factions of a congregation struggle over which hymnal to adopt; various factions attempt to exercise coercive power to make another group yield to their demands.

The state is a formal system of rules and relationships that determines who decides the fundamental allocation of social resources and further enforces such decisions.[20] It includes functions such as legislation (rule making), administration (execution of rules), and adjudication (policing and enforcing of rules). Various forms of government—that is, the formal set of institutions of the state—exist that arrange these functions in different forms. Constitutional democracies ground authority within the citizenry and establish a clear set of written rules with checks and balances that give those subject to laws the ability to influence them. Personalist autocracies concentrate such authority within a person or small group of individuals who have the ability to enforce their will over others. Of course, these polar opposites represent ideal types; actual governments exhibit great variation in their combination of democratic and autocratic tendencies. Who is in charge and how much power they control are always in a state of flux.

With these definitions, it should come as no surprise that religion and politics, and church and state, have always been entangled and will continue to be. Individuals hold religious beliefs (including atheism[21]) that shape preferences for how society should be organized, who should be in positions of authority, and how resources should be distributed. This is unavoidable. Asking someone to keep her or his religion out of politics is akin to asking grocery shoppers to disregard their food preferences and simply pick items at random. This is not to say that religion is *the only thing* that shapes political preferences; professional status, education, and class standing (among other things) also exert influence. However, conceptions of eternity, moral codes, and the purpose of life factor into how we prefer society to operate. Furthermore, the ability to organize into groups (congregations) and express religious beliefs is influenced by laws and regulations created by the state and thus have an impact on how individuals pursue their religious beliefs. Leaders of these groups (e.g., priests, rabbis) and their adherents thus have a stake in how those laws are written and enforced. The state, as we shall see, can exert great pressure on the content and practice of religion, though (as noted above) political rulers seem unable to *completely dominate* the authority and persistence of faith in the divine.

AN EVOLVING UNDERSTANDING OF RELIGION AND POLITICS, CHURCH AND STATE

While study of politics dates back to the time of Aristotle, the modern academic discipline of political science only emerged with increasing specialization of the social sciences during the late 1800s and early 1900s. What follows is a general survey of how the topic of religion has figured into our understanding of politics and government since then, especially secularization theory, which has tended to permeate the field in general. Most attention is placed on scholars within the United States, who have tended to be more interested in religion during this period than their European counterparts. At the time when political science departments were being created in modern universities, Europe was seeing a stagnation of religious practice (not to mention two major wars that disrupted everything). As one might expect, European scholars have devoted even less attention to religion and politics than their American counterparts.

With renewed study of religion and politics, there have emerged two general camps into which analyses have fallen: an ideational perspective emphasizing the importance of theological ideas and values, and an economic school of thought that examines the interests motivating both clergy and laity. While these two schools of thought are not necessarily mutually exclusive—both ideas and interests can motivate humans—they have nonetheless remained fairly separate. We will examine each general paradigm separately with an eye toward possible points of connection in the future.

Religion and Politics from an Ideational Perspective

Given that religions and religious organizations trade in the currency of ideas about God and other philosophical questions, it is not surprising that political scientists assume that the most interesting aspect of religion with respect to politics would be in the area of ideas and values. Theologies shape our understanding of the world, including our core values, and thus humans take these values to the ballot box or barricades in an effort to shape their political surroundings. Ideational perspectives, putting beliefs at the center of human action, seem custom-made for those studying religion and politics. In essence, when faced with decisions, often under conditions of uncertainty, individuals dip into their preexisting stockpile of knowledge to inform their choices. The nature of their knowledge and how it was imparted via cultural institutions such as religious organizations determine what choices are made and the political results. It is expected that individuals raised in a Catholic culture will hold different views of the world than Jews or Muslims. Those differences are translated into the types of political institutions and policies that they prefer, and how they go about advocating for them. Changing political outcomes, therefore, is a function of changes in worldviews and theologies. Thus, from this perspective, a great deal of emphasis is placed upon intellectual history as well as the stated religious preferences of individuals via survey research.

Of particular interest early on was the role that religious thought played in the founding of the American republic. As the first constitutional democracy to appear in modern times, and with a great deal of interest paid to the rise of democracy (or its demise), political scientists and historians emphasized the role that Puritanism played in shaping the U.S. Constitution and America's subsequent political culture. Earlier scholars such as Perry Miller[22] and Sydney Ahlstrom[23] emphasized how Calvinism shaped an emphasis on individual rights that permeated revolutionary rhetoric in the late 1700s, becoming codified in the U.S. Constitution. All this was in the growing tension with Enlightenment philosophy and deism, and these scholars emphasized how intellectual debates between these two worldviews shaped the structure of government.

These arguments have been furthered recently by a number of other scholars who have argued that the institutional framework governing the United States emanated from the religious ideas of a broad set of constitutional architects who have gone unrecognized, such as Roger Sherman and John Jay.[24] These authors write in contradistinction to others who claimed that the rise of secular Enlightenment ideas combined with a denominationally neutral deism were more foundational in determining the governmental structure of the new nation.[25] Beneke[26] posits that the rise of religious freedom and toleration, a cornerstone policy of the new republic, was the result of a vigorous intellectual debate that was invariably won by the separationists who combined Calvinist ideas with the heritage of Enlightenment thinkers like John Locke. For all of these authors, the critical role that religion plays comes through the ideological milieu of the time; religion influences politics via the avenue of intellectual ideas and debate.

Another branch of the ideational perspective on religion and politics arose with the "behavioral revolution" in political science during the mid-twentieth century, dominated by the increasing cost effectiveness and use of public opinion polling. The logic here is that, if we ask individuals their political preferences and match them with a set of characteristics, we may find patterns in the data suggesting explanations. Taking a quantitative approach to research, these studies used correlation as a first step in determining causation. Researchers asked a battery of questions about political issues followed by a set of "usual suspect" demographics, including age, gender, income, education, and religion. Here we do have an instance where scholars at least had some suspicion that religion might be important prior to 2001. The logic behind these studies was that, if a substantial portion of Catholics, for example, tend to hold similar preferences for candidates or policies, other factors held constant (via regression analysis), then there must be something innate to Catholicism that prompts such views.

This logic was similarly extended to all religious faiths. Indeed, early survey research dating back to the 1950s, combined with studies linking voting patterns to ethnoreligious precincts, did show a fairly strong connection between denominational affiliation and political preferences, with Protestants leaning toward the Republican party and Catholics and Jews favoring Democrats.[27] These partisan affiliations have not been static, though, and one of the more interesting findings in this literature has been a significant political realignment among religious adherents that began manifesting itself in the 1970s.

Whereas voting and policy preferences were drawn largely along denominational lines, religious attendance and intensity of belief are now more closely aligned with political divisions creating a new secular-religious divide. Atheists, agnostics, and individuals who do not attend church very often tend to lean Democrat, whereas regular churchgoers and those that consider religion to be an important aspect of their life favor Republicans.[28] In other words, a Catholic who attends services weekly is as likely to vote Republican as is a regular-attending evangelical Protestant. Even Jews who live a more Orthodox religious lifestyle are trending in a Republican direction.

Explanations for this phenomenon usually date the divide to the controversial *Roe v. Wade* Supreme Court case over abortion rights and the Democratic Party's embrace of a more secular platform. While Jimmy Carter, a self-declared evangelical Christian, did forestall this trend temporarily in the mid-1970s, it seems to have solidified in the latter two decades of the twentieth century.[29] The continued relevance of religiosity has led a number of other scholars to investigate the ideological influence wielded by clergy members and religious networks,[30] expanding research on religious and political attitudes to examine how religious and political ideas are formed within churches. Their research has taken the study of religious ideas beyond mere correlation and inductive guessing, and they have started to examine the underlying theoretical linkages as to how spiritual attitudes change and can have an influence on political behavior.

While most of the early work on the connection between religious ideas and political outcomes focused on America, a new wave of scholars has extended this perspective into global affairs, explaining both the politics within and between other countries. Granted, there had always been curiosity about the religious creeds of other nations among sociologists and anthropologists. However, the surprise success of the 1979 Islamic Revolution in Iran prompted political scientists to think more carefully about religion, including some individuals who had previously looked at the world exclusively through a secular lens.

In writing about that event, Theda Skocpol, a noted secular-materialist theorist of social revolutions, admitted that "the networks, the social forms, and the central myths of Shi'a Islam helped to coordinate urban mass resistance and to give it the moral will to persist in the face of attempts at armed repression."[31] The Islamic Revolution in Iran remained a curiosity, though, and the influence of religion on world affairs was not considered much beyond that case until another famous scholar who had previously ignored religion fired the next salvo. Samuel Huntington's 1993 article in *Foreign Affairs*, entitled "A Clash of Civilizations?,"[32] set off a firestorm of controversy by claiming that political conflict would be defined by relatively incompatible cultural worldviews (or civilizations), notably between Islam and Christianity. While coming under intense criticism for his assertion, the attacks of September 11, 2001, and the subsequent war on terror (including the current rise of the Islamic State in Syria and Iraq) may have proven Huntington prophetic. Prompted further by a major research project on the causes and consequences of the global resurgence in fundamentalist religion spearheaded by Marty and Appleby,[33] more scholars began examining the role of theology in promoting social tension.

During the mid-1990s, a group of sociologists, political scientists, and religious studies scholars began to examine the connection between religious fundamentalism and political violence. In examining events in the Middle East, Mark Juergensmeyer[34] and James Piscatori[35] advanced the argument that, while secular nationalism had been used to create nation-states in Western Europe, similar attempts to do so during the latter half of the twentieth century in Europe failed dramatically. Regimes such as Abdel Nasser's Egypt and the Baathist systems in Syria and Iraq were unable to deliver on the promises of improved socioeconomic conditions among populations that were intensely religious. This gave rise to a "confrontation of two ideologies of order"[36] wherein secular nationalists battled with Islamists to define the ideological framework of governance. The Pan-Arabism of the 1960s and 1970s eventually gave way to the Pan-Islamism of the 1980s and beyond. Even leaders who had strong secular leanings in their early careers, such as Yasser Arafat and Saddam Hussein, began adopting religious symbolism and rhetoric to appease a restless religious population. Juergensmeyer extended his analysis in both his seminal article[37] and his later book[38] to include Hindu and Christian fundamentalism, with the general thesis being that secular modernization will prompt intense backlash from religious citizens who felt left behind in the march of economic progress nationally or worldwide. With entrenched autocrats still wielding power in many of these areas, and globalization reminding people of their economic backwardness relative to the West, it was not surprising that the fundamentalist response to secular rule manifested itself in political violence.[39]

The observations made by Huntington, Juergensmeyer, Barber, and others necessarily prompted more scholarly soul searching as to whether or not certain theologies were compatible with democracy and a peaceful civil society. Not surprisingly, given where most of the violent action was, the attention was turned toward Islam.

Bernard Lewis, a prominent Princeton professor, is the most well-known author to argue that Arab Islamic culture is difficult to square with modern notions of liberal democracy and capitalism.[40] His analysis largely echoes the themes of Huntington, but the exact causal mechanisms between a general religious worldview and the implementation of actual political and economic institutions remain relatively vague.[41] John Esposito and John Voll,[42] who actually picked up this question earlier, argue that there is nothing inherent to Islam that would make it inimical to democratic governance. Indeed, many of the early Muslim forms of governance revolved around inclusive councils that solicited debate and consensus building, and Islamic thinking includes such democratic forms of participation.[43] It is not the theology per se that has led primarily to autocratic outcomes in postcolonial Muslim states but rather the historical legacies of imperialism that have been hard to overcome, particularly in the Arab world,[44] or the actions of rulers who have through repressive policies politicized Islam in a way that gives it the appearance of autocracy.[45] Many of these scholars have noted that democracy has been relatively successful in some Muslim nations such as Turkey, Malaysia, and Indonesia.[46] Recent work by González[47] goes to a more grassroots level and notes that Islam is not incompatible with democracy per se, pointing out that there are rumblings from society advocating for greater social freedoms in various demographic pockets, including the promotion of women's rights, though not necessarily in the manner in which Western feminists may expect.

The study of Islam has not been the only area where scholars have used ideational models to explore connections between religion and politics around the world. Ideological battles fought in the past have had a significant impact in structuring church–state relations throughout Europe, demonstrating that religious ideas are fairly malleable and can accommodate different forms of government.[48] How religious and political leaders are willing to understand the relationship between church and state in Europe has also affected the ability to accommodate new faiths.

Fetzer and Soper[49] argue that Britain's ideological preference for handling religious affairs at the local level has allowed for greater accommodation of Muslims than has the French system, which seeks to impose a national ideology of laicism uniformly across the entire country. Kuru[50] echoes this claim with a sophisticated historical analysis showing how different conceptualizations of "secularism" have led to policies that are more accommodating to religious minorities in the United States but less accommodating in France and, ironically, to the majority Muslim population in Turkey. And Daniel Philpott[51] has extended the examination of religious ideas beyond the realm of domestic politics to show how the Protestant Reformation intellectually shaped the system of international relations coming out of the Peace of Westphalia. His work has led a number of scholars to look critically at how religion and theology matter in the realm of foreign affairs[52] and civil and international conflict.[53]

The ideational perspective on religion and politics has blossomed in the past decade, moving beyond simple correlational analysis of voting behavior to look seriously at how religious ideas affect everything from political protest to domestic governmental institutions, to the structure of international relations. The recent work of scholars such as Philpott, Owen, Hall, and Kuru has rooted many of their analyses in a deep historical context showing how ideas do shape the political options available to various actors. The one crucial weakness of many of these studies, particularly those that work on a very broad level,[54] is that they never explain clearly why certain ideas win over others.

While it might seem logical that the best idea always wins in a free and fair intellectual debate, rarely is the playing field level. Individuals who have a self-interested stake in certain ideas and have the power to coerce others to their position may often win a debate regardless of any intellectual merits of the arguments being proffered. For many centuries, the Catholic Church was able to tamp down theological dissenters either by buying them off with their own monasteries or by burning them at the stake.[55] The imposition of certain ideas about Islamic theology in different countries, such as Saudi Arabia, with its preference for Wahhabism, may also revolve around the exercise of self-interested power by well-situated individuals. As such, an understanding of the progress of ideas and how they shape the world of religion and politics is not complete without an examination of the incentives faced by different religious actors. We now enter the world of political economy.

Religion and Politics from an Economic Perspective

While ideational perspectives on religion and politics have tended to reign supreme in the political science literature, a new source of theoretical inspiration began emerging in the late 1980s from an unlikely source: economics. During the 1950s and 1960s, the economic profession itself witnessed a broadening of its scope, away from narrow topics such as banking and employment statistics and toward using economic theories to examine all sorts of human behavior, including criminal behavior, marriage, and religion. While many individuals were involved in this endeavor, Nobel Laureate Gary Becker, who pioneered the use of economic reasoning in "nontraditional" economic topics, deserves the most credit. While not writing on religion explicitly, his theoretical approach inspired one of his students Larry Iannaccone to make the explicit link between religion and rational choice theory.[56] But even before Iannaccone began his work, it was a sociologist—Rodney Stark—who popularized the term *religious economies*[57] and set in motion a stream of research that would reshape the way scholars understood religion and, eventually, religion and politics.

Beginning as a standard sociologist of religion in the 1960s and 1970s, Stark began rethinking some of the dominant understandings of religion at the time and applying something known as exchange theory as a means of challenging secularization theory.[58] Dissatisfied with secularization theory's highly abstract theorizing about cultural milieus and an inevitable decline of faith (which he observed was most apparently not occurring), Stark promoted the idea that people in a religious context behave like people in any other environment. This gelled well with economic theories wherein individuals make choices (or trade-offs) under scarcity that serve to maximize their benefit, whether in terms of financial income or spiritual enlightenment.

Simply put, this was a game changer in the study of religion in that it situated interests at the center of understanding a variety of religious behaviors, including the actions of individuals, the formation and operation of organizations (churches), and how such organizations interact in a larger marketplace. Along with his former student Roger Finke, another early and critical player in this new paradigm, he wrote what could be considered the seminal work summarizing these new ideas in their book *Acts of Faith: Explaining the Human Side of Religion*.[59] Stark, Finke, and Iannaccone wrote on a wide array of topics related to religion, including the decline of Catholic vocations, the success of strict sects, the attraction of certain cults to secularists, and religious intermarriage, to name just a few of the topics they put under the microscope.[60]

The temporal concurrence of Stark, Finke, and Iannaccone writing and collaborating on similar topics helped to shape a new direction in the study of religion and politics. One of their most important contributions to this effort came with the observation that religious pluralism and competition coincided with greater religious practice.[61] This finding actually reinforced an assertion made by none other than the eighteenth-century economist Adam Smith, perhaps the first economist of religion, who noted that, when granted a religious monopoly over a citizenry, church leaders could be found "reposing themselves upon their benefices" and became negligent in cultivating the faith of the populace.[62] Stark[63] asserted that religious preferences in society are naturally pluralistic and that the ability of any denomination to hold a dominant market share requires the coercive power of the state; natural religious monopolies could not exist without government intervention.[64] Enter politics.

At the time when this small group of sociologists (Stark and Finke) and economists (Iannaccone) were shifting the paradigm on our understanding of religious behavior, a number of political science graduate students were picking up these economic insights and bringing them over to their discipline. Stathis Kalyvas[65] integrated rational choice theory, which underpinned the work of Iannaccone, Stark, and Finke, to explain the rise of Christian Democratic parties in a number of countries throughout Europe. He argued that the interests of Catholic leaders in protecting their institutions amid growing calls for democratic governance prompted them to become engaged in the political process by founding and supporting auxiliary

organizations that funneled lay leaders into forming political parties. While Christian Democratic parties have distinct ideologies, it
was the reactive *interests* of the Catholic hierarchy that shaped the
political landscape. Interests held sway over theology.

Kalyvas further extended this approach to look at how organizational structures can have a profound impact on the ability of
religious institutions to pursue their interests. In a fascinating comparative study, he argued that it was the strong hierarchical nature of
Catholicism that allowed the Vatican to eliminate its most theologically radical members who were in opposition to democracy in late
nineteenth-century Belgium. He contrasts this with similar Islamic
opposition to democratization in late twentieth-century Algeria,
wherein the decentralized nature of Sunni Islam made it impossible
to control radical dissenters leading Algerian military leaders to
abort the incipient attempts at creating a liberal democratic polity.[66]

Carolyn Warner[67] expanded such an interest-based analysis in her
examination of the fates of the Catholic Church's efforts to engage
in partisan politics in France, Germany, and Italy. Using a rational
choice approach, Warner explored how the church operated as an
interest group seeking to bolster its institutional power and influence over society, but strategic choices made during and after World
War II acted as significant constraints on the ability of hierarchs
to build political alliances. The interesting thing to note about her
innovative use of historical institutional analysis was that, although
the theology of the church was essentially constant across all three
cases, the differing outcomes in the three nations was determined
much more by cost-benefit constraints. The importance of this work
stands to remind us, just as Stark and Finke have noted, that the
personal and institutional incentives of clergy and their followers
are theoretically similar to individuals acting in another context;
the tools of interest-based analyses can be extended to the realm of
religion and politics to great effect.

A third scholar and present author of this chapter, Anthony Gill,
also directly applied the insights of Stark, Finke, and Iannaccone to
understand varying Catholic responses to dictatorship in Latin America
during the 1970s and 1980s. Whereas the dominant theory was that
theological changes introduced during Vatican II and the corresponding rise of a Marxist-based liberation theology changed the mindset
of church leaders and set them in opposition to right-wing military

dictatorships, Gill[68] noticed that such opposition was not uniform across the region, as the ideational perspective would predict. Some bishops adopted the rhetoric of Vatican II, while others continued with their decades-long support of the ruling regimes. He adopted the religious competition model of Stark and Iannaccone to argue that, where religious competition between Protestants and Catholics was most intense (namely Brazil and Chile), bishops needed to signal their concern for the weakest in society by opposing the excesses of dictators and undertake a preferential option for the poor. Indeed, the tactics of the Catholic Church at the pastoral level were similar to the efforts of Protestant missionaries, thereby providing additional evidence to the religious-pluralism-equals-religious-vitality thesis, but the institutional history of the Catholic Church required an additional political response to break with oppressive governments.

Gill further explored the microeconomic rationale behind religious competition in Latin America by noting, in accordance with the predictions of Iannaccone[69] and Chaves and Cann,[70] that Protestant competition to Catholic hegemony in Latin America was most likely to arise in countries that had deregulated religious markets. In other words, religious liberty gave rise to religious pluralism/competition, which in turn prompted greater amounts of religious activity in society. All these works presented a significant challenge to the age-old secularization theory that claimed that the decline of religion was a demand-side phenomenon (i.e., parishioners stopped believing). Instead, it was the ability of organizations to supply religious services to the population that mattered more in creating a more religiously dynamic environment, and government policy played an important role in shaping the nature of the supply, be it monopolistic (bad for religious faith) or pluralistic (good for it).

Inspired by a seminal article by Finke,[71] Gill[72] introduced a theory of why governments would ever deregulate religious markets when it would seemingly be in their interests not to. Compared to earlier theories of religious liberty that linked greater freedoms to intellectual innovations during the Enlightenment, Gill argued that politicians are constantly tinkering with the rules and regulations that affect churches and that this tinkering is motivated by political ambition and economic concerns. Whereas previous studies of religion and politics tended to ignore the influential role that public policy had on the overall level of religious practice and belief, Gill put this connection at center stage.[73]

The political economy approach to religion has not caught on as rapidly as rational choice approaches have in sociology and economics.[74] However, younger scholars are beginning to take this perspective in new directions by examining how Russia and China have regulated their religious minorities,[75] how dictatorships have restricted the rights of religious minorities,[76] and the role of religion in ethnic conflict.[77] Ironically, it is economists and sociologists who have more readily picked up the torch of studying political influences on religion.

Fenggang Yang[78] examines how the revival of religion in communist China, a major challenge to ideational perspectives and secularization theory in and of itself, is largely a matter of how government regulates the religious marketplace, allowing religious groups that do not challenge the party's hegemony to operate in a "gray market" while crushing those that appear as a mobilizing threat against the regime. Eli Berman[79] builds on a seminal paper by Iannaccone[80] to show how the organizational structure of radical religious groups makes them prime candidates for conducting terrorist operations. Here the argument is that more fanatical forms of religion that require high levels of sacrifice and stigmatizing behavior control the free-riding problem that many clandestine groups face and allow them to carry out seemingly impossible tasks such as suicide bombings. Rather than relying upon a theory of why a particular theology gives rise to extremism, Berman shows that there is an underlying organizational logic that can be explained by economic theory—and that has dramatic political consequences.

Finally, the innovative work of economic historian Timur Kuran[81] has demonstrated how legal restrictions placed on entrepreneurs by Islamic religious leaders has shaped the differential economic outcomes observed in the Middle East compared to Western Europe. Kuran's work is unique because he shows how ideas do matter, but in the context where they can affect the economic and political incentives of various actors who have an influence in enacting those ideas in policy. He further demonstrates that, while many of these ideas are meant to shape political outcomes, they are extremely malleable, and economic interests often override the best intentions of those ideas, particularly in the arena of Islamic prohibitions on charging interest.[82] Creative mechanisms to circumvent such restrictions show that people can live by the "spirit of the theological law" while violating it in practice.

In contrast to ideational perspectives, a more economic (interest-based) approach has expanded our knowledge of religion and politics by putting forth the observation that people acting in a religious context are not uniquely different from any other situation. Clergy and laity exist within a world of scarcity and must make difficult trade-offs in how to use resources to best achieve their goals. Such goals might include lofty objectives such as seeking spiritual enlightenment, but they also often involve accumulating wealth and power, just as any organization must do. Priests, rabbis, and imams must all contend with resource scarcity and power relations within their own religious organizations and must also manage relations with political actors that seek to manipulate these religious organizations for their own purposes. And, of course, spiritual leaders have been known to appeal to political powers for their own objectives, often restricting religious competitors or seeking subsidies to help them carry out their evangelical mission. This is not to say that ideas do not matter in the grand scheme of things. Sociologists who have made great use of an economic approach to religion, such as Stark, have repeatedly noted that ideas do matter and have incorporated them into their studies.[83] However, political scientists have yet to plow this field, which could yield a great harvest for any budding graduate student so inclined to take on that challenge.

CONCLUSION: AN AWAKENING AND THE ROAD AHEAD

Political science has undergone a "great awakening" when it comes to the topic of religion. Since 2001, not only has there been growing interest in studying the relation between religious extremism and terrorism, but also many scholars are now aware that the influence of religious beliefs and institutions extends to all facets of social and political life. Not only has the empirical scope of our attention increased tenfold, but the theoretical tools used to understand the religious-political nexus have expanded as well. No longer is religion understood as a mindset among increasingly irrelevant believers who may occasionally bring their values to bear on political action; now, we are open to approaches that see religious actors and organizations influenced by a whole host of incentive structures, many of which have commonalities with other political phenomena (e.g., political parties, protest movements) but also may have a certain uniqueness. We now recognize sincerely that individuals and groups may be motivated by more than concerns over wealth and power and that the pull of worshiping one's God may be of equal or greater importance in many situations. Such a realization provides us with a more complete understanding of the world that we live in.

Despite, or perhaps a result of, the grand awakening that has occurred, many roads not yet travelled have opened new horizons for scholars who are interested in this field. One promising side street entails examining how different confessional structures affect the ability of religious actors to be successful in the political realm. Kalyvas[84] provides a significant step in this direction by comparing the relative success of the hierarchical Catholic Church in nineteenth-century Belgium being able to signal a commitment to democracy and quell its dissidents compared to Muslim radicals in late twentieth-century Algeria who existed in a more decentralized organizational structure where dissidents acted more as spoilers. Andrew Gould[85] and Carolyn Warner[86] also make significant strides on this frontier by examining how religious institutional structures act as interest groups. And Kollman[87] also examines the internal organizational dynamics of the Vatican and how it may affect its overall political placement. While these latter three works mostly focused on the Catholic Church, where organizational lines of authority are generally clear, they point to what is possible by extending their superb analyses toward other organizational forms, from more congregational styles of leadership to thinking about how highly decentralized faiths like Sunni Islam might affect their surroundings.

While those studying the topic have tended to examine how religion influences politics, there is comparatively less work on the reverse causation: how politics influences religion. Early work in the 1990s by Stark, Iannaccone, Finke, and others has prompted more recent efforts to explore how the level of government regulation and a variety of other policies can play an important role in determining how easy it is for seemingly minor regulations such as registration requirements or zoning laws to have an impact on how effectively religious leaders can organize their potential congregants.[88] Fox[89] and Grim and Finke[90] have taken this examination further by using sophisticated data gathering and statistical analysis to show how governments encourage religious persecution worldwide.

A burgeoning literature on religious liberty, including its determinants and impact, is currently on the cutting edge of examining how government affects not only religious organizations but also socioeconomic conditions more generally. A working group of scholars at the Religious Freedom Project at Georgetown University have decided to examine whether religious liberty translates into long-term economic growth.[91] This latter project owes an immense debt to the pioneering work of Robert Woodberry,[92] who provided one of the most quantitatively rigorous articles linking Protestant missionary activity to the rise of liberal democracy, as noted above. That article, appearing as the lead in the *American Political Science Review*, the discipline's flagship journal, finally brought the study of religion and politics to its due prominence and has garnered the attention not only of those interested in religion but also those who have long neglected its influence.

To conclude, the roads still left to explore are numerous. Many paths remain completely unknown and will only be discovered by intrepid graduate students and independent scholars who are willing to recognize the full social and political potential that religion has always exercised.[93] To this, all the faithful believers in social science say . . . amen.

NOTES

1. Early in his life, Stalin was a seminarian studying for the priesthood. One could plausibly wonder if he was truly an atheist. Perhaps he harbored personal beliefs about God throughout his life. This we will never know, but it is fairly evident that his public actions did not indicate he was all that "churchy."

2. Defining what constitutes a "nonreligious" institution might be a bit tricky here. While state-run institutions such as the University of Washington or Michigan State University would obviously be secular schools, places such as Princeton, Harvard, and the University of Chicago all have divinity schools associated with them, but finding any religious flavor outside the halls of the seminary building would be a hard task indeed.

3. Compare Kenneth D. Wald and Clyde Wilcox, "Getting Religion: Has Political Science Discovered the Faith Factor?," *American Political Science Review* 100 (2006): 523–29; and Daniel Philpott, "Has the

Study of Global Politics Found Religion?," *Annual Review of Political Science* 12 (2009): 183–202.

4. See Anthony J. Gill and Steven J. Pfaff, "Acting in Good Faith: An Economic Approach to Religious Organizations as Advocacy Groups," in *Advocacy Organizations and Collective Action*, ed. Aseem Prakash and Mary Kay Gugerty (Cambridge, UK: Cambridge University Press, 2010), 58–90. Some folks may be surprised by the religious influence in the women's suffrage movement. However, this should not be surprising given that evangelicals in the early twentieth century were agitating to ban the sale of liquor. One strategic means of doing this would be to allow wives to vote because they would likely vote to take booze away from their husbands. That strategy proved successful, as Prohibition followed quickly on the heels of women being granted the franchise.

5. Gill and Pfaff, "Acting in Good Faith."

6. A recent notable exception has been Ken Kollman's *Perils of Centralization: Lessons from Church, State, and Corporation* (Cambridge, UK: Cambridge University Press, 2013), a study comparing the Catholic Church to other political and economic entities, including the U.S. government, the European Union, and General Motors. Kollman explicitly uses the tools of political economy to show that religious organizations need not be studied apart from political entities but can be used to enhance understanding of secular institutions.

7. Whether one dates the Catholic Church back 2,000 years to the time of Jesus, or 1,700 years to the First Council of Nicaea, it has out-survived even the longest-lasting Chinese, Egyptian, and Mayan dynasties, not to mention any currently existing nation-state. While many scholars have touched upon the influence of Catholicism in politics, Eric O. Hanson's *The Catholic Church in World Politics* (Princeton, NJ: Princeton University Press, 1987) stands out as the one work to take the Vatican seriously as a major "nation-state" player in world history, though even his book focused mostly on events in the twentieth century. A serious study using the tools and theories of political science for the Catholic Church as "historical nation-state" has yet to be written and would make an ideal dissertation for an enterprising graduate student.

8. Anna Grzymala-Busse, "Why Comparative Politics Should Take Religion (More) Seriously," *Annual Review of Political Science* 15 (2012): 421–42.

9. José Casanova, *Public Religions in the Modern World* (Chicago: University of Chicago Press, 1994); Anthony Gill, *Rendering unto Caesar: The Catholic Church and the State in Latin America* (Chicago: University of Chicago Press, 1998); Jeff Haynes, *Religion in Global Politics* (London: Longman, 1998); and Mark Juergensmeyer, *Terror in the Mind of God: The Global Rise of Religious Violence* (Berkeley: University of California Press, 2000).

10. On a personal note, I was asked by a colleague in the mid-1990s whether I would move on to a different topic after I published my dissertation in book form (see Gill, *Rendering unto Caesar*) since (to paraphrase) "that religion thing was going nowhere." Shortly after 9/11, a well-known scholar gave a talk at the University of Washington and during the presentation mentioned that he thought our discipline had ignored the influence of religion on politics and that our department should consider hiring somebody who studied that topic. Having just published an article on the importance of taking religion seriously ("Religion and Comparative Politics," *Annual Review of Political Science* 2001 [4]: 117–38), I wanted to bang my head repeatedly against the chair in front of me.

11. Émile Durkheim, *The Elementary Forms of Religious Life* [1912] (London: George Allen & Unwin, 1976), quotation on p. 47.

12. Robert N. Bellah, "Civil Religion in America," *Daedalus* 96, no. 1 (1967): 1–21.

13. See Paul Froese, *The Plot to Kill God: Findings from the Soviet Experiment in Secularization* (Berkeley: University of California Press, 2008).

14. See Rodney Stark and William Sims Bainbridge, "Secularization, Revival, and Cult Formation," *Annual Review of the Social Sciences of Religion* 4 (1980): 85–119.

15. Rodney Stark, *For the Glory of God: How Monotheism Led to Reformations, Science, Witch-Hunts, and the End of Slavery* (Princeton, NJ: Princeton University Press, 2003), quotations on p. 4 (emphasis in original).

16. This does not exclude the notion that humans interpret the will of God and that conflicting interpretations by humans can arise. That is obvious by the multiplicity of faiths in existence. It could also mean that all religions are simply a human construct, a popular notion in anthropology. See Rodney Stark's *Discovering God: The Origins of the Great Religions and the Evolution of Belief* (New York: HarperOne, 2007) for a unique counterargument. What it does say, though, is that those who do interpret scriptures understand that there is an eternal force standing outside their manipulation, which also implies, in many cases, a nonhuman judge and arbitrator for all actions. The central claim that a God exists, regardless of human interpretations of what God is, creates the crucial difference between a religion and a secular ideology.

17. For the sake of simplicity, I use the term *church* to refer to a wide array of confessional organizations, which encompass synagogue, mosque, or temple. While some may object to such a Christian-centric approach, I use it for rhetorical simplicity.

18. Sunni Muslims do organize cooperative and authoritative entities larger than the individual mosque, much like Pentecostals do at times.

Theological training via seminaries may also help define the scope of authority within these more decentralized faith traditions, as training from particular schools may lend greater legitimacy to some pastors or imams and also create informal networks of influence among them.

19. It may seem unusual to consider elections to be a form of coercion. However, as the literature in public choice points out, constitutions and other laws in society obligate the loser in any election to yield to the desires of the winner. If 55 percent of the population votes to use public funds to build a football stadium, everyone—including those who voted against the stadium—must financially support its construction. Use of the term *coercion* might also shock a few readers who see politics as a means of compromising toward the goal of some mutually agreeable outcome. However, that outcome needs to be enforced and deviations from the cooperative agreement need some form of punishment. Such punishment can range from something as innocuous as shaming to things more severe such as monetary fines, imprisonment, or death.

20. I use the terms *state* and *government* interchangeably in this chapter. While some political scientists see a conceptual distinction between the two, the arguments to this effect are too esoteric for present purposes.

21. While atheism would seem to be outside Stark's definition of religion, it simply represents the null set of beliefs about the supernatural. Atheism is a religion to the extent that it rests on the assertion that the supernatural is nonexistent and that meaning is determined by nongodly forces. This would seem to bring Marxism and other secular ideologies back into the mix of religions, and it could be debated whether this is true, but we will treat atheism simply as a single faith tradition representing the no-god option.

22. Perry Miller, *Errand into the Wilderness* (Cambridge, MA: Belknap Press, 1956).

23. Sidney Ahlstrom, *A Religious History of the American People* [1972], 2nd ed. (New Haven, CT: Yale University Press, 2004).

24. Daniel Dreisbach, Mark David Hall, and Jeffry H. Morrison, eds., *The Forgotten Founders on Religion and Public Life* (Notre Dame, IN: University of Notre Dame Press, 2009); and Jonathan J. Den Hartog, *Patriotism and Piety: Federalist Politics and Religious Struggle in the New American Nation* (Charlottesville: University of Virginia Press, 2015).

25. See Isaac Kramnick and Laurence Moore, *The Godless Constitution: The Case Against Religious Correctness* (New York: W.W. Norton & Company, 1996).

26. Chris Beneke, *Beyond Toleration: The Religious Origins of American Pluralism* (New York: Oxford University Press, 2008).

27. E. J. Dionne, Jr., "Catholics and the Democrats: Estrangement but Not Desertion," in *Party Coalitions in the 1980s*, ed. Seymour Martin Lipset

(San Francisco: Institute for Contemporary Studies, 1981), 307–25; and Robert Booth Fowler, *Religion and Politics in America* (Metuchen, NJ: Scarecrow Press, 1985).

28. Lyman A. Kellstedt, John C. Green, James L. Guth, and Corwin E. Smidt, "Has Godot Finally Arrived?: Religion and Realignment," in *Religion and the Culture Wars: Dispatches from the Front*, ed. John C. Green, James L. Guth, Corwin E. Smidt, and Lyman A Kellstedt (Lanham, MD: Roman and Littlefield, 1996), 291–99; Louis Bolce and Gerald De Maio, "Secularists, Antifundamentalists, and the New Religious Divide in the American Electorate," in *From Pews to Polling Places: Faith and Politics in the American Religious Mosaic*, ed. J. Matthew Wilson (Washington, DC: Georgetown University Press, 2007), 251–76; and Kenneth D. Wald and Allison Calhoun-Brown, *Religion and Politics in the United States*, 6th ed. (Lanham, MD: Rowman and Littlefield, 2010). The literature on religious voting patterns is vast, but a core group of political scientists including Paul Djupe, John Green, James Guth, Allen Hertzke, Ted Jelen, Lyman Kellstedt, Laura Olson, Corwin Smidt, and Ken Wald has contributed regularly in recent years. Many of these individuals, though not all, were students of Robert Booth Fowler at the University of Wisconsin and this survey research approach to understanding religious-political affiliations could be called the Wisconsin School.

29. John C. Green, *The Faith Factor: How Religion Influences American Elections* (Westport, CT: Praeger Press, 2007).

30. For example, David E. Campbell, John C. Green, and J. Quin Monson, *Seeking the Promised Land: Mormons and American Politics* (New York: Cambridge University Press, 2014); and Paul A. Djupe and Christopher P. Gilbert, *The Political Influence of Churches* (New York: Cambridge University Press, 2009).

31. Theda Skocpol, "Rentier State and Shi'a Islam in the Iranian Revolution," *Theory and Society* 11 (1982): 265–83, quotation on p. 275.

32. Samuel P. Huntington, "The Clash of Civilizations?," *Foreign Affairs* 72 (1993): 22–49, especially 31–32.

33. Martin E. Marty and R. Scott Appleby, eds., *Fundamentalisms and the State: Remaking Polities, Economies, and Militance* (Chicago: University of Chicago Press, 1993). This was one of a series of five edited volumes produced in the 1990s under the title of *The Fundamentalism Project*.

34. Mark Juergensmeyer, "The New Religious State," *Comparative Politics* 27 (1995): 379–91.

35. James Piscatori, "Accounting for Islamic Fundamentalisms," in *Accounting for Fundamentalisms: The Dynamic Character of Movements*, ed. Martin E. Marty and R. Scott Appleby (Chicago: University of Chicago Press, 1994), 361–73.

36. Juergensmeyer, "The New Religious State," quotation on 379.
37. Juergensmeyer, "The New Religious State."
38. Juergensmeyer, *Terror in the Mind of God.*
39. See Benjamin R. Barber, *Jihad vs. McWorld: Terrorism's Challenge to Democracy* (New York: Ballantine Books, 1995).
40. Bernard Lewis, *What Went Wrong?: The Clash Between Islam and Modernity in the Middle East* (New York: Harper Perennial, 2002).
41. As will be noted below, Timur Kuran (see *The Long Divergence: How Islamic Law Held Back the Middle East* [Princeton, NJ: Princeton University Press, 2011], and *Islam and Mammon: The Economic Predicaments of Islamism* [Princeton, NJ: Princeton University Press, 2004]), who fits more squarely in the "economic perspective" on religion, also acknowledges the roles that ideas matter and examines how historical and contemporary Islamic ideas of economics and law can affect governing outcomes. However, he situates his theory of ideas into a more institutional context, wherein different individuals have various incentives to choose some ideas over another. His work is probably the best example of the blending of ideational and economic perspectives of religion, and he is one of the most exciting scholars to study religion.
42. John L. Esposito and John O. Voll, *Islam and Democracy* (New York: Oxford University Press, 1996).
43. Abdulaziz Sachedina, *The Islamic Roots of Democratic Pluralism* (New York: Oxford University Press, 2001); and Graham E. Fuller, "The Future of Political Islam," *Foreign Affairs* 81 (2002): 48–60.
44. See Alfred C. Stepan, "Religion, Democracy, and the 'Twin Tolerations,'" *Journal of Democracy* 11 (2002): 37–57.
45. Jocelyne Cesari, *The Awakening of Muslim Democracy: Religion, Modernity, and the State* (New York: Cambridge University Press, 2014).
46. I am neglecting some recent work on what has been called the Arab Spring, given that early expectations that this would lead to a flowering of democracy in the Middle East have largely been dashed by the replacement of one autocracy with another and by a civil war in Syria that appears to be spilling over into neighboring countries. Claims about a phenomenon that are so fluid at present are somewhat dangerous for any social scientist.
47. Alessandra L. González, *Islamic Feminism in Kuwait: The Politics and Paradoxes* (New York: Palgrave Macmillan, 2013).
48. Stephen V. Monsma and J. Christopher Soper, *The Challenge of Pluralism: Church and State in Five Democracies* (Lanham, MD: Rowman and Littlefield, 1997); and Bryan T. McGraw, *Faith in Politics: Religion and Liberal Democracy* (New York: Cambridge University Press, 2010).

49. Joel S. Fetzer and J. Christopher Soper, *Muslims and the State in Britain, France, and Germany* (Cambridge, U.K.: Cambridge University Press, 2005).

50. Ahmet T. Kuru, *Secularism and State Policies toward Religion: The United States, France, and Turkey* (New York: Cambridge University Press, 2009).

51. Daniel Philpott, *Revolutions in Sovereignty: How Ideas Shaped Modern International Relations* (Princeton, NJ: Princeton University Press, 2001).

52. Thomas F. Farr, *World of Faith and Freedom: Why International Religious Liberty Is Vital to American National Security* (New York: Oxford University Press, 2008); and John M. Owen IV, *Confronting Political Islam: Six Lessons from the West's Past* (Princeton, NJ: Princeton University Press, 2015).

53. Monica Duffy Toft, Daniel Philpott, and Timothy Samuel Shah, *God's Century: Resurgent Religion and Global Politics* (New York: W.W. Norton, 2001).

54. For example, Huntington, "The Clash of Civilizations?"; and Lewis, *What Went Wrong?*

55. See Stark, *For the Glory of God.*

56. See Larry Witham, *Marketplace of the Gods: How Economics Explains Religion* (New York: Oxford University Press, 2010), particularly chap. 6, for a colorful history of how the economics of religion became a major paradigm in the study of religion.

57. Rodney Stark, "Religious Economies: A New Perspective," paper presented at the Conference on New Directions in Religious Research, University of Lethbridge, Lethbridge, AB, Canada, 1983.

58. Rodney Stark, "The Economics of Piety: Religion and Social Class," in *Issues in Social Inequality*, eds. Gerald W. Theilbar and Saul D. Feldman (Boston: Little, Brown, 1972), 483–503; and Rodney Stark and William Sims Bainbridge, *A Theory of Religion* (New York: Peter Lang Publishing, 1987).

59. Rodney Stark and Roger Finke, *Acts of Faith: Explaining the Human Side of Religion* (Berkeley: University of California Press, 2000).

60. The ideas advanced by these scholars and a handful of others in the late 1980s and early 1990s represented a Cambrian explosion of new thinking on religion, leading some scholars to call it the emergence of a new paradigm. The amazing scope of the topics studied is too broad to cover here. Indeed, it would take a book itself just to document the contributions each of these individuals made. Our focus instead is on how they advanced the football in political science by inspiring a new generation of scholars willing to risk deviating from the dominant stream of thinking in the profession.

61. Rodney Stark, Roger Finke, and Laurence R. Iannaccone, "Pluralism and Piety: England and Wales, 1851," *Journal for the Scientific Study of Religion* 34 (1995): 431–44; Rodney Stark, "Do Catholic Societies Really Exist?," *Rationality and Society* 4 (1992): 261–71; and Rodney Stark and Laurence R. Iannaccone, "A Supply-Side Reinterpretation of the 'Secularization' of Europe." *Journal for the Scientific Study of Religion* 33 (1994): 230–52.

62. Adam Smith, *The Wealth of Nations* [1776] (New York: Bantam Classic, 2003), quotation on p. 995. See also Laurence R. Iannaccone, "The Consequences of Religious Market Structure: Adam Smith and the Economics of Religion," *Rationality and Society* 3 (1991): 156–77.

63. Two publications by Stark: "Do Catholic Societies Really Exist?"; and *For the Glory of God.*

64. See Mark Chaves and David E. Cann, "Regulation, Pluralism, and Religious Market Structure: Explaining Religion's Vitality," *Rationality and Society* 4 (1992): 272–90.

65. Stathis N. Kalyvas, *The Rise of Christian Democracy in Europe* (Ithaca, NY: Cornell University Press, 1996).

66. Stathis N. Kalyvas, "Commitment Problems in Emerging Democracies: The Case of Religious Parties," *Comparative Politics* 32 (2000): 379–98.

67. Carolyn M. Warner, *Confessions of an Interest Group: The Catholic Church and Political Parties in Europe* (Princeton, NJ: Princeton University Press, 2000).

68. Gill, *Rendering unto Caesar.*

69. Iannaccone, "The Consequences of Religious Market Structure."

70. Chaves and Cann, "Regulation, Pluralism, and Religious Market Structure."

71. Roger Finke, "Religious Deregulation: Origins and Consequences." *Journal of Church and State* 32 (1990): 609–26.

72. Anthony Gill, *The Political Origins of Religious Liberty* (New York: Cambridge University Press, 2008).

73. While this assertion may seem a bit pompous, the present author is extremely proud of having made this case for two full decades amid great criticism that this type of economic analysis should not be done. As such, I feel a little touchdown celebration is warranted. Consider this my spiking of the theoretical football.

74. Evidence of this paradigm's growing influence is seen in the efforts of Larry Iannaccone to craft an association of scholars who examine religion from an economic perspective. While you could count on one hand the people who adopted this approach in 1990, the Association for the Study of Religion, Economics, and Culture (one of Iannaccone's institutional creations) now hosts an annual conference with hundreds of participants. Alas, the most underrepresented group at these confabs

is political science, to which the present author has no one to blame but himself for his general lack of evangelical fervor.

75. Karrie J. Koesel, *Religion and Authoritarianism: Cooperation, Conflict, and the Consequences* (New York: Cambridge University Press, 2014).

76. Ani Sarkissian, *The Varieties of Religious Repression: Why Governments Restrict Religion* (New York: Oxford University Press, 2015).

77. Matthew Isaacs, "For God or Country?: Examining the Salience of Religion in Ethnic Conflict" (Ph.D. dissertation, Department of Political Science, Brandeis University, Waltham, MA, 2017).

78. Fenggang Yang, *Religion in China: Survival and Revival Under Communist Rule* (New York: Oxford University Press, 2012).

79. Eli Berman, *Radical, Religious, and Violent: The New Economics of Terrorism* (Cambridge, MA: The MIT Press, 2009).

80. Laurence R. Iannaccone, "Sacrifice and Stigma: Reducing Free-Riding in Cults, Communes, and Other Collectives." *Journal of Political Economy* 100 (1992): 271–91.

81. Kuran, *The Long Divergence*.

82. Kuran, *Islam and Mammon*.

83. See two books by Stark: *For the Glory of God* and *Discovering God*.

84. Kalyvas, "Commitment Problems in Emerging Democracies."

85. Andrew C. Gould, *Origins of Liberal Dominance: State, Church, and Party in Nineteenth-Century Europe* (Ann Arbor: University of Michigan Press, 1999).

86. Warner, *Confessions of an Interest Group*.

87. Kollman, *Perils of Centralization*.

88. See Finke, "Religious Deregulation"; Chaves and Cann, "Regulation, Pluralism, and Religious Market Structure"; Stark and Iannaccone, "A Supply-Side Reinterpretation of the 'Secularization' of Europe"; and Anthony Gill, "Septics, Sewers and Secularization: How Government Regulation Flushes Religiosity down the Drain," ARDA Guiding Paper Series, Association of Religion Data Archives, 2010, accessed at http://www.thearda.com/rrh/papers/guidingpapers/Gill.pdf.

89. Jonathan Fox, *A World Survey of Religion and the State* (New York: Cambridge University Press, 2008).

90. Brian Grim and Roger Finke, *The Price of Freedom Denied: Religious Persecution and Conflict in the 21st Century* (New York: Cambridge University Press, 2011).

91. Anthony Gill, "Religious Liberty and Economic Development: Exploring the Causal Connections," *The Review of Faith and International Affairs* 11 (2013): 5–23. This is part of a larger set of essays in *The Review of Faith and International Affairs* examining this topic as part of a symposium. This article and critical responses were the starting point of a much larger, ongoing project that involves many of the authors

cited in this chapter, including Karrie Koesel, Ani Sarkissian, Daniel Philpott, John Owen, Allen Hertzke, Timothy and Rebecca Shah, and Brian Grim.

92. Robert D. Woodberry, "The Missionary Roots of Liberal Democracy," *American Political Science Review* 106 (2012): 244–74.

93. Although this chapter has focused on the academic writing of scholars working in colleges and universities, a great deal of wisdom is being revealed by people who live out their lives in the worlds of religion and politics. Scholars would be well advised to listen to what they have to say, not only for the questions that they raise but also for the answers that they provide.

SUGGESTED READINGS

Berman, Eli. *Radical, Religious, and Violent: The New Economics of Terrorism*. Cambridge, MA: The MIT Press, 2009. Berman applies the theories of religious economies to explain how and why many terrorist organizations have religious linkages. It is not the theology per se but the organizational structure of religious groups that plays a vital role. A highly accessible book for non-economists.

Djupe, Paul A., and Christopher P. Gilbert. *The Political Influence of Churches*. New York: Cambridge University Press, 2009. Going beyond mere survey data and looking at the political preferences of religious voters, Djupe and Gilbert explore how preferences are formed and turned into political action. A landmark book for pointing out new research directions in American religion and politics.

Esposito, John L., and John O. Voll. *Islam and Democracy*. New York: Oxford University Press, 1996. One of the first books to explore seriously whether Islamic theology is compatible with political democracy. While much has transpired since this book's publication, Esposito and Voll set the standard for research in this area.

Fowler, Robert Booth. *Religion and Politics in America*. Metuchen, NJ: Scarecrow Press, 1985. Fowler is perhaps the godfather of modern survey research applied to the study of religion and politics in the United States. He trained two generations of scholars who followed in his footsteps and demonstrated that religion should be taken seriously in political science. This work offers a good summary of his major contributions.

Froese, Paul. *The Plot to Kill God: Findings from the Soviet Experiment in Secularization*. Berkeley: University of California Press, 2008. This book offers the first serious, and humorous, study exploring whether a society can be secularized by an atheist ideology and coercive force. Froese's work implicitly undermines many of the claims of secularization theory and highlights the enduring role religion plays in society.

Gill, Anthony. *The Political Origins of Religious Liberty*. New York: Cambridge University Press, 2008. Building upon the early work of Roger Finke, Gill offers a comprehensive theory of why governments would want to deregulate their religious markets. Rather than proposing an ideational theory of why policy makers consider religious liberty an inherently good idea, Gill argues that political and economic interests played a vital role.

Huntington, Samuel P. "The Clash of Civilizations?" *Foreign Affairs* 72 (1993): 22–49. Huntington's thesis that international relations in the twenty-first century would be dominated by conflicts between differing religious cultures looks prescient today. His controversial article has become the focal point of debate on religion around the world within political science.

Iannaccone, Laurence R. "Sacrifice and Stigma: Reducing Free-Riding in Cults, Communes, and Other Collectives." *Journal of Political Economy* 100 (1992): 271–91. While not political science per se, the study of politics is dominated by theories of collective action. This seminal article represents a major contribution to the theories of cooperation and is highly generalizable to all sorts of political and social behavior.

Koesel, Karrie J. *Religion and Authoritarianism: Cooperation, Conflict, and the Consequences*. New York: Cambridge University Press, 2014. An important recent work that takes the economics of religious perspective into new empirical areas, namely, into the autocratic world of China and Russia.

Kuran, Timur. *The Long Divergence: How Islamic Law Held Back the Middle East*. Princeton, NJ: Princeton University Press, 2011. Using an institutional analysis, Kuran demonstrates how economic interests and concerns over political power can explain the divergent development outcomes between Europe and the Arabic world. A work that should be of relevance not only to students of religion but also to economic and political historians.

Marty, Martin E., and R. Scott Appleby, eds. *Fundamentalisms and the State: Remaking Polities, Economies, and Militance*. Chicago: University of Chicago Press, 1993. One of the first collective research projects to note the continuing (and perhaps increasing) influence that religion plays in all facets of social life. This edited volume contains a number of critical pieces by individual scholars who would continue developing this research agenda.

Stark, Rodney. *For the Glory of God: How Monotheism Led to Reformations, Science, Witch-Hunts, and the End of Slavery*. Princeton, NJ: Princeton University Press, 2007. More than any single scholar in the past half century, Stark resurrected the study of religion within sociology and also left an indelible impression on other fields. Although ostensibly historical sociology, this book provides a wide array of insights into the politics of the past and today. Stark's entire catalogue should be included, but if there is one book most important for political scientists, it is this.

Woodberry, Robert D. "The Missionary Roots of Liberal Democracy." *American Political Science Review* 106 (2012): 244–74. A very bold theory explaining how critical Protestant missionaries were in sowing the seeds of civil liberties and political democracy in the developing world. One of the most methodologically detailed articles ever to appear in the discipline's flagship journal and one that will undoubtedly set a standard for decades to come.

4

The Economics of Religion

———— ◆◆◆ ————

Charles M. North

Over the past two decades, there has been tremendous growth in the number of economists studying various aspects of religion. Iannaccone provided an article-length introduction to the field,[1] and Iyer delivered another article-length update almost two decades later.[2] McCleary edited a book-length handbook on the economics of religion,[3] and yet it failed to cover some important topics.[4] Indeed, the economics of religion has grown so much that the *Journal of Economic Literature* has given the field its own code: Z12.

Much early work in the economics of religion studied religion-as-dependent-variable topics: Why do people choose to participate in religion? What factors affect that choice? Why do strict religions succeed? How does government involvement affect the market for religion? All of these questions treat religion itself as the outcome of interest. Yet in recent years, economists have paid much more attention to religion-as-independent-variable questions: How does religion affect education, health, crime, work, earnings, migration, and more? Given the diversity of religious topics now studied by economists, the economics of religion is best defined as the use of the tools of economic analysis to study phenomena related to religion, where religion can be either the outcome of interest or the influencing factor on the outcome of interest.

In this chapter, I cannot hope to provide a full overview of the economics of religion, precisely because it has become so broad and multifaceted. Instead, I will focus mostly on how economists have analyzed religion-as-dependent-variable topics. Specifically, I will address individual religious choice, the behavior of religious organizations, and the nature of religious markets. In addition, I will discuss one religion-as-independent-variable topic: the link between religion and economic growth. This leaves out a wide array of topics in the religion-as-independent-variable category. For introductions to some of these other topics in the economics of religion, I recommend Iannaccone,[5] McCleary,[6] Part IV of Oslington,[7] and Iyer.[8]

In Section I of this chapter, I present a model of individual religious choice and explain how the addition of the concept of religious capital can refine the basic model. Section II summarizes the research on the behavior of religious organizations, and Section III discusses religious markets and regulation thereof. Section IV provides an introduction to research on religion and economic growth, and Section V concludes.

I. RELIGIOUS CHOICE OF INDIVIDUALS

Economists analyze human behavior through mathematical models of the decisions of individual agents. Based on these models, they derive predictions about human behavior in the face of changing incentives, and they test these predictions using observed and experimental data. Therefore, I will begin by presenting a model of individual religious choice and explaining how we can derive testable hypotheses from it. Thereafter, I will discuss some basic empirical results related to the model.

In the economics of religion, the seminal article on individual religious choice is by Azzi and Ehrenberg,[9] who modeled religious participation at the household level. In their model, households consisted of a husband and a wife (no children) who live for T periods. The household used time and a secular good to produce consumption in each period of the present life, and it could also devote time in each period of the present life to religious activities to generate afterlife consumption. Thus, the utility function of the household was represented by $u(C_1, C_2, \ldots, C_T, q)$, where C_t represented the household's secular consumption in period t of this life and q represented afterlife consumption.

Azzi and Ehrenberg acknowledged that, by modeling religious devotion as producing only afterlife consumption value, they were limiting their analysis of the value of religious participation to what they called the "salvation motive."[10] They recognized at least two other reasons why people might participate in religious activities: a "consumption motive" and a "social pressure motive." The consumption motive arises because people obtain this-life satisfaction from religious participation, both because they enjoy religious services and activities and because they enjoy the social aspect of activities in religious groups. The social pressure motive arises if people gain benefits in reputation, business, or other areas of life from being perceived as being devoutly religious. Though Azzi and Ehrenberg derived many interesting insights into the religious behavior of households using a model of afterlife consumption,[11] they left open how to model more general utility from all three motives for religious consumption in this life.

In an underappreciated article, Sullivan provided a simple yet valuable modification to the Azzi–Ehrenberg afterlife consumption model.[12] For one thing, he modeled religious consumption as an individual decision rather than a household one. Also, instead of distinguishing between consumption in this life and consumption in the next, Sullivan assumed that religious consumption in this life yields satisfaction in this life that might stem from any of the motives for religious consumption. Made operational, his modified assumptions led to an individual utility function of $u(C_1, C_2, \ldots, C_T; S_1, S_2, \ldots, S_T)$, where C_t represents consumption bundles of a secular good in period t and S_t represents consumption bundles of a religious service in period t. Both the secular and religious consumption bundles were produced by the individual using time and goods purchased in the market.

A Model of Individual Religious Choice

Having described the model's origins, I now present a full model of individual religious choice that merges the strengths of both Azzi and Ehrenberg[13] and Sullivan[14] into a single framework.[15] An individual who lives for T periods gains utility according to a utility function $u(C_1, C_2, \ldots, C_T; S_1, S_2, \ldots, S_T)$. The individual allocates all available time H in each period among three activities: production of a secular consumption bundle C_t using a secular good x_t and time h_t, production of a religious consumption bundle S_t using a religious service y_t and time r_t, and work for time l_t at wage w_t. The secular and religious consumption bundles are produced according to production functions $C_t(x_t, h_t)$ and $S_t(y_t, r_t)$.[16] Assuming a discount rate i, the individual's utility maximization problem can be represented as

$$\max_{h_t, r_t, l_t, x_t, y_t} U\big[C_1(x_1, h_1), C_2(x_2, h_2), \ldots, C_T(x_T, h_T);$$

$$S_1(y_1, r_1), S_2(y_2, r_2), \ldots, S_T(y_T, r_T)\big]$$

subject to the individual's income constraint

$$\sum_{t=1}^{T}\left[\frac{p_x x_t + p_y y_t}{(1+i)^{t-1}}\right] = \sum_{t=1}^{T}\left[\frac{w_t l_t}{(1+i)^{t-1}}\right]$$

and time constraint

$$h_t + r_t + l_t = H$$

for all t. The income constraint ensures that the individual earns over his or her lifetime an amount sufficient to purchase the goods used in producing the secular and religious consumption bundles, and the time constraint ensures that no time available for production is wasted.

To solve this problem, we can substitute the time constraint into the income constraint and write the individual's Lagrangian function:

$$\max_{h_t, r_t, x_t, y_t} L = U\big[C_1(x_1, h_1), C_2(x_2, h_2), \ldots, C_T(x_T, h_T);$$

$$S_1(y_1, r_1), S_2(y_2, r_2), \ldots, S_T(y_T, r_T)\big]$$

$$+ \lambda\left\{\sum_{t=1}^{T}\left[\frac{w_t(H - h_t - r_t)}{(1+i)^{t-1}}\right] - \sum_{t=1}^{T}\left[\frac{p_x x_t + p_y y_t}{(1+i)^{t-1}}\right]\right\}$$

There are four first-order conditions (plus the budget constraint arising as a first-order condition to ($\partial L / \partial \lambda$), and they can be arranged in a variety of ways to generate predictions on matters of interest. Here, I will highlight a couple of predictions derived from the model's first-order conditions as examples of how economists use this model.

First, if year-over-year wages grow faster than the discount rate i, then the individual will work more hours over time and consume fewer of both the secular and religious consumption bundles. To see this, take the first-order conditions for $\partial L/\partial h_t$ and $\partial L/\partial r_t$ for any two consecutive periods t and $t-1$, and calculate ratios to obtain the following equation:

$$\frac{(\partial U/\partial S_t)\,(\partial S_t/\partial r_t)}{(\partial U/\partial S_{t-1})\,(\partial S_{t-1}/\partial r_{t-1})} = \frac{(\partial U/\partial C_t)\,(\partial C_t/\partial h_t)}{(\partial U/\partial C_{t-1})\,(\partial C_{t-1}/\partial h_{t-1})} = \frac{w_t}{w_{t-1}(1+i)}$$

If $w_t > w_{t-1}(1+i)$, then the numerators of these ratios will exceed their denominators, which would imply lower optimal values of r_t and h_t—that is, the time devoted to producing and consuming both the religious and the secular good—and a higher value of l_t, the time devoted to working.

Second, if there is some degree of substitutability between time and money in the production of the religious consumption bundle, then an increase in earnings will lead to less time, more money, or both being spent in producing the religious bundle. Again, drawing on first-order conditions from the Lagrangian, we can divide $\partial L/\partial y_t$ by $\partial L/\partial r_t$ to yield

$$\frac{\partial S_t/\partial y_t}{\partial S_t/\partial r_t} = \frac{py}{w_t}$$

If w_t increases, then the individual's optimal solution will involve either spending more money (an increase in y_t to decrease $\partial S_t/\partial y_t$) on the religious service or spending less time (a decrease in r_t to increase $\partial S_t/\partial r_t$) producing it.[17]

The two examples just highlighted give a glimpse into the general flexibility of the Azzi/Ehrenberg/Sullivan model of individual religious choice. This model provides a general framework that can be modified as needed to develop theoretical predictions about how various factors might have an impact on religion. For example, interpretation of the equations derived above could change depending on the assumptions made about whether money and time are substitutes or complements for each other in the production of the secular and religious consumption bundles. It might be intuitively pleasing to think of time and money as substitutes in producing the secular bundle because people can spend more money to save time in acquiring food, clothing, housing, and so on. However, time and money might be complements in producing the religious bundle; after all, it is generally the case that more active church members donate higher percentages of their incomes to the church.[18] Similarly, the model could allow for an investigation into the effects of changes in the "price" of the religious good used to produce the religious consumption bundle, though this would require more specificity about the nature of that price than I have discussed here. The larger point, though, is that most economists begin their thinking about matters of individual religious choice with the framework of this model in mind. Understanding the Azzi/Ehrenberg/Sullivan framework is essential to understanding the economic approach to religion.

There are some empirical regularities in the factors correlated with higher religious attendance. As shown in Iannaccone:[19]

- Women attend religious services more often than men.
- Older people attend religious services more often than younger people.
- Married people attend religious services more often than single or divorced people. This is especially true where the husband and wife are of the same religion.
- More educated people attend church more often than less educated people.[20]
- Catholics, conservative Protestants, and sect members such as Latter-Day Saints, Jehovah's Witnesses, and Seventh-day Adventists attend church more often than "mainline" Protestants.

The Azzi/Ehrenberg/Sullivan model can be used to derive predictions of these effects, which can assist in interpreting the results—and in assessing how changes in the various prices might change the traditionally observed relationships.

Having described the basic model of individual choice, I next discuss two related items. First, I discuss how the concept of religious capital can be incorporated into the model. Second, I discuss how the availability of secular choices can affect religiosity.

Religious Capital

In discussing the production of any type of good or service, economists usually refer to inputs such as labor and capital that are used to produce outputs. In this sense, the term *capital* refers to physical capital–human-made items used in the production of something else. Physical capital includes tools, equipment, buildings, and similar physical items used to make some sort of output. Spurred by Becker,[21] economists have carried this concept of physical capital over to human beings using the concept of human capital. Put simply, human capital is the set of knowledge and skills that has built up over time and is passed on to new generations. Like physical capital, human capital is a human-made set of ideas that can be used to produce other things. Workers with more human capital are generally more productive because they have learned the best ways to accomplish their tasks.

Iannaccone extended the idea of human capital to religion,[22] sparking the religious capital approach to analyzing individual religious choice. In general, the religious capital approach views religious activities as both consumptive behavior and as an investment in religious capital. For example, a person attending a church service may directly benefit because she enjoys the service, but she is also learning more about her religion in a way that will make her an even more productive participant in the future. Such learning may be about the general tenets of the faith, about the institutional features of the religious organization, or about the particulars of the church's rituals. Each time that person returns to church, though, she will likely get more out of the service and understand better how to participate in and contribute to the service than she did the time before. In terms of our general model of individual religious choice, participating in religious activities builds religious capital, which can be added into the model through the religious production function S. Specifically, let $R_t = \sum_{t=1}^{t} r_t$. We can modify the production function for religious goods to $S(y_t, r_t, R_t)$. This is a simple and direct way to incorporate past time devoted to religion into the present production of the religious good.

To see how the model is modified by the inclusion of religious capital, note that the only change is in the calculation of the marginal product of time devoted to religious production, r_t. In the previous version of the model, $MP_r = \partial S_t / \partial r_t$. Adding in religious capital means that $MP_r = \partial S_t / \partial r_t + \partial S_t / \partial R_t$. Under the reasonable assumption that $\partial S_t / \partial R_t > 0$, then past time spent in religious production will increase today's marginal productivity of time devoted to religion.

The higher productivity of religious time will increase the marginal utility earned from additional r_t to

$$\frac{\partial U}{\partial r_t} = \frac{\partial U}{\partial S_t}\left(\frac{\partial S_t}{\partial r_t} + \frac{\partial S_t}{\partial R_t}\right)$$

instead of $\partial U/\partial r_t = (\partial U/\partial S_t)\,(\partial S_t/\partial r_t)$.

In the previous section, I showed how the basic model of individual religious choice predicts that an increase in earnings will lead to less time spent in religious participation and more time spent working. However, the predicted reduction in hours devoted to religion might not occur if we incorporate religious capital into the model. Because past religious participation builds religious capital, the marginal utility of time spent in religion will increase in period t, perhaps enough to offset the effect of w_t increasing faster than i. With regard to consumption of secular goods, it is likely that time spent producing the secular consumption bundle will decline for basic tasks such as cooking, cleaning, home maintenance, and so on. On the other hand, any secular consumption that has a human capital component (such as hobbies and avocations) may also see no decline in time devoted to it. This means that secular activities with strong human capital components—volunteer work, jogging, Sunday morning golf—should also be considered as competition for religious activities.

Of course, these effects work in reverse when wages began to flatten, which usually happens as workers approach the end of their work lives. As the individual gets older and his wage growth declines, he spends more time in both religious participation and production of the secular consumption bundle and less time at work. If the marginal products of religious capital and the time spent in religious production increase, then there will be an even more distinct increase in religious participation as people get older than the model above predicts. Thus, regardless of how particular parameters might change, introducing religious capital into the Azzi/Ehrenberg/Sullivan model generates higher predicted levels of religious participation over time because of the investment effect of current religious consumption.

Secular Consumption Options

While we have so far contemplated facets of the individual's religious choice, we have not explicitly considered the possibility that attractive secular consumption options will crowd out religious production and consumption. A pair of empirically oriented papers by Jonathan Gruber and Daniel Hungerman have explored this question.[23]

Religious organizations have long provided social welfare services to people in need. This has been true of churches in the United States for much of its history. Indeed, the availability of welfare services through religious organizations generates the potential for free riders that motivates the club goods model presented in the next section. However, the growth of government-supported welfare programs raised the possibility that church programs might be crowded out. Gruber and Hungerman examined the extent of crowd-out of church charitable spending during the New Deal's expansion of the welfare state.[24] Their dependent variable was state-level charitable spending by six denominations from 1929 to 1939. To avoid endogeneity problems caused by economic conditions affecting both church charitable spending and New Deal spending, they used a state's representatives' tenure on Appropriations Committees of the U.S. Congress as an instrument for state-level New Deal spending. They concluded that each dollar of New Deal spending crowded out 2.9 cents of church charitable spending. Annual church charitable spending between 1929 and 1932 was about 10 percent of annual New Deal spending from 1933 to 1939, and it declined by about 30 percent during the New Deal. Thus, Gruber and Hungerman calculated that nearly all of the observed decline in church charitable spending between 1933 and 1939 was attributable to crowding out by New Deal spending.[25] Gill and Lundsgaarde found a negative correlation between religious attendance and government welfare spending in a cross-sectional sample of 22 nations,[26] thus finding a crowd-out effect on church attendance rather than just church spending. However, their findings are not as carefully identified as Gruber and Hungerman's results.

In a study focused more directly on church attendance, Gruber and Hungerman studied the effect on religious attendance of relaxing secular options.[27] They used the repeal of state blue laws to identify the effect of increased Sunday options on church attendance. Blue laws outlaw shopping and other forms of commerce on Sundays; with their repeal, people could choose additional Sunday activities beyond going to church. Gruber and Hungerman found that church attendance declined following repeal of blue laws; about 15 percent of weekly church attendees began attending only two or three times a month.[28] Other attendance categories showed similar drop-offs, so that the overall effect of blue law repeal was a general downward shifting of the distribution of church attendees from more frequent to less frequent categories. Gruber and Hungerman also concluded that both church contributions and church spending declined following repeal of blue laws.[29]

Taken together, these studies indicate that secular options are legitimate alternatives to religious consumption. This result is fully consistent with the Azzi/Ehrenberg/Sullivan model of individual religious choice in that decreases in the overall price of producing the secular good should induce shifts toward producing and consuming the secular good. It also frames the discussion in Section III about religious competition, reminding us that providers of secular alternatives to religion are part of the competition for religious providers.

II. THE BEHAVIOR OF RELIGIOUS ORGANIZATIONS

Some of the earliest work in the economics of religion focused on the puzzle of why stricter religious groups enjoyed higher attendance rates and higher donations as a percentage of income. Traditional economic thinking about consumption of goods and services expects higher prices to lead to reduced quantity demanded. Applied to churches, the question is why would people have higher religious consumption in groups that impose greater monetary and/or behavioral costs? Or why would someone choose to join a religious group that requires costly and unproductive behaviors? Iannaccone provided an intriguing answer to such questions: Stricter religious groups use stigma and sacrifice to screen out less-committed potential members.[30]

Examples of the sacrifices imposed by religious groups run the gamut from relatively mild to very extreme. Conservative Protestants often expect their members to abstain from pre- and extramarital sex, and many abstain from alcohol, dancing, and other common activities. Latter-Day Saints abstain from caffeine, while Seventh-day Adventists often follow only vegetarian diets. Many Jews keep kosher diets, while Muslims refrain from eating pork and from drinking alcohol. At the other extreme are groups such as the Amish, with their traditional attire and limitations on technology uses, and Hasidic Jews, with their traditional attire and side locks. Berman described how Ultra-Orthodox Jewish men in 1980s and 1990s Israel were staying out of the labor force into their forties to spend extended time studying in *yeshiva*,[31] a religious education with very low returns in the secular job market. At the same time, fertility rates were increasing: Israeli Ultra-Orthodox women experienced an increase in total fertility rate from 6.5 children per woman in the mid-1980s to 7.6 children per woman by the mid-1990s. Thus, the choices of Ultra-Orthodox Jews were leading to high rates of poverty in very large families with able-bodied fathers voluntarily staying out of the labor force in order to pursue a purely religious education.

To answer questions about these sorts of costly and unproductive behaviors, Iannaccone proposed a model of the church as a club good.[32] Conceptually, in a club, all members contribute to the production of the club good, whose benefits are shared by everyone in the club. The members can exclude nonmembers from consuming the club good.[33] A religious organization produces community services and activities, as well as varying forms of social insurance. To implement the club goods model in the religious context, Iannaccone modified the individual's utility function in an Azzi/Ehrenberg/Sullivan model to include a variable Q that measures the quality of the club.[34] Thus, the individual's utility function became $U(S,R,Q)$, where S represents a quantity of secular goods, R represents a quantity of religious services, and Q represents the quality of the religious club. As in the Azzi/Ehrenberg/Sullivan setting, S and R are produced through household production functions. In contrast, the value of Q is determined by the average R of all other members and by the number of other club members.

With this modified utility function, Iannaccone derived equilibrium conditions very much in line with other club goods models.[35] Higher levels of participation by members would generate higher-quality Q; the opportunity to free-ride this higher Q would attract less-committed members, whose participation would reduce the value of Q for the more-committed members. As a result, all members would reduce their commitment levels, thereby lowering overall commitment levels and weakening the church. In theory, effective monitoring of commitment levels could eliminate free riding, but the types of inputs needed for an effective religious service—commitment, effort, and enthusiasm, for example—are intrinsically hard to monitor. Thus, Iannaccone showed how religious organizations could use sacrifice of secular goods or opportunities to screen out less-committed individuals such that voluntary self-sorting led to only high-commitment individuals in high-commitment churches.[36]

Mathematically, the key to Iannaccone's result was that the secular good to be sacrificed had to be a close substitute for the religious services being offered. For example, a night of socializing in pubs and restaurants is a close substitute for a night of socializing with other church members at a potluck, so church members might place a heavy emphasis on the importance of coming to the church social if you want to be part of the group. If high attendance at the church social (an increase in R) is strongly productive of higher quality (an increase in Q), then some highly committed people will forego barhopping for the church social, even as people less committed to the church will choose not only to go barhopping but also not even to attempt to free-ride other activities of the church. Once the sacrificed secular good is established, the potential church member's choice is between barhopping without joining the church and being part of the church without barhopping. For the highly committed person (who, truth be told, might enjoy some occasional barhopping), the activities of the strict church are valuable enough to make it worth giving up socializing in pubs altogether; for the less-committed person, joining the church becomes unappealing if it means no more Friday or Saturday nights in the pubs. In this way, a rule about drinking alcohol or an expectation of not socializing outside the church group turns into a mechanism whereby the most committed choose to join the group while the least committed choose not to join. The outcome is a higher-quality club experience, a higher Q in terms of the model, which increases the utility of club members relative to the free-riding outcome.

Berman used the club goods model to understand the puzzles associated with Ultra-Orthodox Jews in Israel in the 1990s:[37] Why were their working-age men impoverished and in *yeshiva* rather than working, and why were their women having more babies in an era where women in most demographic groups in Israel and around the world were having fewer babies? Berman argued that the answers flowed from increased subsidies to the Ultra-Orthodox that began after the 1977 election of a right-center coalition government in which Ultra-Orthodox parties were the swing voters.[38] For a strict religious group with a heavy social insurance component, the subsidies to the Ultra-Orthodox in the 1980s and 1990s made free riding more appealing. As a result, the Ultra-Orthodox responded by increasing the sacrifice expected of committed members. For men, that meant more years in *yeshiva* and out of the workforce. For women, that meant expectations of larger families and more babies.

In another intriguing extension of the club goods model, Berman contemplated why radical religious groups were more effective terrorists than their secular counterparts.[39] Examples included the Taliban in Afghanistan, Hamas in Gaza, and Hezbollah in southern Lebanon, each of which arose as a religious movement with no particular expertise in fighting or terrorism. What they did effectively was provide social services in places with weak states. In so doing, they learned how to use sacrifice and stigma to screen out less-committed members. The club good implication was that the members of these radical religious groups were highly committed to the group and unlikely to defect, traits that make radical religious groups more effective if they decide to turn to terrorism.

The largest theoretical advancement in the economics of religious organizations since Iannaccone[40] has been McBride's model of optimal free riding.[41] One puzzle for anyone familiar with both the club goods model and actual churches is why so many actual churches tolerate so much free riding. It is common for large numbers of people to be loosely connected to a church, while a small minority of highly committed members (or a group of paid clergy) does most of the work of the church. McBride addressed the puzzle of why free riders might still be tolerated in a club setting by adding two elements to the model: a dynamic setting and religious capital. McBride introduced a simple two-generation model where agents have a childhood period and an adulthood period, and where religious capital enhances the agent's utility from joining a church. The key result is that churches will optimally allow some level of free riding in order to generate the church members of tomorrow. In addition, McBride split churches into the categories of nonstrict, strict, and ultrastrict and made predictions by church type. First, though all churches have some free riders, strict and ultrastrict churches have fewer free riders than nonstrict churches. Second, members' contributions to the work of the church will be unequal for all churches, but contributions will be less skewed as strictness increases. Finally, the ultrastrict churches (such as Amish or the Hasidim) rely primarily on fertility for survival rather than on conversion of nonmembers.

Overall, McBride's two simple additions to the club goods model[42] made it far more consistent with stylized facts about religious organizations in competitive environments such as the United States.

One useful future direction for the study of both individual religious choice and religious organizations involves the functioning of megachurches. These churches are often defined as having at least 1,000 members, and they tend to be fairly strict in their expectations. Future studies can look into the use of small groups with strict expectations as a way to overcome the free-rider problem. Where are free-riding costs most problematic? It may be that free riders do not pull down the quality of a large worship service, especially compared to those who do not contribute to small group meetings and lessons. Also, megachurches have begun providing goods generally available in secular form, such as gyms, coffee bars, dieting programs, and financial education. Is this a way for churches to create close substitutes for secular goods in order to create a means for sacrifice of secular options? The previous two sections provide a fertile theory for analyzing such questions.

III. RELIGIOUS MARKETS

Individuals and religious organizations interact in religious markets, which may or may not feature government involvement. In general, economists think of markets as the processes by which the buyers and sellers of goods or services come together to trade. A religious market is no different—there must be some mechanism by which religious services are allocated among potential adherents. In a market, the allocation occurs through voluntary exchange between the individual and the religious organization. Though it is possible to allocate religious services through nonmarket means—such as mandatory attendance at an assigned parish—it is more common in modern developed nations for people to participate in religious services voluntarily and for the religious organizations to welcome that participation so long as the individual complies with the organization's expectations.

The simplest economic approach to modeling a market is the well-known model of supply and demand. There are problems with using a simple supply-and-demand model to study religion, though. For one, at its core, the supply-and-demand model assumes a homogeneous good and relies upon an equilibrium solution where every consumer pays the same price for the good. Religion simply does not fit this basic model. Different religious organizations have different teachings and different expectations of their members, leading to differentiated products and prices. Plus, there continues to be the problem of determining exactly what the concept of "price" represents when religion is the good. Instead of a basic supply-and-demand model, what is needed is a model rooted in differentiated products. One of the handiest models for that purpose is the Hotelling location model,[43] where differentiation is based on each firm's location in some type of space.

To date, the most complete model of religious markets is by McBride,[44] who adapted the Hotelling model to a linear space measuring the degree of strictness of religion on a [0, 1] interval. Each religious consumer has an endogenously determined, ideal level of religious strictness, and the consumer prefers a religious denomination with strictness levels close to her own ideal value. A strictness level of zero represents the choice of being nonreligious. Denominations provide religious services with a goal of maximizing their memberships while at least breaking even financially. Thus, denominations choose whether to enter the religious market and what strictness level to adopt if they do. McBride reached several conclusions about competition in religious markets. First, the individual's preferred level of strictness decreased as income increased. Second, the number of denominations and their membership sizes depended on the fixed cost of providing religious services, the profit that the denominations' resources could generate in nonreligious uses, and the technology used in providing the religious service. Third, he examined the relationships between economic growth and both religious participation and pluralism, yielding complex results.

For example, McBride concluded that a growing economy could affect religious suppliers by increasing the opportunity cost of supplying religious services, by improving the technology through which religious services are delivered, and by decreasing the direct costs of providing religious services.[45] On one hand, an increased opportunity cost of the resources of a denomination (such as increases in the secular income that clergy could earn or the rents possible from denominational land and buildings) tends to lead to fewer suppliers and less religious participation. On the other hand, improved technology and lower direct costs would encourage more entry by denominations and higher levels of religious participation. As a result, there was no clear prediction about how economic growth would affect religion.

Similarly, McBride showed that a higher return for individuals from secular activities, such as the ability to earn a higher wage from secular work, would lead to declining demand for strict religion across the entire distribution of potential adherents.[46] If the decline is strong enough, then a number of individuals are likely to choose the nonreligious alternative at the zero-strictness end of the Hotelling space. On the other hand, if increased returns from secular activities are unequal across the population, then it is likely that the beneficiaries of economic growth will demand less strict religion (and maybe even no religion), whereas those who share less in economic growth may demand even more strict denominations.

McBride's analysis[47] provided a nuanced response to the secularization hypothesis—which contends that societies move away from religious belief and practice as they get wealthier—and to critics of that hypothesis, who generally contend that freer religious markets increase religious participation.[48] Specifically, McBride demonstrated how the predicted outcomes of each side of the secularization debate could come to pass so that there are offsetting effects on religiosity from expanding wealth. His model provides an excellent response to anyone who would argue that economic development has only a unidirectional effect on religion.

Though McBride's model[49] is indeed the most complete model of a religious market developed to date, it still leaves much room for further development. For example, the strategic goals of the government are not specified, so actions of a self-interested government cannot be analyzed. Also, with only a single dimension for product differentiation, the model is not designed to study denominational choice among denominations of similar strictness levels.

Regulation of Religious Markets

So far, we have discussed religious markets in an unregulated setting. But most religious markets have some level of government involvement, ranging from support (such as state church and subsidies) to hindrance (such as restrictions and outright bans). In this section, I discuss the research on regulation of religious markets.[50] As with the study of religious markets generally, there is not yet a well-specified model of strategic decisions by individuals, religious organizations, and governments. The final section of McBride examines the choices of individuals and organizations in the context of government restrictions on both religious and secular goods.[51] I will conclude this section with insights from that model after describing the literature as it currently stands.

Sociologists conducted the earliest empirical research on the regulation of religious markets. They mainly allowed a Herfindahl-based measure of religious pluralism to proxy for government regulation, implicitly reasoning that restrictions on disfavored religions would lead to a single or small number of dominant churches. Specifically, if s_i is church i's share of all church members in a place (such as a city, county, or country),[52] then the Pluralism Index is defined as

$$PI = 1 - \sum_{t=1}^{N} s_i^2,$$

where N is the total number of churches in the market and $0 \leq s_i \leq 1$. A Pluralism Index of 0 indicates a highly concentrated market; if there is only one church, then its share is equal to 1 and the Pluralism Index is equal to 0. In contrast, a religious market with many small churches will have a Pluralism Index near 1.

Some very prominent sociologists conducted a large number of studies on the relationship between religious participation and religious pluralism, beginning with Finke and Stark[53] and Breault.[54] In a summary article, Chaves and Gorski concluded that there were numerous studies split between finding positive and negative relationships between participation and pluralism.[55] The entire stream of literature came to an abrupt end when Voas, Crockett, and Olson demonstrated that many results were simply a mathematical artifact of calculating the pluralism and participation measures from the same data series.[56]

There was a benefit from the sociologists' decade-long debate over pluralism and participation. Voas and associates cleared the way for social scientists to think about religious competition in the same way that economists think about competition in markets for other types of goods: in terms of barriers to entry and other forms of imperfect competition.[57] North and Gwin examined the relationship between religious attendance and several types of government intervention in religious markets.[58] With a cross-section of fifty-nine countries from the first three waves of the World Values Survey (WVS), they created dummy variables for nine factors reflecting government intervention in religious markets, including official state religion, restrictions on foreign missionaries, censoring of religious beliefs and media, government financial support for churches, and so on. They constructed a simple regulation index equal to the sum of the nine dummy variables,[59] which across countries ranged in value from zero to six. North and Gwin found a significant negative correlation between this index and religious attendance, such that a one-point increase in the index was associated with a reduction in attendance by 3.3 percent of the total population.[60]

North and Gwin also constructed a variable measuring years of religious freedom, defined as the survey year minus the first year that a country created formal legal protection of religious freedom.[61] They found that each decade of religious freedom was associated with increased attendance of 1.2 percent of the population. Similarly, an official state religion was associated with a 14.6 percentage point reduction in attendance. Overall, they concluded that state restrictions on religious competition had substantial negative effects on religious participation.

Two other papers addressing regulation of religious markets were by McCleary and Barro.[62] Both papers used similar methodologies on somewhat different datasets. In the first paper, the data represented a cross-section of sixty-eight countries drawn from the first three waves of the WVS, the 1991 and 1998 waves of the International Social Survey Programme, and the 1999 Gallup Millennium Survey; the second paper analyzed a total of eighty-one countries by adding the fourth wave of the WVS. In both papers, McCleary and Barro found that state religion had a positive effect on religious attendance, while state regulation had a negative effect. The most reasonable interpretation is that their state religion variable was capturing a subsidy effect such that the two variables effectively offset each other. That is, most countries with a state religion also have restrictions on competition with the state church, and the two interventions offset each other.

The most recent literature on the regulation of religious markets is taking advantage of better measures of government regulation. Both Jonathan Fox's Religion and State (RAS) project[63] and Grim and Finke's International Religion Indexes provide more carefully constructed measures of government's intervention in religious markets.[64] Fox's RAS project constructed an index of government involvement in religion, comprised of subindices measuring "official support" for religion, "general restrictions" on some or all religions, "religious discrimination" against minority religions, "religious regulation" on most or all religions, and "religious legislation" whereby government enforces religious teachings through law. Grim and Finke used the U.S. State Department's International Religious Freedom reports to construct indices measuring government regulation of religion, government favoritism of religion, and social regulation of religion.

Economic research is still limited in this area following the creation of the newer indices of governmental involvement. Using the same sample as McCleary and Barro,[65] Fox and Tabory found that the RAS measures of religious involvement were generally negatively correlated with religious attendance, including their "official support" index.[66] Similarly, they found little evidence that the RAS indices affected measures of beliefs in God, heaven, hell, or an afterlife. In a preliminary look at both the RAS and the Grim/Finke indices, Swift was able to expand his sample to ninety-two countries with the fourth and fifth waves of the WVS, and to 116 countries from the Gallup World Poll.[67] It is important to note that his sample included more non-Western and non-Christian countries than prior research. Contrary to most of the previous research, he found few correlations between religious attendance and the various measures of government intervention when analyzing the whole sample. On the other hand, when he limited his analysis to the smaller samples from earlier papers, he found the same negative effects on attendance as prior research. One implication is that the negative effect of government involvement in religion may be a phenomenon of only Western countries, and perhaps only Protestant ones.

This set of empirical results draws us back to the final section of McBride,[68] in which he used his model to examine how government regulation of markets for both religious and secular goods might affect religious participation. In a country where regulations prohibit entry of new churches but fail to punish nonattendees, he predicted that the state-run monopoly church would embrace a minimal level of strictness, that most people would affiliate with the state church, but that attendance would be low. This describes well the Protestant state churches of Scandinavia, and even the current-day versions of the Catholic Church in southern Europe. Finally, he turned his attention to state-religion countries that prevent entry by religious competition and that also place substantial restrictions on secular goods and activities. In such a setting, McBride predicted that a state monopoly religion could adopt higher levels of strictness and still maintain high levels of affiliation and attendance. This result harkens back to the crowd-out findings of Gruber and Hungerman[69] in that high-cost secular activities are less attractive than religious ones, even in the face of a strictness level higher than an individual might desire.

To conclude this section, I note that the nature of competition in religious markets can be as varied and complicated as the nature of competition in markets for secular products such as soap, gasoline, pharmaceuticals, and legal services. As a result, there is much room for work by economists who specialize in studying market structures. At a minimum, we know that religious markets can see a wide variety of outcomes from seemingly similar shocks and government interventions. Even so, at least in developed countries, state intervention in religious markets appears to reduce religious participation. Tied back to the concept of religious capital, this means that succeeding generations might grow up less "churched" than their ancestors, thereby lowering their utility from church participation and making it harder to draw them back to the churches. McBride's model[70] suggests that lax regulation of secular activities (such as the blue law repeal studied by Gruber and Hungerman[71]) can have a similar depressive effect on church attendance, which then reverberates through subsequent generations via the channel of low religious capital. It may well be that the apparent proliferation in recent years of religious "nones" (adults who claim no religious affiliation) is an outgrowth of greater secular competition in the last few decades, thus crowding out the childhood church attendance, and thus the religious capital, of several generations.

IV. RELIGION AND ECONOMIC GROWTH

The relationship between religion and economic growth has generated much heat and some light among economists and other social scientists. The seminal volley came from Max Weber in *The Protestant Ethic and the Spirit of Capitalism*.[72] Weber contended that the modern capitalist economy arose because of a "spirit of capitalism," an ethos that viewed profit and hard work as ends in themselves rather than as means to some other goal. The spirit of capitalism meant that people did not choose to earn money for hedonistic purposes; rather, frugality amid wealth was the guiding virtue. Weber attributed the spirit of capitalism to the predestination theology of Calvinists, the idea that God had already determined each person's salvation and that the individual was powerless to alter God's already-made choice. Weber thought that individual Calvinists (and other Protestants to a lesser degree) would have a psychological need to demonstrate to themselves and others that they were among God's chosen. Combined with Martin Luther's idea of calling, Weber contended that Protestants embraced the virtues of work and success in a calling as evidence of their salvation. Thus arose the spirit of capitalism among certain Protestants, which Weber believed led to an accumulation of capital and wealth in places where Protestantism was dominant. In Weber's eyes, this spirit of capitalism was an essential ingredient in the growth of modern capitalism and, by extension, what modern economists think of as economic growth.

A number of authors have disputed Weber's hypothesis on both theological and empirical grounds.[73] In a recent study of the connection between religious affiliation and economic success, Cantoni examined preindustrial economic growth of 272 cities in Germany from 1300 to 1900,[74] focusing on whether they became Protestant or remained Catholic during the Reformation. Using population growth as a proxy for economic growth, he found no significant differences in population growth rates between cities that became Protestant and those that remained Catholic. These findings suggest that, at least in this one place prior to the Industrial Revolution, variations in religious affiliations may not have affected economic outcomes.

Even so, contemporary gross domestic product (GDP) per capita varies substantially across countries when sorted by their largest religious groups. Table 4.1 reports the mean GDP per capita in 2001 for groups of countries based on their largest religious groups in the year 1900. Countries whose largest religious group was Protestant, Catholic, or an Asian ethnic religion had higher GDP per capita than countries whose largest groups were other religions. Table 4.1 does not prove that religion has any causal effect on economic growth and development, but it raises questions about whether certain religions might have a positive effect on economic growth.

Table 4.1. GDP per capita in 2001, by largest religious group in country*

Largest Religious Group	Number of Countries	Mean GDP per Capita in 2001
African ethnic religion	36	$2,067
Asian ethnic religion	8	15,088
Buddhist	8	6,025
Catholic	53	13,030
Hindu	4	4,800
Islam	41	6,091
Orthodox	13	7,223
Protestant	38	16,545

*This table shows the unweighted mean GDP per capita in 2001 for different countries based on their largest religious group in 1900. GDP per capita is measured in PPP dollars.

Source: Table 2 of Charles M. North, Wafa Hakim Orman, and Carl R. Gwin, "Religion, Corruption, and the Rule of Law," *Journal of Money, Credit and Banking* 45 (2013): 757–79.

A prominent exploration of religion's effect on economic growth was by Barro and McCleary.[75] They examined the role of religious attendance, beliefs in heaven and hell, and religious denomination on country-level growth rates in GDP per capita for a sample of forty-one countries in the second half of the twentieth century. Employing reduced-form linear estimations of ten-year growth rates, they found that religious beliefs (especially strength of the belief in hell) were positively correlated with economic growth, while religious attendance was negatively correlated with economic growth. They rightly viewed attendance as an input into the production of beliefs, so their results can best be explained in this way: Given a certain level of attendance, higher religious beliefs reflect more efficient religious productivity and are associated with more economic growth. In sum, Barro and McCleary showed that strong correlations exist between measures of religiosity and ten-year economic growth outcomes, and they speculated that "stronger religious beliefs stimulate growth because they help sustain specific individual behaviors that enhance productivity."[76] However, their statistical analysis was not sufficient to prove this claim, leaving open a variety of possible avenues by which religion might affect economic growth.[77]

Current research suggests several plausible mechanisms by which Protestant regions in Europe and elsewhere may have become more economically developed than Catholic regions. However, these mechanisms generally are not direct effects of theological differences, as Weber had argued.[78] Instead, the most plausible avenues by which Protestantism may have fostered economic growth involve secondary effects of Protestantism: changes in nonreligious attitudes, changes in allocation of resources, changes in education and literacy, and changes in compliance with rule of law. The next several paragraphs present examples of each of these mechanisms.

One possibility is that at least some religions foster progrowth beliefs, as Weber contended.[79] In a thorough analysis of WVS data, Guiso, Sapienza, and Zingales concluded that, on balance, religious people exhibited beliefs and attitudes conducive to economic growth.[80] The WVS was a sample of thousands of individuals across sixty-six countries, many of them high- and middle-income. Guiso and associates examined correlations between religion and survey responses on attitudes toward cooperation, the role of women in society, government, legal rules, market economies, and thrift. Key findings included that religious people were generally more trusting of others and of the government, and they were more inclined to comply with the law and to believe that markets are fair. The positive correlation with trust in others was driven by churchgoing Christians, with the effect among Protestants more strongly positive than among Catholics, and no significant effect among other denominations. All denominations except for Buddhists were associated with higher trust in government, the effect being strongest among Hindus and Muslims. Overall, the authors concluded, "Christian religions are more positively associated with attitudes conducive to economic growth, while religious Muslims are the most anti-market. Within Christian denominations, the ranking is unclear: Protestants are more trusting and favor incentives more, Catholics are thriftier and favor private property and competition more."[81]

Two possible mechanisms linking Protestantism to economic growth are Reformation-era shifts of resources and changes in legal institutions that favored the expansion of commerce. Ekelund, Hébert, and Tollison argued that the medieval Roman Catholic Church functioned as a monopolist that could price-discriminate across believers,[82] charging prices near the maximum that each person was willing to pay.[83] Part of the reason that the Protestant Reformation succeeded, they contended, was that it undermined the ability of the Catholic Church to extract wealth through price discrimination.[84] While the Catholic Church successfully used limit-pricing strategies in regions of Europe where land rents were the biggest source of income, it had less information about ability and willingness-to-pay of the merchants and other commercial interests who predominated in the areas that became Protestant. The consequence of this process was that areas that became Protestant would have had less extractive rules of property and contract. Following this logic, it was the shift toward commerce that paved the way both for Protestantism and for institutions that foster economic growth.

Another consequence of the Protestant Reformation, as described by Ekelund and associates, was a reduction in the number of religious holidays ("holy days"), which permitted more days of work and thus greater productivity of labor.[85] This idea was substantially expanded by Cantoni, Dittmar, and Yuchtman,[86] who looked at the interplay between competition in the religious market and competition in the market for political legitimation of rulers. They proposed that political leaders relied heavily on religious leaders for legitimation in the decades before and after the Reformation, and that the Reformers offered legitimation to rulers at a lower price than the Catholic Church. The shifting of political legitimation in Germany from the Catholic Church to Lutherans had several effects, all of which shifted resources from religious functions to secular ones. First, graduates from German universities that became Protestant shifted toward earning a higher number of degrees in secular subjects (especially law and the arts) rather than theology. Second, these same graduates were more likely after the Reformation to work in secular (especially government) occupations than before. In both instances, graduates of the universities that remained Catholic continued to earn theological degrees and embark on careers in the Catholic Church at the same rates as before the Reformation. Third, the authors found that German cities and towns that became Protestant increased construction of secular projects, especially palaces for the rulers and administrative buildings for their growing governments. The Catholic towns did not experience the same growth in secular construction. All in all, Cantoni and colleagues concluded that the Protestant Reformation allowed rulers to obtain religious legitimation at a lower price, which in turn shifted more elite human and physical capital to secular production uses.[87]

In a related argument, Rubin contended that rulers in areas that became Protestant also shifted their sources of legitimation from religious authorities to parliaments composed of economic elites primarily engaged in commerce, such as merchants, craftspeople, money changers, commercial farmers, and others engaged in production for markets.[88] To win the approval of the economic elites, rulers embraced laws and other institutions that benefited commercial activity. For Rubin,[89] Cantoni and associates,[90] and Ekelund and colleagues,[91] the links between Protestantism and economic growth ran through secondary effects: the shifting of human and physical capital to secular uses, an increase in the number of productive workdays, and the adoption of new legal institutions more favorable to commerce. None of these was a tenet of Protestant theology; rather, they were consequences, perhaps unintended, of the Reformation.

Another channel by which Protestantism could have caused economic growth is increased human capital. Martin Luther and his followers emphasized the importance for each believer of being able to read the Bible on his or her own, without mediation through the church or a priest. As a result, Luther advocated universal schooling in order to increase literacy of the German population. Relying on this Lutheran emphasis on schooling, Becker and Woessman examined whether Protestantism induced higher rates of literacy in nineteenth-century Prussia.[92] To avoid potential reverse causality (that higher literacy rates may have led to more Protestants), they used distance to Wittenberg as an instrumental variable for the Protestant share of the population in each Prussian county. Using data from the 1871 Prussian census, Becker and Woessman found a strong effect of Protestant population share on literacy rates in Prussian counties. Additional analysis suggested that much—or perhaps all—of the differences in incomes between Protestant and Catholic counties could be explained by differences in human capital.

Woodberry provided a global analysis[93] of the links between nineteenth- and early twentieth-century "Conversionary Protestant" missionaries[94] and the growth of democracy. He argued that, in country after country, Conversionary Protestant missionaries created written alphabets in the vernacular where none existed, translated the Bible and wrote other pamphlets and tracts to spread their messages, and began mass printing of those materials in order to convert new believers. Through both historical and statistical analysis, Woodberry showed that, all over the world, such missionaries were positively associated—and likely causally connected—with the introduction of mass printing, the expansion of mass education,[95] the emergence of civil society, and the imposition of rule of law on colonial governments. The first two factors reinforce Becker and Woessman's conclusion that Protestants caused higher literacy rates in Prussia,[96] and the latter two factors provide support for the idea (discussed in the next few paragraphs) that Christianity had important consequences for the rule of law and other institutions favorable to economic growth.

The rule of law is the final mechanism linking religion and economic growth that I will discuss. Perhaps maintaining the rule of law is easier or less expensive among a religious population. For example, followers of a religion with a strong moral code might be more inclined to comply with secular laws restraining immoral behavior; Guiso, Sapienza, and Zingales found such effects in their analysis of WVS data.[97] Beyond personal compliance with the law, followers of a morality-based religion might demand that their governments enact laws upholding their moral tenets. From the government's perspective, enforcing the law is less expensive when there are fewer violators to catch. For these reasons, North, Orman, and Gwin examined the relationship between religious affiliation and the rule of law in a sample of 207 countries.[98] They concluded that a country's largest religious group in 1900 A.D. was significantly correlated with its rule of law in 2004, with Protestant and Catholic religions having more positive effects on rule of law than Islam, African ethnic religions, and Orthodox Christianity. These findings raised a puzzle though—why would the two Western Christian religions be so favorable toward rule of law, while Eastern Christianity had the most negative correlation of all religions examined? The basic theology of interpersonal behavior and trust is not dramatically different between the Western and Eastern branches, so how could any link between religion and the rule of law flow from theological teachings?

These questions prompted North and Gwin to sketch an outline of answers.[99] They argued that the medieval Roman Catholic Church created its own judicial system, which over time developed the types of limitations on government power central to modern conceptions of the rule of law. The medieval Roman Catholic Church had substantial wealth, especially in its monastic landholdings, and many rulers were tempted to appropriate those lands. The ecclesiastical courts of the eleventh and twelfth centuries used the credibility and transnational influence of the church to set up legal doctrines that protected the wealth of landowners against an arbitrary state. In the process of protecting itself, though, the church incidentally began developing a body of law limiting the state more generally, and this body of law eventually made its way in various forms into the secular laws of Western Europe. North and Gwin contended that this body of law was the foundation on which modern rule of law was built.[100]

So far, this section has paid much attention to the differential effects on economic growth of Protestantism versus Catholicism. However, another set of literature focuses on broader comparative development questions related to religion. Some of these have already been mentioned.[101] One very important contributor is Timur Kuran and his analysis of the underdevelopment of the Islamic Middle East.[102] Though he has made numerous contributions to this literature, much of it is summarized in *The Long Divergence*.[103] Kuran first noted that the Middle East fell behind Europe economically at some point between 1000 A.D. and 1750 A.D. Thereafter, he provided detailed explanations of numerous legal institutions that likely hindered economic development in the Middle East. For example, the Islamic inheritance system established in the Qur'an required division of the deceased's assets across numerous heirs. The effect over time was to inhibit the concentration of productive capital in the hands of any continuing commercial enterprise. The problem was magnified by the lack of efficient business structures beyond simple partnerships that dissolved on the exit or death of any partner, a structure not directly mandated in the Qur'an. Instead, the most common enduring form of business organization was the *waqf*, which was a charitable trust that could endure in perpetuity but also was not permitted to change its purpose.

Why was the *waqf* a less effective form of business organization than a corporation? Consider a family who chose to avoid dispersion of its wealth (and taxation) by donating land and other productive assets to a *waqf* that supported a charitable purpose, such as a caravansary (a fortified inn along a trade route). The family wealth could be preserved, and succeeding generations could continue to manage the caravansary. Over time, though, trade routes change, and the need for a caravansary might diminish, yet the legal rules governing the *waqf* prohibited diverting productive resources away from the obsolete caravansary. Thus, the *waqf*, intended to provide beneficial social services, became a hindrance to adapting property to more efficient uses in response to changing circumstances.[104]

To summarize this section, evidence suggests that religion is related in meaningful ways to economic growth. Contrary to the Weber hypothesis, the main effect of religion does not appear to flow through doctrines and beliefs. Instead, religion has altered other factors—increased schooling, individual rights, laws limiting state power, laws enabling commerce—in numerous ways, which in turn have an important impact on the ability of a macroeconomy to grow. Research on the Weber hypothesis in its widest sense continues, and opportunities abound to explore pathways by which religion may advance or inhibit economic growth.

V. CONCLUSION

The economics of religion is still a young field, though it has matured into one too large to describe in a single chapter. For this reason, I have focused on four areas of research within the economics of religion. Three of them are at the core of the religion-as-dependent-variable scholarship: individual religious choice, religious organizations, and religious markets. The fourth—religion and economic growth—is a popular example of religion-as-independent-variable scholarship. While many opportunities remain for future work, much of the growth in the field has been through religion-as-independent-variable research; examples from recent conferences include studies of the effects of religion on health, education, gender norms, U.S. Supreme Court voting, political outcomes, trust among individuals, and more. There is a tremendous need for improvement in theory and measurement, and unexplored topics in all categories abound. Religion is still alive in our modern world, and economic research into religion and its effects promises fascinating future insights.

ACKNOWLEDGMENTS

In writing this chapter, I am drawing on insights from conversations over many years with numerous friends and fellow researchers in the economics of religion. I cannot possibly name all of those who have played a role in this chapter, but I would be remiss in not acknowledging the following people who have had a profound influence on my understanding of the application of economic theory to the study of religion: Anthony Gill, Carl Gwin, Daniel Hungerman, Laurence Iannaccone, Timur Kuran, Michael Makowsky, Michael McBride, Robert Mochrie, Wafa Orman, Rodney Stark, and Marc von der Ruhr. To those that I have failed to mention, I apologize. For any errors that may appear in this chapter, I accept full responsibility.

NOTES

1. Laurence R. Iannaccone, "Introduction to the Economics of Religion," *Journal of Economic Literature* 36 (1998): 1465–96.
2. Sriya Iyer, "The New Economics of Religion," *Journal of Economic Literature* 54 (2016): 395–441.
3. Rachel M. McCleary, ed., *The Oxford Handbook of the Economics of Religion* (New York: Oxford University Press, 2011).
4. See Charles M. North, "*The Oxford Handbook of the Economics of Religion*, Rachel M. McCleary, ed., 2011" [Book review], *Faith & Economics* 63 (2014): 60–64, for a review of McCleary, *The Oxford Handbook of the Economics of Religion*.
5. Iannaccone, "Introduction to the Economics of Religion."
6. McCleary, *The Oxford Handbook of the Economics of Religion*.
7. Paul Oslington, ed., *The Oxford Handbook of Christianity and Economics* (New York: Oxford University Press, 2014).
8. Iyer, "The New Economics of Religion."
9. Corry Azzi and Ronald Ehrenberg, "Household Allocation of Time and Church Attendance," *Journal of Political Economy* 83 (1975): 27–56.
10. Ibid.
11. Ibid.
12. Dennis H. Sullivan, "Simultaneous Determination of Church Contributions and Church Attendance," *Economic Inquiry* 23 (1985): 309–20.
13. Azzi and Ehrenberg, "Household Allocation of Time and Church Attendance."
14. Sullivan, "Simultaneous Determination of Church Contributions and Church Attendance."
15. I will follow the exposition of Charles M. North and Carl R. Gwin, "Religious Freedom and the Unintended Consequences of State Religion," *Southern Economic Journal* 71 (2004): 103–17. My co-author Carl Gwin did much of the hard work in synthesizing the two models and developing the modeling approach that I now present.

16. The functional forms of $C_t(\,\cdot\,)$ and $S_t(\,\cdot\,)$ do not change over time. The subscripts are included to identify each particular year t.
17. Note that this result mirrors an intuitively pleasing conclusion regarding the secular consumption bundle. A similar calculation for the secular good would yield the following equilibrium condition:

$$\frac{\partial C_t / \partial x_t}{\partial C_t / \partial h_t} = \frac{p_x}{w_t}$$

This equation implies that an increase in the wage w_t would lead an individual to shift production of the secular consumption bundle toward spending more on the good x_t and using less time h_t to produce it. In lay terms, when income goes up, people spend more money to consume meals that require less time to prepare and clean up.
18. For example, Charles M. North, Wafa Hakim Orman, and Carl R. Gwin, "Giving: The Rich, the Poor, and the Widow's Mite," in *What Americans Really Believe: New Findings from the Baylor Surveys of Religion*, ed. Rodney Stark (Waco, TX: Baylor University Press, 2008), 95–100. In contrast, Jonathan Gruber, "Pay or Pray? The Impact of Charitable Subsidies on Religious Attendance," *Journal of Public Economics* 88 (2004): 2635–55, concluded that religious giving and religious attendance were substitutes.
19. Iannaccone, "Introduction to the Economics of Religion."
20. For a contrary result, see Daniel M. Hungerman, "The Effect of Education on Religion: Evidence from Compulsory Schooling Laws," *Journal of Economic Behavior and Organization* 104 (2014): 52–63.
21. Gary S. Becker, *Human Capital: A Theoretical and Empirical Analysis, with Special Reference to Education* (New York: National Bureau of Economic Research, 1964).
22. Laurence R. Iannaccone, "Religious Practice: A Human Capital Approach," *Journal for the Scientific Study of Religion* 29 (1990): 297–314.
23. Two papers by Jonathan Gruber and Daniel M. Hungerman: "The Church Versus the Mall: What Happens When Religion Faces Increased Secular Competition?," *The Quarterly Journal of Economics* 123 (2008): 831–62; and "Faith-Based Charity and Crowd-Out during the Great Depression," *Journal of Public Economics* 91 (2007): 1043–69.
24. Gruber and Hungerman, "Faith-Based Charity and Crowd-Out during the Great Depression."
25. Ibid.
26. Anthony Gill and Erik Lundsgaarde, "State Welfare Spending and Religiosity: A Cross-National Analysis," *Rationality and Society* 16 (2004): 399–436.

27. Gruber and Hungerman, "The Church versus the Mall."

28. Ibid.

29. Ibid.

30. Laurence R. Iannaccone, "Sacrifice and Stigma: Reducing Free-riding in Cults, Communes, and Other Collectives," *Journal of Political Economy* 100 (1992): 271–91.

31. Eli Berman, "Sect, Subsidy, and Sacrifice: An Economist's View of Ultra-Orthodox Jews," *The Quarterly Journal of Economics* 115 (2000): 905–53.

32. Iannaccone, "Sacrifice and Stigma."

33. Excludability distinguishes club goods from public goods.

34. Iannaccone, "Sacrifice and Stigma."

35. Ibid.

36. Incurring a stigma has the same effect. In religious settings, stigma can take the form of distinct modes of dress and other appearance, such as a *yarmulke* for Orthodox Jews or the distinctive dress of the Amish.

37. Berman, "Sect, Subsidy, and Sacrifice."

38. Ibid.

39. Eli Berman, *Radical, Religious, and Violent: The New Economics of Terrorism* (Cambridge, MA: The MIT Press, 2009).

40. Iannaccone, "Sacrifice and Stigma."

41. Michael McBride, "Why Churches Need Free-Riders: Religious Capital Formation and Religious Group Survival," *Journal of Behavioral and Experimental Economics* 58 (2015): 77–87.

42. Ibid.

43. Harold Hotelling, "Stability in Competition," *The Economic Journal* 39 (1929): 41–57.

44. Michael McBride, "Religious Market Competition in a Richer World," *Economica* 77 (2010): 148–71.

45. Ibid.

46. Ibid.

47. Ibid.

48. An early presentation of the secularization hypothesis is Peter L. Berger's *The Sacred Canopy: Elements of a Sociological Theory of Religion* (Garden City, NY: Doubleday, 1967). For a vigorous rejection of the secularization hypothesis, see chap. 3 of Rodney Stark and Roger Finke, *Acts of Faith: Explaining the Human Side of Religion* (Berkeley: University of California Press, 2000).

49. McBride, "Religious Market Competition in a Richer World."

50. A more complete treatment of the regulation of religious markets is available in Charles M. North, "Regulation of Religious Markets,"

in *The Oxford Handbook of Christianity and Economics*, ed. Paul Oslington (Oxford, UK: Oxford University Press, 2014), 489–511.

51. McBride, "Religious Market Competition in a Richer World."

52. Note that S_t is defined as a share of the population that is churchgoing, not of the total population.

53. Roger Finke and Rodney Stark, "Religious Economies and Sacred Canopies: Religious Mobilization in American Cities, 1906," *American Sociological Review* 53 (1988): 41–49.

54. Kevin D. Breault, "New Evidence on Religious Pluralism, Urbanism, and Religious Participation," *American Sociological Review* 54 (1989): 1048–53.

55. Mark Chaves and Philip S. Gorski, "Religious Pluralism and Religious Participation," *Annual Review of Sociology* 27 (2001): 261–81.

56. David Voas, Alasdair Crockett, and Daniel V.A. Olson, "Religious Pluralism and Participation: Why Previous Research Is Wrong," *American Sociological Review* 67 (2002): 212–30.

57. Ibid.

58. North and Gwin, "Religious Freedom and the Unintended Consequences of State Religion."

59. This index mimicked an earlier one used by sociologists Mark Chaves and David E. Cann in "Regulation, Pluralism, and Religious Market Structure: Explaining Religion's Vitality," *Rationality and Society* 4 (1992): 272–90.

60. North and Gwin, "Religious Freedom and the Unintended Consequences of State Religion."

61. Ibid.

62. Two papers by Rachel M. McCleary and Robert J. Barro: "Religion and Political Economy in an International Panel," *Journal for the Scientific Study of Religion* 45 (2006): 149–75; and "Religion and Economy," *The Journal of Economic Perspectives* 20 (2006): 49–72.

63. Jonathan Fox and Shmuel Sandler, "Quantifying Religion: Toward Building More Effective Ways of Measuring Religious Influence on State-Level Behavior," *Journal of Church and State* 45 (2003): 559–88; Jonathan Fox, *A World Survey of Religion and the State* (Cambridge, UK: Cambridge University Press, 2008); and Jonathan Fox and Ephraim Tabory, "Contemporary Evidence Regarding the Impact of State Regulation of Religion on Religious Participation and Belief," *Sociology of Religion* 69 (2008): 245–71.

64. Brian J. Grim and Roger Finke, "International Religion Indexes: Government Regulation, Government Favoritism, and Social Regulation of Religion," *Interdisciplinary Journal of Research on Religion* 2 (2006): Article 1.

65. McCleary and Barro, "Religion and Economy."
66. Fox and Tabory, "Contemporary Evidence Regarding the Impact of State Regulation of Religion on Religious Participation and Belief."
67. Matthew Swift, "Reexamining the Effects of State Religion on Religious Service Attendance," honors thesis (Waco, TX: Baylor University, 2010).
68. McBride, "Religious Market Competition in a Richer World."
69. Gruber and Hungerman, "Faith-Based Charity and Crowd-Out during the Great Depression," and "The Church versus the Mall."
70. McBride, "Religious Market Competition in a Richer World."
71. Gruber and Hungerman, "The Church versus the Mall."
72. Max Weber, *The Protestant Ethic and the Spirit of Capitalism* [1904–1905], trans. Talcott Parsons [1930] (London: Routledge, 1992).
73. Kurt Samuelsson, *Religion and Economic Action: A Critique of Max Weber* [1957], trans. E. Geoffrey French (New York: Basic Books, 1961); Jacques Delacroix and François Nielsen, "The Beloved Myth: Protestantism and the Rise of Industrial Capitalism in Nineteenth-Century Europe," *Social Forces* 80 (2001): 509–53; Benito Arruñada, "Protestants and Catholics: Similar Work Ethic, Different Social Ethic," *The Economic Journal* 120 (2010): 890–918; and two works by Rodney Stark: "SSSR Presidential Address, 2004: Putting an End to Ancestor Worship," *Journal for the Scientific Study of Religion* 43 (2004): 465–75, and *The Victory of Reason: How Christianity Led to Freedom, Capitalism, and Western Success* (New York: Random House, 2005).
74. Davide Cantoni, "The Economic Effects of the Protestant Reformation: Testing the Weber Hypothesis in the German Lands," *Journal of the European Economic Association* 13 (2015): 561–98.
75. Robert J. Barro and Rachel McCleary, "Religion and Economic Growth across Countries," *American Sociological Review* 68 (2003): 760–81.
76. Ibid., 779.
77. See Steven N. Durlauf, Andros Kourtellos, and Chih Ming Tan, "Is God in the Details? A Reexamination of the Role of Religion in Economic Growth," *Journal of Applied Econometrics* 27 (2012): 1059–75, who used Bayesian model averaging to analyze whether Barro and McCleary's religion variables belonged in a true model of economic growth. They concluded that none of the variables survived the probabilistic determination of which variables should be included in a model of economic growth.
78. Weber, *The Protestant Ethic and the Spirit of Capitalism*.
79. Ibid.
80. Luigi Guiso, Paola Sapienza, and Luigi Zingales, "People's Opium? Religion and Economic Attitudes," *Journal of Monetary Economics* 50 (2003): 225–82.

81. Ibid., 228.
82. Robert B. Ekelund, Jr., Robert F. Hébert, and Robert D. Tollison, *The Marketplace of Christianity* (Cambridge, MA: The MIT Press, 2006).
83. The argument that the medieval Church was a rent-seeking monopoly was more fully presented in Robert B. Ekelund, Jr., Robert F. Hébert, Robert D. Tollison, Gary M. Anderson, and Audrey B. Davidson, *Sacred Trust: The Medieval Church as an Economic Firm* (New York: Oxford University Press, 1996).
84. Ekelund et al., *The Marketplace of Christianity.*
85. Ibid.
86. Davide Cantoni, Jeremiah Dittmar, and Noam Yuchtman, "Religious Competition and Reallocation: The Political Economy of Secularization in the Protestant Reformation," NBER Working Paper No. 23934 (Cambridge, MA: National Bureau of Economic Research, 2017).
87. Ibid.
88. Jared Rubin, *Rulers, Religion, and Riches: Why the West Got Rich and the Middle East Did Not* (New York: Cambridge University Press, 2017).
89. Ibid.
90. Cantoni et al., "Religious Competition and Reallocation."
91. Ekelund et al., *The Marketplace of Christianity.*
92. Sascha O. Becker and Ludger Woessmann, "Was Weber Wrong? A Human Capital Theory of Protestant Economic History," *The Quarterly Journal of Economics* 124 (2009): 531–96.
93. Robert D. Woodberry, "The Missionary Roots of Liberal Democracy," *American Political Science Review* 106 (2012): 244–74.
94. "*Conversionary Protestants* (1) actively attempt to persuade others of their beliefs, (2) emphasize lay vernacular Bible reading, and (3) believe that grace/faith/choice saves people, not group membership or sacraments. CPs are not necessarily orthodox or conservative" (Woodberry, "The Missionary Roots of Liberal Democracy," 244, n. 1).
95. Francisco A. Gallego and Robert Woodberry, "Christian Missionaries and Education in Former African Colonies: How Competition Mattered," *Journal of African Economies* 19 (2010): 294–329, found positive effects of Protestant missionaries in Africa. This article emphasized the role of competition in encouraging Catholic missionaries to provide more and better schooling in African regions where Protestant competition was allowed on an equal footing, a conclusion that combines the literature on religious competition with the literature on religion and economic growth.
96. Becker and Woessman, "Was Weber Wrong?"
97. Guiso et al., "People's Opium?"

98. Charles M. North, Wafa Hakim Orman, and Carl R. Gwin, "Religion, Corruption, and the Rule of Law," *Journal of Money, Credit and Banking* 45 (2013): 757–79.

99. Charles M. North and Carl R. Gwin, "Religion and the Emergence of the Rule of Law," in *Religion, Economy, and Cooperation*, ed. Ilkka Pyysiäinen (Berlin: De Gruyter, 2010), 127–55.

100. In discussing connections between canon law and modern Western law, North and Gwin drew heavily on Harold J. Berman, *Law and Revolution: The Formation of the Western Legal Tradition* (Cambridge, MA: Harvard University Press, 1983).

101. Rubin, *Rulers, Religion, and Riches*; North et al., "Religion, Corruption, and the Rule of Law"; and Guiso et al., "People's Opium?"

102. Timur Kuran, *The Long Divergence: How Islamic Law Held Back the Middle East* (Princeton, NJ: Princeton University Press, 2011).

103. Ibid.

104. See Kuran, *The Long Divergence*, pp. 110–15, 128–31, and 282–83, for more detailed discussion of the *waqf*.

SUGGESTED READINGS

Azzi, Corry, and Ronald Ehrenberg. "Household Allocation of Time and Church Attendance." *Journal of Political Economy* 83 (1975): 27–56. This article established the basic model used in analyzing individual religious choice and found many of the now-standard empirical relationships between individual characteristics and religious attendance.

Barro, Robert J., and Rachel McCleary. "Religion and Economic Growth across Countries." *American Sociological Review* 68 (2003): 760–81. This article was the first to capture the attention of much of the rest of the economics profession beyond those who work in the economics of religion. When examining state intervention into religion or the relationship between religion and economic growth, it remains a paper to deal with.

Berman, Eli. *Radical, Religious, and Violent: The New Economics of Terrorism*. Cambridge, MA: The MIT Press, 2009. Berman's book provides an excellent explanation of Iannaccone's club goods model in a way that is accessible to non-economists. He also addresses the issue of terrorism in an interesting and often counterintuitive way.

Iannaccone, Laurence R. "Introduction to the Economics of Religion." *Journal of Economic Literature* 36 (1998): 1465–96. This is the first grand summary of the economics of religion and remains the starting point for anyone seeking an entrée into the field. Written by the unquestioned pioneer of the field, the article is a must-read for anyone hoping to learn about the economics of religion.

Iannaccone, Laurence R. "Sacrifice and Stigma: Reducing Free-Riding in Cults, Communes, and Other Collectives." *Journal of Political Economy* 100 (1992): 271–91. This is chronologically the second major theory article in the economics of religion, after Azzi and Ehrenberg, "Household Allocation of Time and Church Attendance." It presents the club model and provides some empirical support for the model's predictions.

Iyer, Sriya. "The New Economics of Religion." *Journal of Economic Literature* 54 (2016): 395–441. Iyer writes the second grand article-length summary of the economics of religion. She does an excellent job of conveying the breadth of the field as of 2016 in a relatively short space. This is the second work (after Iannaccone's "Introduction to the Economics of Religion") to be read by anyone seeking to learn about the economics of religion.

Kuran, Timur. *The Long Divergence: How Islamic Law Held Back the Middle East*. Princeton, NJ: Princeton University Press, 2011. This landmark book presents much of Kuran's earlier works on the underdevelopment of the Islamic Middle East. He shows how the region's economic woes flowed from Islam, even as he explains why Islam need not be a barrier to repairing the lagging economies of the Middle East.

McBride, Michael. "Religious Market Competition in a Richer World." *Economica* 77 (2010): 148–71. This article is another important theoretical contribution to understanding how religious markets function. It is the most complete model to date of the interactions between individuals and religious organizations.

McCleary, Rachel M., ed. *The Oxford Handbook of the Economics of Religion*. New York: Oxford University Press, 2011. This book-length treatment provides numerous contributions from many of the authors cited above. Its best chapters could serve as the basis for a textbook on the economics of religion.

Oslington, Paul, ed. *The Oxford Handbook of Christianity and Economics*. New York: Oxford University Press, 2014. Though much of this book addresses matters at the intersection of theology and economics, Part IV contains six chapters on the economics of religion, including this author's overview of the regulation of religious markets.

5

"Like a Shot"

The Historical Study of (Mostly American) Religion, 1870–2014

Barry Hankins

In 1989, intellectual historian Henry F. May reminisced that in the 1930s, when he was in graduate school, the progressive school of history dominated the field. "Part of the progressive ideology," May wrote, "was the assumption that religion was and must be declining. . . . Religion was dependent on a series of dogmas and legends that no serious intellectual could entertain."[1] In other words, religion was giving way to modern progress, which entailed an increasingly secular and scientific view of the world. As May put it, "Democracy and progress were closely associated with the liberation of mankind from superstition."[2] And religion fit in the category of superstition because it was unverifiable by the scientific method. May was hardly the first historian to note this. As early as 1968, Paul Carter recalled an era when "a historian of the Protestant churches in America felt that he had to make excuses for his subject-matter's very existence."[3] May and Carter both pointed to a deep and unacknowledged epistemological paradigm shift that had been underway since the Enlightenment of the eighteenth century. By the

early twentieth century, only data amenable to scientific quantifica-
tion could properly be classified as knowledge. Everything else was
subjective at best and superstitious at worst.

The belief that religion would invariably decline in modern societies was later dubbed the secularization thesis by sociologists. For
the history profession, this meant that religion was truly an artifact
of the past, worthy of study only if one could glean something
from it that contributed to the development of modern America.
Colonial Americans had been highly religious, everyone acknowledged, but their religion itself had little lasting importance. Rather,
what interested historians were certain ways of thinking that just
happened to take place within religious categories. By the time
of the American Revolution, the story went, secular forces of the
Enlightenment increasingly supplanted religion. The revivals of the
nineteenth century served as a remnant of a bygone era. Likewise,
the fundamentalist spasms of the early twentieth century represented
an outburst of status anxiety on the part of religious reactionaries
who intuited subconsciously that history had passed them by. May
entered graduate school roughly a decade after the Scopes trial of
1925, which served symbolically as the last gasp of traditional religion in America. The trial, or at least its interpretation as popular
history, served as the death knell of fundamentalism, and the victory
of the secular scientific worldview. That the trial came on the heels of
modernist victories over fundamentalists in the northern Baptist and
Presbyterian denominations only made the end of fundamentalism
seem more imminent. In covering the battles in those denominations,
the *Christian Century* editorialized in 1926 that fundamentalism "is
henceforth to be a disappearing quantity in American religious life."[4]

THE CHURCH HISTORY ERA

In this era when attention to religion declined in university graduate schools and among those working in the history profession, the
serious study of religion proceeded among those known as church
historians. Church history formed as a discipline in the nineteenth
century largely in seminaries, not in the newly formed research universities. Philip Schaff was arguably the most influential founder of
the discipline and a key figure in forming the American Society of
Church History in 1888. Church historians saw their craft as largely

ecclesiastical, denominational, and confessional. Each denomination had its own historians who documented the group's institutional history and attempted to place it within a broad history of Christianity written by a few of the leaders in the field. Chief among the leaders were Schaff, whose eight-volume *History of the Christian Church* appeared from 1892 to 1894, and Williston Walker's 1918 *A History of the Christian Church.*[5] Presbyterians, Methodists, Baptists, Congregationalists, Episcopalians, and so on, wrote their own history, situated it within the larger history of Christianity, and taught it to young ministerial candidates who trained in their denominational seminaries. Catholic historians proceeded in similar fashion in their schools. Among Catholic historians, Peter Guilday led the effort to form the American Catholic Historical Association in 1919. During this same period a few historians, following the lead of Robert Baird's 1856 book *Religion in America*, specialized in church history in the United States.

In an effort to enter the mainstream of scholarship, church historians in the first half of the twentieth century appropriated the dominant "scientific history" that had been pioneered in Germany and adopted by research universities in the United States. Essentially, they tried to make the study and interpretation of history as scientifically objective as possible. Church historians in the leading seminaries eschewed providentialism as they laid out the historical facts and drew modest conclusions. In other words, while working on religious topics, they used the same methods as secular historians working in the research universities. Reflecting on this secularization of church history, Albert Outler noted a significant loss and a very limited gain in "suppressing" the idea of providence. "Our loss has been that church history, in this century, has largely ceased to count as a *theological* discipline," he wrote in 1965. "Yet even the most resolute secularization of church history has not gained for us that status of full membership in the guild of general historians to which we think we are entitled—and this is a pity, for us and for them."[6]

In the second and third decades of the century, church historians also moved away from the grand narratives, the *History of the Christian Church* approach, toward narrower, more specialized monographs. Following this development, in the 1920s and 1930s, church historians began to broaden or eliminate the theological parameters for what counted as Christian. Historians began to accept as "Christian" those groups and individuals who claimed to be so. In the 1930s, the so-called Chicago School of church history began to utilize a sociohistorical approach that sought to understand how politics, culture, economics, and geography shaped religious influences. This, too, reflected larger trends taking place in secular research universities where interpretation became a more salient feature of scientific history.[7]

The dominance of church history served the positive purpose of advancing the study of religion in the United States at a time when secular historians tended to ignore it. But the church history approach also created a ghetto for the study of religion, relegating it to the periphery of the academy. In response, a few church historians took note of the need to relate the study of American religion to the larger enterprise of American history generally. Appropriating the frontier thesis of Frederick Jackson Turner, Peter G. Mode produced his *The Frontier Spirit in American Christianity* in 1923.[8] Turner had argued in an influential and famous 1893 essay that the frontier and the need to adapt to it made America unique. Turner mentioned religion several times in the book-length expansion of his essay that appeared in 1921. But he left serious treatment of the topic to others, and Peter Mode became the first to apply the frontier thesis to the study of religion in a serious way. Mode wrote that "the Americanizing of Christianity has been the process by which it has been frontierized," by which he meant that religion in the United States had adjusted to meet the needs of the frontier.[9] Following in the line of Mode, William Warren Sweet made the frontier thesis central. In addition to writing four volumes in the *Religion on the American Frontier* series—one each on the Baptists, Presbyterians, Congregationalists, and Methodists—his synthetic work *The Story of Religion in America* (1939) became a classic standard text. He showed not only how the frontier shaped American Christianity but also how the churches served to help civilize and domesticate Americans as they pushed across the frontier.[10]

By the mid-twentieth century, some church historians called for a shift away from objective, scientific history to a focus on "the actualization of the gospel in history" and an effort to track the "subtle indications of the presence of the Risen Christ to his adopted brethren."[11] Such an explicitly theological approach was made possible by the post–World War II "revival of religion," as it was called.

In the early postwar years, increased birthrates (baby boom), growth of the suburbs, and the rise of the white middle class all contributed to a surge in church membership. During this same period, Billy Graham became a household name and American religious icon. But the theological force most in vogue among the intellectual class was Neo-Orthodoxy, or, more accurately, the theological realism of Reinhold Niebuhr.

After Dresden, Hiroshima, and most of all Auschwitz, the platitudes of progress from theological liberals and secular progressives seemed passé or even naïve. Following in the wake of Karl Barth's Neo-Orthodox theology in Europe, Niebuhr helped move consideration of humankind's sinful nature back into public consciousness. Niebuhr even appeared on the cover of *Time* magazine in 1948. The popularity of Neo-Orthodoxy had several different effects in different quarters of society, but for our purposes here it pushed theological conversation back into academic and popular discourse. A few emboldened church historians raised theological issues once again, even if only briefly.

To summarize thus far, church historians served to keep the study of religion alive in an era when the secular academy largely ignored it. Sweet complained in 1946 when he was winding down his career at the University of Chicago Divinity School that in the early part of the century when he did his Ph.D. at the University of Pennsylvania, no student dared write a dissertation on religion. Such a statement was consistent with Harold Stearns's slight exaggeration in 1922 when he claimed he could find no one interested in writing an article on religion for his *Civilization in the United States*. Stearns acknowledged that the omission of religion in the text was so "strange" that it required "a paragraph of explanation." Americans were a churchgoing people with many sects and creeds, he acknowledged. And he claimed to have thought more about the omission of an essay on religion than about the essays that were actually included in the volume. "The bald truth is," he claimed, "it has been next to impossible to get anyone to write on the subject." When he broached the topic with his team of scholars they were nearly unanimous in their view that "real religious feeling in America had disappeared."[12] Church history was fine in the seminaries and divinity schools, but scholars in the secular academy found themselves preoccupied with seemingly more important things.

THE MOVE INTO THE ACADEMY

Even during the era when church history dominated the study of religion, however, change was underway. A few scholars in research universities began to pay attention to religious ideas. A trend toward intellectual history took place in the 1930s and can be illustrated with reference to two works by Reinhold Niebuhr's brother H. Richard Niebuhr. In 1929, he published *The Social Sources of Denominationalism*. In it, he argued that the best way to understand the proliferation of Protestant denominations was to track their ethnicity, economics, and geography. These social forces explained denominational pluralism more than theological ideas. Just eight years later, Niebuhr repented, as some have put it. In *The Kingdom of God in America*, he sought to track the way the idea of the kingdom shaped American religion. This shift from social to intellectual forces was part of a growing interest in intellectual history.[13]

But Niebuhr was an ordained minister who taught theology and ethics at Yale. By far the most important secular historian to promote the study of religious ideas was Perry Miller. Educated at the University of Chicago, Miller joined the faculty at Harvard in 1931 where Henry May would become a graduate student a few years later. Miller himself was an atheist but nevertheless became interested in the Puritans in the late 1920s. This was a time when journalist H. L. Mencken's view of religion, prejudice really, tended to dominate secular circles. Mencken supposedly once described Puritanism as the "haunting fear that someone, somewhere, may be happy." By contrast, Miller concluded the Puritans were people of ideas worthy of academic study. As one historian has put it, "Miller rebutted the methodological bias that elevated tracking what colonists bought over deciphering what they thought."[14] In 1939, he published his second book, *The New England Mind*. So profound was his work that some would say he "discovered" the Puritans, while critics would "almost say later," according to May, that he "created" them.[15] One of Miller's students, Edmund Morgan, also became an influential historian of the Puritans. In the preface to his biography of seventeenth-century Massachusetts governor John Winthrop, Morgan credited Miller with overthrowing what one might call the Menckenesque caricature that Puritans "were killjoys in tall crowned hats whose main occupation was to prevent each other from having fun and whose sole virtue lay in their furniture."[16] A more recent historian of colonial America has written that Miller "vivified the study of American Puritanism [and] refigured theologian Jonathan Edwards from raging arachniphobe into enlightened intellect."[17]

Even Miller operated within the secularization thesis, however, interpreting the Puritans' covenant theology largely as a strategy for dealing with the decline of religion in the face of modern forces, from Puritan to Yankee as it were.[18] Paul Carter predicted in 1968 that, as important as Miller was for rehabilitating the Puritans, someday historians may conclude that he had "translated a previous generation's psycho-socio-economic interpretations of Puritan religious ideas into philosophical and rhetorical categories more subtle but no less secular."[19]

Although influenced by Miller, May wrote his doctoral dissertation with Arthur Schlesinger, Sr. While not interested in religion himself, Schlesinger nevertheless recognized its importance in American history and encouraged May and other graduate students to consider religious influences. May's dissertation became his first book, *Protestant Churches and Industrial America* (1949). In his own words, May wrote from a "thoroughly secular point of view," interested in the effects of religion on society, not the ideas of religion.[20] In other words, religion was significant only to the extent it had influence on something nonreligious.

By the 1960s, May detected a significant upsurge in the interest in religion beyond the fraternity of church historians. He called this "The Recovery of American Religious History" and made the somewhat daring proclamation, "For the study and understanding of American culture, the recovery of American religious history may well be the most important achievement of the last thirty years."[21] He attributed the recovery to church historians, sociologists, Neo-Orthodox theologians, and the general revival of popular interest in religion in the 1950s. He also cited secular historians in the academy who had included consideration of religion in their broader works, and chief among them, of course, was Perry Miller.

Two years after May's "recovery" proclamation Edwin Scott Gaustad published *A Religious History of America*. Previous texts surveying religion over the entire sweep of American history had been written by church historians such as William Warren Sweet and Winthrop S. Hudson, both of whom taught in divinity schools. Gaustad, by contrast, served in the history department of the

University of California, Riverside. Having studied for the Ph.D. in colonial America at Brown University with Edmund Morgan, Gaustad stood in the lineage of Perry Miller. In addition to serving as a leading textbook, *A Religious History of America* signaled that being a historian at a secular state university far from the Ivy League proved no bar to a successful career in religious history. Indeed, the line between church history in the seminaries and divinity schools and religious history in the secular academy blurred significantly by the 1970s. In addition to historians in history departments, the rise of religious studies departments also played a role in narrowing the gap between church history and religious history.[22]

While Sweet, Hudson, and Gaustad's texts were all valuable in their own right, Sydney Ahlstrom's *A Religious History of the American People* (1972) became the most comprehensive and magisterial survey of American religious history by far. Running roughly 1,200 pages, Ahlstrom's book has served for nearly two generations as a virtual reference work. From his post at Yale, where he served as the Samuel Knight Professor of American History and Modern Religious History, Ahlstrom utilized almost all the approaches to the study of religion in America discussed thus far—intellectual, sociological, economic, cultural, and so forth. Gaustad and Ahlstrom's texts showed that American religious history had moved into the mainstream of the academy.

FROM THE NEW SOCIAL HISTORY
TO THE EVANGELICAL PARADIGM

The recovery of religious history that May cited not only continued, the pace quickened. As we have seen, Perry Miller made serious study of the Puritans safe for historians in the academy. Similarly, Johns Hopkins professor and ordained Nazarene minister Timothy Smith discovered in the revivals of the Second Great Awakening the social reform influences that shaped American voluntarism.[23] Other historians began to analyze the Social Gospel of the early twentieth century as the urban expression of Protestant reform—the Progressive Era at prayer, one might say. The history of African American religion also emerged as a significant subfield. Pioneered in the first half of the century by black sociologists W. E. B. Du Bois and then E. Franklin Frazier, in 1973 seminary professor Gayraud Wilmore helped move Black religion into the realm of church history with his influential book *Black Religion and Black Radicalism*. Five years later, Ahlstrom's student Albert Raboteau helped bring the study of Black religion into the larger academy with his first book *Slave Religion: The "Invisible Institution" in the Antebellum South*.[24]

The 1970s also saw the rise of the New Social History, followed in the 1980s and 1990s by the New Cultural History. Both facilitated an increase in scholarship on religion. The first attempted to get at lives of common people, which sometimes included the ways that religion remained vital, or at least epiphenomenal, for them even as it declined among elites. The second, the so-called cultural turn, was associated with postmodernism. It revived issues of agency and the use of language by historical actors, including the ways people used religious language. As it turned out, the New Social History and New Cultural History fostered the recovery of American religious history that May identified in 1964. As two historians wrote in the late 1990s, "Once social and cultural history recovered religion and displaced intellectual history as the subject of choice for aspiring young graduate students, religion would be at the heart of the American history enterprise." The study of religion could now move beyond the Puritans and the revivals of the nineteenth century, into the twentieth, and even to the near present. The New Social History and the New Cultural History therefore facilitated religious history's move from the divinity schools into university history and religious studies departments in the mainstream of academy.[25]

Some subjects proved more attractive than others, however. The area that lagged in historical treatment became after 1980 the one with the most prolific output, the history of evangelicals and fundamentalists. It was one thing to study Puritans, nineteenth-century revivalists, and progressive-minded Protestants of the Social Gospel. The first two movements resided safely in the past and could be studied as historical relics, while the Social Gospel presented a religion that had adapted to modernity. Early twentieth-century fundamentalists, by contrast, were a bit too close for comfort and way too antimodern. There were even rumors of a few fundamentalists still living in the United States. As for evangelicals, they seemed to be everywhere, apparently having not gotten the post-Scopes memo that they were supposed to die out or go away. It was as if what Mencken had said about fundamentalists in the 1920s had come true of evangelicals in the 1950s: "Heave an egg out a Pullman window and you will hit [one] almost anywhere in the United States today."[26] Historians were beginning to notice that the sort of religion that resisted modernity was not disappearing as the secularization thesis insisted it should. This needed explaining.

But the Scopes trial had complicated, retarded, and distorted the treatment of fundamentalism. Almost every American historian knew that the Northern Baptists and the northern Presbyterian Church (U.S.A.) experienced intense battles between conservatives and liberals from 1890 to 1925. And anyone who studied these fundamentalist-modernist controversies also knew that the liberals won in the Northern Baptist Convention and the northern Presbyterian Church. Following on the heels of the controversies, the Scopes trial of 1925 served as public notice that the secular, scientific worldview had triumphed in the culture just as liberal theology had triumphed in the mainline denominations. This was, of course, as progressive historians believed it should be. Liberal Protestantism was the modernization of Protestant theology in accord with the challenges of science. That adjustment saved it from extinction. Fundamentalism represented the theological resistance to modernism and would of course die out. Actually, as Edward Larson showed in a Pulitzer Prize–winning book in 1997, few initially interpreted the Scopes trial as a defeat for the fundamentalists. But beginning with Frederick Lewis Allen's 1931 popular history *Only Yesterday: An Informal History of the Nineteen-Twenties*, the trial became fundamentalism's Waterloo. Antievolution served as the essence of fundamentalism, which had been humiliated in Dayton, Tennessee, so the story went.[27] Allen's view moved even more firmly into the American imagination nearly thirty years later in the play, and then film, *Inherit the Wind*. As a result of this interpretation of Scopes, fundamentalism, like Puritanism, came to be viewed as a historical relic. Unlike Miller's intellectually astute Puritans, however, there was nothing of worth to salvage from fundamentalism's brief history.

The first history of fundamentalism appeared the same year as Allen's *Only Yesterday*. The attitude of liberal church historian Stewart Cole can be characterized as something like the following: Now that fundamentalism is over, we need to analyze it historically and psychologically. The fundamentalist effort to defend traditional orthodoxy in the face of progress, Cole argued, began in earnest at the end of the first decade of the century. It gathered momentum during the 1910s, strengthened and became militant during World War I, and experienced something of a revival after the war. But following the denominational battles of the 1920s, then the Scopes trial, fundamentalists became a remnant. Cole described nearly every fundamentalist organization or individual after Scopes as "an ineffective agent," "inconsequential," "near collapse," having "run its course," "inoperative," or "disheartened." At one point he even said fundamentalists appealed "to the principles of magic rather than those of science or religion."[28]

From Cole onward, a handful of historians portrayed fundamentalism as part of the political far right or lunatic fringe of American life, while a few scholars tried, somewhat in vain, to take fundamentalism more seriously. For the most part, the standard view portrayed fundamentalism as a form of American anti-intellectualism. In his Pulitzer Prize–winning book *Anti-Intellectualism in America Life* (1963), Richard Hofstadter followed Cole's lead in calling fundamentalism "frantic," "desperate," and in the "waning phase of its history" in the 1920s. He lumped together fundamentalism, the Ku Klux Klan, the failed defense of Prohibition, and the campaign against Catholic presidential candidate Al Smith. This *Kulturekampf*'s only victory was the defeat of Smith, and even here the conservative Protestants lost because the campaign led to the reorganization of the Democratic Party along urban, cosmopolitan lines.[29] In this view, fundamentalists could best be understood not as having ideas but reacting against them. Like other late nineteenth-century populist movements, fundamentalists experienced what Hofstadter and others called status anxiety. As they lost their authority in the face of modernism's turn toward science, they reacted with a vengeance in an effort to stop the clock.

In 1970, this anti-intellectual view of fundamentalism began to change with the appearance of Ernest Sandeen's *The Roots of Fundamentalism*.[30] Sandeen attempted to do for fundamentalists what Miller did for Puritans. He took their ideas seriously. As an intellectual historian, Sandeen was not part of the New Social History, and after his book appeared, the rest of the 1970s remained pretty quiet in terms of the study of fundamentalism. That all changed after 1980, and George Marsden led the way with his book *Fundamentalism and American Culture*.[31] This refutation of Sandeen helped launch what Yale historian Jonathan Butler called "the evangelical paradigm," opening the door for a torrent of scholarship on evangelicalism and fundamentalism.[32] By 1987, Marsden had become what Leonard Sweet called "the closest thing one can imagine to a pontiff of evangelical history."[33] What is most significant about such a statement is not calling Marsden "a pontiff" but identifying a distinct "evangelical history." Before 1980, the term might well have been viewed as something akin to astrology. By the end of the decade, it was commonplace, leading to Henry May's reflection on how different the 1980s were from the 1930s when he was in graduate school.

Like Sandeen, Marsden believed fundamentalists were people of ideas. But he believed Sandeen had discovered only two of the roots of fundamentalism, mistaking them for the whole tree. Where Sandeen focused on British millenarianism and the Princeton theology of Charles Hodge and B. B. Warfield, Marsden argued that fundamentalism was also fed by nineteenth-century forces such as Scottish Common Sense Realism, Baconian science, revivalism, holiness impulses, pietism, and Baptist traditionalism, as well as Sandeen's Reformed confessionalism (Princeton theology) and dispensational premillennialism (British millenarianism). In addition to Marsden's more comprehensive approach, his book was perhaps the timeliest book ever published. Marsden worked on the book for about ten years, essentially the 1970s. When he started, he, of course, had no way of knowing that the same year the book appeared in print, Ronald Reagan would be elected president with the backing of America's most popular fundamentalist Jerry Falwell and his recently founded organization, the Moral Majority. In other words, the same year that fundamentalism emerged from its post-Scopes slumber and burst back into public consciousness, Marsden's book rolled off the press explaining where fundamentalists came from.

It is hard to overstate the significance of *Fundamentalism and American Culture*, but let me try.[34] Marsden utilized a wealth of mostly printed primary sources to document his story, and the book also provided a broad synthesis that sketched the big picture of fundamentalism from 1870 to 1925. But rather than being the final word on the subject, the book instead called forth a whole scholarly industry. Hardly any of the individual fundamentalist leaders Marsden covered had been subjected to scholarly biography. Young scholars began to pick off these subjects as dissertation topics that became books. Marsden also showed that early fundamentalism was a largely urban movement in the Northeast. Only later did the center of gravity shift to the South. Such regional awareness created another lens for further study. Along with biographies and regional studies came the standard scholarly categories of race, class, and gender, which Marsden hardly touched. A cadre of women historians began to address gender issues in early fundamentalism. There seemed to be no end to the scholarly possibilities for studying evangelicals, all of which were fueled by the resurgent evangelical influence in politics and culture during the so-called Reagan revolution. If *Fundamentalism and American Culture* cracked open a window and legitimized the serious study of evangelicalism, the culture wars made such study seem important and relevant, just as the postwar revival of the 1950s brought theological considerations back into the church history of that era.

The resurgence of conservative or traditional religion appeared to be a worldwide phenomenon. For better or worse, many scholars lumped American fundamentalism with the rise of fundamentalist Islam, Hinduism, Judaism, and other faiths in a series of interdisciplinary scholarly endeavors. In his role as something like the dean of American scholars of religion, Martin Marty along with R. Scott Appleby convened a series of conferences from 1987 to 1995 that became known as the Fundamentalism Project and resulted in five volumes of essays, studies, charts, statistics, and so forth.[35] This international and interdisciplinary *tour de force* focused on how fundamentalism's militant defense of tradition against the onslaught of modernity cut across religious cultures.

Marty's leadership gave the Fundamentalism Project an authority no other historian of the era could have provided. His career serves as a biographical testament to the transition from church history to mainstream religious history. He joined the faculty of the University of Chicago Divinity School in 1963, the year before Henry May identified "the Recovery of American Religious History." He eventually held appointments not only in the Divinity School but also the Department of History and the Committee on the History of Culture, serving as the Fairfax M. Cone Distinguished Service Professor. At various times he served as president of the American Society of Church History, the American Academy of Religion, and even the American Catholic Historical Association, although he himself is an ordained Lutheran minister. His Wikipedia entry (https://en.wikipedia.org/wiki/Martin_E._Marty) claims he published an authored book and an edited book for every year he was a full-time professor (1963–1998). No historian would find this surprising or bother to check whether it is exactly accurate. For thirty-five years historians simply expected to see a couple of books per year from Marty. His highly influential *Righteous Empire* appeared in 1970, between Gaustad and Ahlstrom's texts, and from 1986 to 1996 he published three of a projected four volumes of his *Modern American Religion*. He interpreted twentieth-century American Protestantism as shaped by its encounter with modernity, in the process tracking the often ironic ways that secularization and religious revival proceed in tandem. Whether inadvertently or intentionally, Marty also gave the field the "two-party system," which viewed the split between conservatives and liberals within Protestantism as more significant than particular denominational labels. Still, he warned against focusing on models, urging historians instead to look for anomalies and exceptions to whatever interpretation prevailed.[36]

The evangelical paradigm launched by Marsden produced one historian who rivals Marty, and that is Mark Noll. Even as Leonard Sweet called Marsden the pontiff, he acknowledged that Noll was the most prolific of the evangelical historians, and that was when Noll was less than fifteen years into his career. Beginning with books on religion and the American Revolution and early Republic, Noll's scholarly and popular books range across the scope of American history. His intellectual history *America's God: From Jonathan Edwards to Abraham Lincoln* is perhaps his magnum opus. His 1992 textbook entitled *A History of Christianity in the United States and Canada* signaled his growing interest in religious history across cultures. He followed with books on evangelicalism in the English-speaking world and then situated American religion within global Christianity. Along the way he has written or edited books on religion and politics, religion and science, religion and money, religion and race, biblical criticism, the Bible and culture, evangelical views of Catholics, Christian hymnody, American piety, and other topics. In addition to his strictly scholarly works, he has written a number of books aimed at helping evangelicals think more clearly about some of the same topics. The historical documentation and contextualization of evangelical history in these works is of such high quality that they are often cited as scholarly works. Chief among these popular works are *Between Faith and Criticism*, *The Scandal of the Evangelical Mind*, and *Jesus Christ and the Life of the Mind*.[37] Noll long ago transcended the evangelical paradigm and took his place alongside Marty and Ahlstrom as one of most well recognized and respected religious historians in the entire historiography of religion in the United States from its beginnings to the present.

The explosion of historical scholarship on evangelicals and fundamentalists expanded quickly to include increased attention to Pentecostals. Other largely ignored areas of religious experience in American history piqued historians' curiosity as well. Mormon history, for example, went from a cottage industry among Mormon scholars to a new subfield attracting the attention of many non-Mormons. And on and on. None of this is to say that Marsden's *Fundamentalism and American Culture* necessarily caused the great upsurge in religious history after 1980. Rather, he treated exactly the right topic at just the right time. Forces that had been coalescing since the 1960s converged in the 1980s, and the historical study of religion moved to an altogether higher plane.

RELIGIOUS HISTORY AND POINT OF VIEW

Not only was Marsden's book timely and immensely influential, it was also an early example of the sort of point-of-view religious scholarship we now take for granted. In the wake of postmodernism's now widely accepted dictum that all knowledge is at least perspectival, if not indeed relative, Marsden's acknowledgment that he was an evangelical writing about evangelicalism seems unremarkable today. But in 1980, it was nearly unheard of. Historians have had a penchant for knowing and at the same time denying that historical interpretation is subjective. As we have already seen, "scientific history" dominated even the field of church history in the early twentieth century. In 1931, Carl Becker gave an American Historical Association presidential address entitled "Every Man His Own Historian," where he frankly acknowledged that the facts of history do not speak for themselves but must be interpreted. "The history written by historians," he said, "like the history informally fashioned by Mr. Everyman, is thus a convenient blend of truth and fancy, of what we commonly distinguish as 'fact' and 'interpretation.'"[38] Church historian Albert Outler wrote in 1965 that in certain ways the historian's work is "incurably subjective."[39] Edward Carr's classic little book *What Is History?* became one of many venues for discussing whether history was a science. Carr had difficulty deciding just how subjective historians should be.[40] Still, with all these caveats in place, historians such as G. R. Elton continued to press for objectivity. In 1967, Elton published *The Practice of History* as a response to Carr, arguing that the historian's task was to gather the facts empirically and interpret them objectively.[41] Peter Novick attempted to resolve the impasse by calling objectivity "a noble dream."[42] Taken together, one might say that historians strive to be objective while acknowledging that objectivity functions as a good myth.

When postmodernism hit with full force, some in the history profession were alarmed, Elton among them. The most thoroughgoing postmodernists denied there was anything objective that could be subjectively interpreted, anything that could be known at all. They also denied the stock and trade of historians—causality. Where Enlightenment skeptic David Hume said causality could not be proven, postmodernists seemed to say it did not even exist.[43]

Marsden and others, however, saw postmodernism as a window of opportunity for those with religious perspectives. The reasoning was logical enough. Postmodernists utilized theories based on race, class, and gender. If these can influence historical interpretation, why not theological views. Even as more traditional historians pursued the noble dream of objectivity, the profession came to accept the obvious fact that women and people of color could, would, and should see things differently than white males. But religion was something different. Race, class, and gender were measurable categories and so still amenable to the Enlightenment, scientific enterprise. Religion was not, so the argument went. But when postmodernism offered a devastating critique of the values of the Enlightenment, arguing that everything from liberal democracy to science was premised on background beliefs that could not be proven by the scientific method, there seemed no reason other than prejudice, preference, and power for excluding religion. *Fundamentalism and American Culture* became the most significant and very nearly the first scholarly historical monograph in which the author identified himself as an evangelical, an heir to fundamentalism, and also said that this made a difference. Several reviewers noted this self-revelation. Some were puzzled or miffed, others saw it as refreshing, while a few viewed such self-disclosure as a harbinger of the future.[44] The latter were closest to the mark as most books on evangelicals and fundamentalists since Marsden's begin with some truth-in-advertising preface, situating the author. Marsden's participant-observer scholarship was nothing new for church historians, as Outler's quote above shows. But in the mainstream academy, in a book published by Oxford University Press, it was surprising. And within a decade, scholars were talking about evangelical history and the evangelical paradigm.

Like the history of evangelicals and fundamentalists in general, the history of evangelical women also captured the interest of a growing cadre of historians who were themselves women and evangelicals. The broader rise of women's history began in the 1960s and 1970s. Still, the rise of the Christian Right and the resurgence of evangelical groups that promote traditional, prefeminist views of gender roles caught the interest of historians and religious studies scholars in new ways. Women historians, sociologists, and anthropologists led the way in ethnographic studies, the best of which combined immersion in the life of a particular community with keen insights from the past that contextualized and explained these contemporary groups in fruitful ways.[45] Women's religious history has been immensely diverse, resulting in studies of Protestant women, Catholic women, evangelical women, Jewish women, Mormon women, Native American women, slave women, black Muslim women, female preachers, female spiritual mediums, and so forth. In 1989, the American Society of Church History began offering a prize annually for the best essay on women in the history of Christianity. By that time, several universities, divinity schools, and seminaries had degrees or certificates in women's religious studies. The proliferation of such scholarship made possible the first textbook on women's religious history in 1996, Susan Hill Lindley's *You Have Slept Out of Your Place: A History of Women and Religion in America*.[46]

Still, as late as 2007, historian Catherine Brekus made a compelling case that women's religious history had not yet joined the mainstream of religious history. Women continued to be underreported in the survey texts written by many of the male historians discussed in this essay. In addition, when included, women's stories often appeared in separate chapters rather than being integrated into the main narrative. A woman preacher from the First Great Awakening, for example, appears in a chapter on women but not in a chapter on the Awakening itself. "The unintended result," Brekus wrote, "is that women often appear marginal to the main story."[47] Such marginality is especially ironic considering that, for the entire sweep of American history, women have made up the majority of church members. This led historian Ann Braude to observe in 1997, "Women's History *Is* American Religious History." The main plot, Braude argues, is the presence of women not the absence of men.[48]

But according to Brekus, the situation worsened after the mid-1980s. As secular women's historians lost interest in religion, the story fell almost wholly on religious historians. Brekus notes the irony of this happening at the same time the Christian Right rose to prominence and religious historians rediscovered fundamentalism and evangelicalism. There may have been a causal connection, she suggests, as secular women saw the nexus between resurgent evangelicalism and conservative politics and concluded that religion did not serve as a liberating force. Women's history had risen to prominence along with and as a result of the feminist movement, which engendered interest in liberal feminists of the past much more than conservative women. "As 'religion' was increasingly equated with 'conservatism' [in the 1980s]," Brekus writes, "many women's historians turned their attention to topics that seemed more useful for nurturing a feminist consciousness."[49] One might say that, whereas the progressive historians of the early twentieth century ignored religion because they thought it was dying out, women's historians of the late twentieth century turned away from religion when they concluded it hindered progress. Some have pointed out that women religious historians face a unique double challenge. They have to convince secular women historians to pay more attention to religion while convincing male historians of religion to pay more attention to women. To slightly tweak Reformation historian Merry Wiesner-Hanks's phrase, women religious historians have been "double missionaries."[50]

The relationship of religion and progress, however, is a contested question. Beginning in the 1970s, religious historians have debated whether religion has been a source of empowerment or control. The social control school argued, for example, that revivals of the nineteenth century were promoted, if not engineered, by factory owners wanting to keep their workers orderly, sober, and hard working. Religion played a conservative role in maintaining class structure. Other historians argued that revivals gave individuals agency and promoted democracy.[51] Women's historians have likewise debated whether religion has on balance empowered women or led to their subjugation and domination. In many secular women's histories, religion nearly disappears after liberal Protestant women helped win suffrage in 1920, in much the same way that religious history nearly disappeared among the progressive historians after Scopes in 1925. Women religious historians have set out to correct this and have leaned to the side of empowerment in doing so.[52]

MAINLINE PROTESTANT AND CATHOLIC HISTORY

By contrast to the great increase in historical scholarship that came in the wake of Marsden's *Fundamentalism and American Culture*, there was no immediate upsurge in scholarship on liberal Protestantism following the 1976 appearance of William R. Hutchison's *The Modernist Impulse in American Protestantism*, even though that book became the standard interpretation of its subject in much the same way Marsden's did. There seemed to be little interest in mainline Protestantism in the 1980s and 1990s in either media or scholarly circles. A survey of religion scholars in the early 1990s found that Catholicism and evangelicalism were by far the religious topics most studied by historians and sociologists.[53] As Leigh Eric Schmidt wrote in 2012, "Evangelicals have stolen the show not only among journalists chronicling the current political landscape, but also among historians trying to make sense of conservatism's resurgence."[54]

But the rising tide of religious influence in public life floated all scholarly boats eventually. As we approach the end of the second decade of the twenty-first century, mainline or liberal Protestantism seems once again a topic of interest. Now that we understand that evangelicals have always been more numerous than liberal Protestants, how do we explain that liberals were far more influential from 1925 to 1980? How did the minority remain the mainline? By 2013, a handful of books on mainline Protestants had appeared, and both Yale and Princeton had held conferences on liberal Protestantism that resulted in an edited volume. The conferences and resulting book focused on three issues within liberal Protestantism: (1) the relationship between religious liberalism and the arts, (2) the piety and politics of liberalism, and (3) the relationship between religious and secular liberalism. These three areas continue as fruitful avenues for further conversation, and they expand the parameters of what counts as liberal religion, a category that includes mainline Protestantism but is not limited by it.[55]

An emerging interpretation argues that while they are the minority numerically, mainline Protestants held disproportionate cultural capital in post–World War II America in the form of the popular literature they produced and causes they promoted. As David Hollinger puts it in the preface to a collection of his essays, they lost Protestantism but won the culture. "In the long run," he writes, "the liberalizers did lose the institutional control of Protestantism they once had, but in return they furthered the causes in the national arena to which they were most firmly committed."[56] Scholars are now exploring the fluidity and intersection between liberal Protestantism and a host of other movements of the twentieth century—New Thought, free thought, Theosophy, the paranormal, ufology, and even occultism. As liberal Protestantism undergoes the current reevaluation, it appears to have maintained its mainstream status in part by finding a comfortable place within a broader religious or even metaphysical liberalism of twentieth-century America. Schmidt, Catherine Albanese, Hollinger, and others currently advocate expanding the boundaries of what counts as religious liberalism to include groups, movements, and individuals outside the bounds of Protestantism or even Christianity. As Jeffrey Kripal argues, histories of American religious liberalism need to get "way, way weirder."[57]

As a general rule of thumb, the "weirder" work is being done mostly by a minority of scholars in religious studies and American studies departments. Historians in the history departments and divinity schools continue to work in more traditional ways. But interdisciplinary conversation and collaboration are on the rise. Just as the circle of scholars doing religious history expanded to include both church historians and historians in secular history departments, so also the growth of religious studies as a discipline has pushed the historical study of religion in new directions, not the least of which is the study of non-Christian religions in the United States. Diana Eck has been a leader in this area, and her 2001 book *A New*

Religious America: How a "Christian Country" Has Now Become the Most Religiously Diverse Nation is a popular text for religion and American history survey courses. In their 2012 *Columbia Guide to Religion in American History*, historian editors Paul Harvey and Edward Blum include essays devoted to Native American religions, Asian American religions, alternative religious movements, American Judaism, and Islam in the United States.[58] The lines between groups of scholars has blurred, as have the parameters for what counts as religious history and what religious historians count as religion. As Schmidt writes, "The precise balancing point—between (to put the tension glibly) a hot-tub harmonialism and a bone-dry Protestant establishment—is elusive."[59]

While liberal Protestantism enjoys renewed attention, scholarship on Catholic history has always been around. But for much of the twentieth century, it ran on a separate historiographical track than the history of Protestantism, even as historians in both groups utilized similar methods and assumptions. Before the New Social History of the 1970s, Catholic history was largely institutional, presenting the Catholic Church as somehow separate from American religious history. Protestant historians had little to turn to that would help them include Catholics in the histories of religion in America. The leading Catholic historians of that era included John Tracy Ellis and Thomas McAvoy. This changed with Jay P. Dolan and others working in the 1960s and 1970s. Dolan began to look at Catholics within American culture, analyzing the role of lay people, women, voluntary Catholic agencies, and forces within Catholic communities that were noninstitutional. Immigrant communities, for example, became an important focus of Dolan's approach. His notion of an "Immigrant Church" could be extended to studies of Puritans or even fundamentalists, he suggested. In other words, what he wrote about Catholics put them in the same conversation with many Protestant groups as to how they experienced American history. It also situated Catholics within the New Social History. Catholics were no longer so different, and surveys of American religion by the likes of Sydney Ahlstrom and Mark Noll included much more extensive coverage of Catholics.[60]

The New Social History approach to Catholics led eventually to the "lived religion work" of Robert Orsi's *The Madonna of 115th Street: Faith and Community in Italian Harlem, 1880–1950.*[61] Incorporating ethnographic participation, interviews, and historical records from the early twentieth century, Orsi portrayed the social, cultural, and spiritual lives of the members of the Catholic community of Mount Carmel Parish in East Harlem as they participated in their annual ritual celebration called the *festa*. Orsi interpreted this event as "deeply Catholic," although not part of institutional Catholicism.[62] Writing in 1997, Catholic historian Patrick Carey called for more social and microhistory monographs of Catholic communities in the hope that someday a broader synthesis might emerge showing what is central and what is peripheral to the American Catholic experience. Carey also called for comparisons between, say, Protestant evangelicals and conservative Catholics in the middle part of the twentieth century, when mainline Protestantism dominated American religion.[63]

Carey also called for a fresh approach to Catholic intellectual history, treating the ways Catholics responded to American intellectual movements. As Carey put it, "What is needed is a history of the American Catholic mentality akin to studies of Puritanism, evangelicalism, liberalism, and fundamentalism."[64] A breakthrough of sorts came six years later in John McGreevy's book *Catholicism and American Freedom*. Building on the work of Catholic social and intellectual historians, McGreevy provided the field with its most satisfying interpretation of the tensions Catholic Americans have experienced in a liberal culture that bases its notion of freedom on the autonomy of the individual.[65]

GLOBAL CHRISTIANITY

Perhaps the most important breakthrough in religious history has been the study of world or global Christianity. There is a sense that this sort of religious history has been around for over a century in the form of missions history, and it is probably no accident that the standard and most comprehensive history of Christianity was authored by Kenneth Scott Latourette, who began his career in 1909 as an agent with the Student Volunteer Movement for Foreign Missions. After teaching briefly in China, Latourette returned to America and eventually joined the faculty at Yale in 1921 as the D. Willis James Professor of Missions and World Christianity.

The study of global Christianity is part of a broader emphasis on global history, but it also emanates from particularly religious, even theological, questions that originated with church historians.

If the study of Christianity is the given, some have asked why historians would divide their scholarly interests according to national boundaries. There is a growing understanding, based on recent scholarship, that even a particular branch of Protestantism such as evangelicalism has been a transatlantic phenomenon from the start. The same can be said about eighteenth- and nineteenth-century revivalism in the English-speaking world. Mark Noll and David Bebbington have taken the lead in this area.[66]

But the real fuel of global Christianity has been global Christianity—that is, the recognition that the faith is growing faster in the southern hemisphere and Asia than in the West. As Lamin Sanneh writes, "Christianity has not ceased to be a Western religion, but its future as a world religion is now being decided and shaped by the hands and in the minds of its non-Western adherents, who share little of the West's cultural assumptions."[67] This raises all sorts of interesting questions as to how and why this is happening and whether or to what degree Western missions efforts from the nineteenth and twentieth centuries played a role. Sanneh points out that Christianity began to explode in the non-Western world at about the same time the Western empires began to recede. He credits Archbishop William Temple as the first to recognize this when, in 1944, he called global Christianity "the new feature of our time."[68] Big picture global Christianity was pioneered by theologian and missiologist Andrew Walls, who began arguing in the 1980s that African Christianity was emerging as a distinct form of the faith. As he concluded in 2002, "For African Christianity is undoubtedly African religion, as developed by Africans and shaped by the concerns and agendas of Africa; it is no pale copy of an institution existing somewhere else." That same year Philip Jenkins called the expansion of Christianity outside the West "the next Christendom."[69]

An African himself, Sanneh grew up as a Muslim, converted to Christianity as a teenager, and eventually received baptism in the Roman Catholic Church. He began his career as a scholar of Islam in Africa then turned his attention to what he prefers to call World Christianity when asked by his colleagues at the University of Aberdeen to teach a course on African Christianity. He now holds the same D. Willis James Chair at Yale once occupied by Latourette. He has teamed with Joel Carpenter on a number of edited projects advancing the study of World Christianity. Carpenter studied with

George Marsden and Timothy Smith and spent most of his career as part of the "evangelical paradigm," interpreting American evangelicals. Gradually, however, he became interested in Christian movements elsewhere in the world. After serving as the provost at Calvin College, he founded the Nagel Institute for the Study of World Christianity in 2006, which sponsors research and academic development projects.

CONCLUSION

As a by-product of the author's focus, expertise, and limitations, this essay has dealt largely with religious history in America done by Americans. If one were to focus on the United Kingdom and the European Continent, the story would have many similarities and a few differences. Of the former would be a decline in interest in religion as religion and certainly a turn away from intellectual history toward economic, social, and political forces. Across the Atlantic there is a much stronger case to be made for decline in religion in the twentieth century. In other words, historians who track secularization in Europe are on a much firmer footing than progressive historians in the 1930s who believed religion was also receding in America. One of the early progenitors of the secularization thesis, Peter Berger, has said that he and others were wrong everywhere but Europe in the belief that religion would decline in the face of modern development. Still, even in the United Kingdom, historians such as Quentin Skinner have urged a return to intellectual history, or perhaps better put, the development of a new intellectual history.[70] This seems to be bearing religious fruit, especially among historians who focus on the Reformation era.

In America, however, the jury is no longer out. As historians Harry Stout and Robert Taylor, Jr. concluded after comparing their 1974 and 1993 studies of historians and religion, "[T]here can be no doubt that a revolution has occurred over the past twenty years, producing a New Religious History. . . . Crucial to this New Religious History is its location at the center of the American history enterprise."[71] Twenty-five years after their second study, the revolution continues.

In 2009, the American Historical Association (AHA) reported, "Specialists in religious history recently surpassed all other topical categories in our annual look at AHA members."[72] As the essays in this volume show, the historical study of religion is just part of a larger trend. Simply put, religious interest has surged all across the academy. In 2005, postmodern theorist Stanley Fish remarked, "When Jacques Derrida died I was called by a reporter who wanted to know what would succeed high theory and the triumvirate of race, gender, and class as the center of intellectual energy in the academy. I answered like a shot: religion."[73]

NOTES

1. Henry F. May, *The Divided Heart: Essays on Protestantism and the Enlightenment in America* (New York: Oxford University Press, 1991), 18.
2. May, *The Divided Heart*, 18.
3. Paul Carter, "Recent Historiography of the Protestant Churches in America," *Church History* 37 (1968): 95.
4. "Vanishing Fundamentalism," *Christian Century* (June 24, 1926): 799.
5. Philip Schaff, *History of the Christian Church* (New York: Scribner's Sons, 1882–1910); Williston Walker, *A History of the Christian Church* [1918] (New York: Scribner's Sons, 1944). Among other historians who wrote general histories of Christianity were G. H. Dryer (1896), G. P. Fisher (1887), J. F. Hurst (1897–1900), A. H. Newman (1900), and H. C. Sheldon (1894). Dryer, Fisher, Hurst, and Sheldon each used the title *History of the Christian Church*, while Newman used *A Manuel of Church History*. See Winthrop S. Hudson, "Shifting Trends in Church History," *Journal of Bible and Religion* 28 (1960): 235–38.
6. Albert C. Outler, "Theodosius' Horse; Reflections on the Predicament of the Church Historian," *Church History* 34 (1965): 259.
7. Hudson, "Shifting Trends in Church History," 236.
8. Henry Warner Bowden, "The Historiography of American Religion," in *Encyclopedia of the American Religious Experience: Studies of Traditions and Movements*, 3 vols., ed. Charles H. Lippy and Peter W. Williams, vol. 1 (New York: Scribner's, 1988), 3–16.
9. Quoted in John Boles, "Turner, the Frontier, and the Study of Religion in America," *Journal of the Early Republic* 13 (1993): 206; Frederick Jackson Turner, "The Significance of the Frontier in American History," *Annual Report of the American Historical Association for the Year 1893* (Washington, DC, 1894), 225–26.
10. Bowden, "The Historiography of American Religion," 7; William Warren Sweet, *The Story of Religion in America* (New York: Harper and Brothers, 1939).

11. James Hastings Nichols, "The Art of Church History," *Church History* 20 (1951): 9. See D. G. Hart, *The University Gets Religion: Religious Studies in American Higher Education* (Baltimore, MD: Johns Hopkins University Press, 1999), 157.

12. Harold E. Stearns, ed., *Civilization in the United States: An Inquiry by Thirty Americans* (New York: Harcourt, Brace, and Co., 1922), v–vi; Henry F. May, "The Recovery of American Religious History," in Henry F. May, *Ideas, Faiths, and Feelings: Essays on American Intellectual and Religious History, 1952–1982* (New York: Oxford University Press, 1983), 70.

13. Hudson, "Shifting Trends in Church History," 237; H. Richard Niebuhr, *The Social Sources of Denominationalism* (New York: H. Holt and Co., 1929); H. Richard Niebuhr, *The Kingdom of God in America* (New York: Willett, Clark and Co., 1937).

14. Charles Cohen, "The Post-Puritan Paradigm of Early American Religious History," *William and Mary Quarterly* 54 (1997): 696.

15. May, *The Divided Heart*, 19.

16. Quoted in Carter, "Recent Historiography," 99. From the preface to Edmund Morgan, *The Puritan Dilemma: The Story of John Winthrop* (Boston: Little, Brown, 1958), xi.

17. Cohen, "The Post-Puritan Paradigm," 695. The term *arachniphobe* comes from Edwards's boyhood fascination with spiders and his use of imagery in his famous sermon, "Sinners in the Hands of an Angry God," where he said, "The God that holds you over the pit of hell, much as one holds a spider, or some loathsome insect over the fire, abhors you, and is dreadfully provoked."

18. Harry S. Stout and Robert M. Taylor, Jr., "Studies of Religion in American Society: The State of the Art," in *New Directions in American Religious History*, eds. Harry S. Stout and D. G. Hart (New York: Oxford University Press, 1997), 17.

19. Carter, "Recent Historiography," 99.

20. Henry F. May, "The Recovery of American Religious History," in Henry F. May, *Ideas, Faiths, and Feelings: Essays on American Intellectual and Religious History, 1952–1982* (New York: Oxford University Press, 1983), 65. This essay was first published in the *American Historical Review* 70 (1964): 79–82. It arose out of a lecture May gave at a 1959 gathering of Protestant church historians from various seminaries, which he delivered again in revised form in 1962 at a meeting of the American Studies Association.

21. May, "The Recovery of American Religious History," 67.

22. See Hart, *The University Gets Religion*.

23. Timothy L. Smith, *Revivalism and Social Reform in Mid-Nineteenth-Century America* (New York: Abingdon Press, 1957).

24. Albert Raboteau, *Slave Religion: The Invisible Institution in the Antebellum South* (New York: Oxford University Press, 1978); Gayraud Wilmore, *Black Religion and Black Radicalism* (Garden City, NY: Anchor Press, 1973); E. Franklin Frazier, *The Negro Church in America* (New York: Schocken Books, 1963).

25. Stout and Taylor, "Studies of Religion in American Society," 17–18. For a somewhat biographical discussion of the New Social History and the New Cultural History, see William H, Sewell, Jr., *The Logics of History: Social Theory and Social Transformation* (Chicago: University of Chicago Press, 2005), in particular chap. 5, "The Political Unconscious of Social and Cultural History, or, Confessions of a Former Quantitative Historian," pp. 22–80.

26. Quoted in George Marsden, *Fundamentalism and American Culture: The Shaping of Twentieth-Century Evangelicalism, 1870–1925* (New York: Oxford University Press, 1980), 188.

27. Edward Larson, *Summer for the Gods: The Scopes Trial and America's Continuing Debate over Science and Religion* (New York: Basic Books, 1997); Frederick Lewis Allen, *Only Yesterday: An Informal History of the Nineteen Twenties* (New York: Harper and Brothers, 1931).

28. Stewart G. Cole, *The History of Fundamentalism* (New York: R.R. Smith, Inc., 1931), 324.

29. Richard Hofstadter, *Anti-Intellectualism in American Life* (New York: Knopf, 1963), 117–19, 123.

30. Ernest R. Sandeen, *The Roots of Fundamentalism: British and American Millenarianism, 1800–1930* (Chicago: University of Chicago Press, 1970).

31. Marsden, *Fundamentalism and American Culture.*

32. Quoted in Stout and Taylor, "Studies of Religion in American Society," 19. The quote is from an unpublished essay by Jon Butler, "Born-Again America? A Critique of the New 'Evangelical Thesis' in Recent American Historiography," unpublished paper, Organization of American Historians, Spring 1991.

33. Leonard I. Sweet, "Wise as Serpents, Innocent as Doves: The New Evangelical Historiography," *Journal of the American Academy of Religion* 56 (1988): 398.

34. I have tried in more detail elsewhere. See Barry Hankins, "Marsden and Modern Fundamentalism," *American Evangelicalism: George Marsden and the State of American Religious History*, eds. Darren Dochuk, Thomas S. Kidd, and Kurt W. Peterson (Notre Dame, IN: University of Notre Dame Press, 2014), 141–65.

35. See Martin E. Marty and R. Scott Appleby, eds., *Fundamentalisms Observed* (Chicago: University of Chicago Press, 1991); *Fundamentalisms and Society: Reclaiming the Sciences, the Family, and Education*

(Chicago: University of Chicago Press, 1993); *Fundamentalisms and the State: Remaking Polities, Economies, and Militance* (Chicago: University of Chicago Press, 1993); *Accounting for Fundamentalisms: The Dynamic Character of Movements* (Chicago: University of Chicago Press, 1994); and *Fundamentalisms Comprehended* (Chicago: University of Chicago Press, 1995).

36. Martin Marty, *Righteous Empire: The Protestant Experience in America* (New York: Dial Press, 1970); Martin Marty, *Modern American Religion*, 3 vols. (Chicago: University of Chicago Press, 1986–1996), vol. 1, *The Irony of It All, 1893–1919*, vol. 2. *The Noise of Conflict, 1919–41*, and vol. 3, *Under God, Indivisible, 1941–1960*. See also Martin Marty, *Pilgrims in Their Own Land, 500 Years of Religion in America* (Boston: Little, Brown, and Co., 1984).

37. Among others see Mark Noll, *Christians in the American Revolution* (Grand Rapids, MI: Christian University Press, 1977); *Princeton and the Republic, 1768–1822: The Search for a Christian Enlightenment in the Era of Samuel Stanhope Smith* (Princeton, NJ: Princeton University Press, 1989); *America's God: From Jonathan Edwards to Abraham Lincoln* (New York: Oxford University Press, 2002); *A History of Christianity in the United States and Canada* (Grand Rapids, MI: Eerdmans, 1992); *The New Shape of World Christianity: How American Experience Reflects Global Faith* (Downers Grove, IL: IVP Academic, 2009); *Between Faith and Criticism: Evangelicals, Scholarship, and the Bible in America* (San Francisco: Harper and Row, 1987); *The Scandal of the Evangelical Mind* (Grand Rapids, MI: Eerdmans, 1994); *Jesus Christ and the Life of the Mind* (Grand Rapids, MI: Eerdmans, 2011); Mark Noll, David Bebbington, and George Rawlyk, eds., *Evangelicalism: Comparative Studies of Popular Protestantism in North America, the British Isles, and Beyond* (New York: Oxford University Press, 1994).

38. Carl Becker, "Every Man His Own Historian," *American Historical Review* 37 (1932): 221–36.

39. Outler, "Theodosius' Horse," 254.

40. Edward H. Carr, *What Is History?* (New York: St. Martin's Press, 1961).

41. G. R. Elton, *The Practice of History* (New York: Crowell, 1967).

42. Peter Novick, *The Noble Dream: The 'Objectivity Question' and the American Historical Profession* (Cambridge, UK: Cambridge University Press, 1988).

43. See Keith Jenkins, *On the Limits of History: Essays on Theory and Practice* (New York and London: Routledge, 2009); or Hayden White, *The Content of the Form: Narrative Discourse and Historical Representation* (Baltimore, MD: Johns Hopkins Press, 1987). For essays on both sides of the postmodern debate among historians, see

Keith Jenkins, ed., *The Postmodern History Reader* (New York and London: Routledge, 1997).

44. Hankins, "Marsden and Modern Fundamentalism," 145–48.

45. See, for example, James Ault, Jr., *Spirit and Flesh: Life in a Fundamentalist Baptist Church* (New York: Vintage Books, 2004); Nancy Ammerman, *Bible Believers: Fundamentalists in the Modern World* (New Brunswick, NJ: Rutgers University Press, 1987); Brenda Brasher, *Godly Women: Fundamentalism and Female Power* (New Brunswick, NJ: Rutgers University Press, 1998), 4; R. Marie Griffith, *God's Daughters: Evangelical Women and the Power of Submission* (Berkeley: University of California Press, 1997); and Alan Peshkin, *God's Choice: The Total World of a Fundamentalist Christian School* (Chicago: University of Chicago Press, 1986).

46. Catherine Brekus, "Introduction: Searching for Women in Narratives of American Religious History," in *The Religious History of American Women*, ed. Catherine Brekus (Chapel Hill, NC: University of North Carolina Press, 2007), 2–3; Susan Hill Lindley, *You Have Slept Out of Your Place: A History of Women and Religion in America*, 1st ed. (Louisville, KY: Westminster John Knox Press, 1996).

47. Brekus, "Introduction: Searching for Women," 6.

48. Ann Braude, "Women's History *Is* American Religious History," in *Retelling U.S. Religious History*, ed. Thomas A. Tweed (Berkeley: University of California Press, 1997), 87–107.

49. Brekus, "Introduction: Searching for Women," 25–26, quotation on 26.

50. Quoted in Brekus, "Introduction: Searching for Women," 24.

51. The classic in this interpretation is Paul E. Johnson, *A Shopkeepers Millennium: Society and Revivals in Rochester, New York, 1815–1837* (New York: Hill and Wang, 1978). The most influential of those who argue that revivals empowered common people is Nathan Hatch, *The Democratization of American Christianity* (New Haven, CT: Yale University Press, 1989). Among others, see also William R. Sutton, *Journeymen for Jesus: Evangelical Artisans Confront Capitalism in Jacksonian Baltimore* (University Park, PA: Pennsylvania State University Press, 1998).

52. Brekus, "Introduction: Searching for Women," 26–27.

53. Stout and Taylor, "Studies of Religion in American Society," 21. Out of 495 respondents in Stout and Taylor's study, 188 listed Catholicism or some aspect of evangelicalism as their focus.

54. Leigh Eric Schmidt, "The Parameters and Problematics of American Religious Liberalism," in *American Religious Liberalism*, eds. Leigh Eric Schmidt and Sally M. Promey (Bloomington, IN: Indiana University Press, 2012), 11–12.

55. Schmidt, "The Parameters and Problematics of American Religious Liberalism," 1–14.

56. David Hollinger, *After Cloven Tongues of Fire: Protestant Liberalism in Modern American History* (Princeton, NJ: Princeton University Press, 2013), xii. See also Matthew Hedstrom, *The Rise of Liberal Religion: Book Culture and American Spirituality in the Twentieth Century* (New York: Oxford University Press, 2013); Elesha Coffman, *The Christian Century and the Rise of the Protestant Mainstream* (New York: Oxford University Press, 2013); and Jennifer Schussler, "A Religious Legacy, with Its Leftward Tilt, Is Reconsidered," *New York Times*, July 23, 2013, accessed at http://www.nytimes.com/2013/07/24/books/a-religious-legacy-with-its-leftward-tilt-is-reconsidered.html.

57. Quoted in Schmidt, "The Parameters and Problematics of American Religious Liberalism," 9.

58. Diana Eck, *A New Religious America: How a "Christian Country" Has Now Become the Most Religiously Diverse Nation* (San Francisco: Harper Collins, 2001); Paul Harvey and Edward J. Blum, eds., *The Columbia Guide to Religion in American History* (New York: Columbia University Press, 2012).

59. Schmidt, "The Parameters and Problematics of American Religious Liberalism," 10.

60. Patrick Carey, "Recent American Catholic Historiography: New Directions in Religious History," in *New Directions in American Religious History*, eds. Harry S. Stout and D. G. Hart (New York: Oxford University Press, 1997), 446–47.

61. Robert Orsi, *The Madonna of 115th Street: Faith and Community in Italian Harlem, 1880–1950* (New Haven, CT: Yale University Press, 1985).

62. Carey, "Recent American Catholic Historiography," 447.

63. Ibid., 452–53.

64. Ibid., 456.

65. John McGreevy, *Catholicism and American Freedom* (New York: W.W. Norton, 2003).

66. See, for example, David Bebbington, *The Dominance of Evangelicalism: The Age of Spurgeon and Moody* (Downers Grove, IL: InterVarsity Press, 2005); David Bebbington, *Baptists through the Centuries: A History of a Global People* (Waco, TX: Baylor University Press, 2010); and David Bebbington, *Victorian Religious Revivals: Culture and Piety in Local and Global Contexts* (New York: Oxford University Press, 2012). For Noll's global approach, see note number 37.

67. Lamin Sanneh, "Introduction: The Changing Face of Christianity: The Cultural Impetus of a World Religion," in *The Changing Face of*

Christianity: Africa, the West, and the World, eds. Joel Carpenter and Lamin Sanneh (New York: Oxford University Press, 2005), 4.
68. Quoted in Sanneh, "Introduction," 4.
69. Quoted in Sanneh, "Introduction," 17, n. 1. See Andrew Walls, *The Cross Cultural Process in Christian History* (Maryknoll, NY: Orbis Books, 2002), 119; and Philip Jenkins, *The Next Christendom: The Coming of Global Christianity* (New York: Oxford University Press, 2002).
70. Alister Chapman, John Coffey, and Brad S. Gregory, eds., *Seeing Things Their Way: Intellectual History and the Return to Religion* (Notre Dame, IN: University of Notre Dame Press, 2009).
71. Stout and Taylor, "Studies of Religion in American Society," 28.
72. Robert B. Townsend, "A New Found Religion? The Field Surges among AHA Members," *Perspectives on History,* December 2009, accessed at http://www.historians.org/publications-and-directories/perspectives-on-history/december-2009/a-new-found-religion-the-field-surges-among-aha-members.
73. Stanley Fish, "One University under God," *Chronicle of Higher Education*, January 7, 2005, accessed at http://chronicle.com/article/One-*University*-Under-God-/45077.

SUGGESTED READINGS

Ahlstrom, Sydney. *A Religious History of the American People*, 2 vols. New Haven, CT: Yale University Press, 1972. The most comprehensive modern survey of religion in America. Running roughly 1,200 pages, the volumes serve as a virtual reference work for the history of religion in America.
Brekus, Catherine, ed. *The Religious History of American Women*. Chapel Hill, NC: University of North Carolina Press, 2007. Collection of essays surveying the historiographical trends, issues, and challenges in studying women and religion in America.
Carpenter, Joel, and Lamin Sanneh, eds. *The Changing Face of Christianity: Africa, the West, and the World*. New York: Oxford University Press, 2005. Collection of essays that helped pioneer recent scholarship on global (or world) Christianity. Sanneh's introductory essay is particularly helpful in framing the conversation. The essays help show the indigenization of Christianity outside the West.
Dolan, Jay. *The American Catholic Experience: A History from Colonial Times to the Present*. Garden City, NY: Doubleday, 1985. Most comprehensive survey of the history of Catholicism in America. Dolan's earlier work brought Catholic history into the mainstream of the study of religion in the United States.

Eck, Diana. *A New Religious America: How a "Christian Country" Has Now Become the Most Religiously Diverse Nation.* San Francisco: Harper Collins, 2001. Narrative of the growth of non-Christian religions in recent American history. Essential for understanding the growth of religious pluralism.

Harvey, Paul, and Edward J. Blum, eds. *The Columbia Guide to Religion in American History.* New York: Columbia University Press, 2012. Collection of historiographical essays covering the major areas of historical scholarship on American religion—colonial, Native American, civil religion, theology, evangelicals, religion and politics, war and peace, gender, race, ethnicity, environment, pop culture, Catholicism, Judaism, Mormonism, and Islam. The place to find expert direction toward the most important historical literature on religion in the United States.

Holifield, E. Brooks. *Theology in America: Christian Thought from the Age of the Puritans to the Civil War.* New Haven, CT: Yale University Press, 2003. Along with Mark Noll's *America's God: From Jonathan Edwards to Abraham Lincoln,* this is one of two comprehensive histories of theology in the United States up to the Civil War. Both are intellectual histories of the highest quality.

Hollinger, David. *After Cloven Tongues of Fire: Protestant Liberalism in Modern American History.* Princeton, NJ: Princeton University Press, 2013. Most recent survey of the history of Protestant liberalism. Helps explain how the liberal minority (there were always more evangelicals) dominated the religious landscape in mid-twentieth-century America.

Hutchison, William R. *The Modernist Impulse in American Protestantism.* Cambridge, MA: Harvard University Press, 1976. The first and now classic interpretation of Protestant liberalism in twentieth-century America.

Jenkins, Philip. *The Next Christendom: The Coming of Global Christianity.* New York: Oxford University Press, 2002. Highly readable narrative of the recent rise of global Christianity in the southern hemisphere and Asia.

Latourette, Kenneth Scott. *A History of Christianity,* 2 vols. New York: Harper and Row, 1975. Originally published in 1953, this is the most comprehensive (over 2,000 pages) modern history of Christianity. With his encyclopedic yet highly readable approach, Latourette's monumental feat of scholarship is best used as a reference work today.

Lindley, Susan Hill. *You Have Slept Out of Your Place: A History of Women and Religion in America,* 1st ed. Louisville, KY: Westminster John Knox Press, 1996. First survey text on the role of women in American religion from the colonial period to the late twentieth century. Shows convincingly how women shaped American religion in decisive ways throughout the sweep of American history.

Marsden, George. *Fundamentalism and American Culture: The Shaping of Twentieth-Century Evangelicalism, 1870–1925*, 2nd ed. (25th year anniversary ed.). New York: Oxford University Press, 1980. New York: Oxford University Press, 2006. The standard interpretation of the rise of Protestant fundamentalism in early twentieth-century America. The book launched what came to be called the evangelical paradigm in the study of religion in the United States.

Marty, Martin. *Modern American Religion*, 3 vols. Chicago: University of Chicago Press, 1986–1996), vol. 1, *The Irony of It All, 1893–1919*, vol. 2, *The Noise of Conflict, 1919–41*, and vol. 3, *Under God, Indivisible, 1941–1960*. Comprehensive history of twentieth-century Protestantism by the most prolific religious historian. Marty created the two-party paradigm (liberal and evangelical) for understanding American Protestantism.

McGreevy, John. *Catholicism and American Freedom*. New York: W.W. Norton, 2003. Best and most accessible interpretation of the tension between a liberal conception of freedom and the doctrine of church authority over all realms of life.

Noll, Mark. *America's God: From Jonathan Edwards to Abraham Lincoln*. New York: Oxford University Press, 2002. Nearly any of the many books by Noll are worthy of mention. *America's God* is one of two comprehensive histories of theology in the United States from the colonial period to the Civil War, the other being E. Brooks Holifield's *Theology in America* (cited above).

Noll, Mark, David Bebbington, and George Rawlyk, eds., *Evangelicalism: Comparative Studies of Popular Protestantism in North America, the British Isles, and Beyond*. New York: Oxford University Press, 1994. An early example of the turn toward the global history of evangelicalism.

Schmidt, Leigh Eric, and Sally M. Promey, eds. *American Religious Liberalism*. Bloomington, IN: Indiana University Press, 2012. Collection of essays marking the recent effort to better understand liberal Protestantism in twentieth-century America.

Walls, Andrew. *The Cross Cultural Process in Christian History*. Maryknoll, NY: Orbis Books, 2002. Walls was a pioneer of the study of global Christianity as early as the 1980s. This book stands with Philip Jenkins's *The Next Christendom* and Joel Carpenter and Lamin Sanneh's *The Changing Face of Christianity* as essential for understanding the rise of global Christianity.

Wilmore, Gayraud. *Black Religion and Black Radicalism*. Garden City, NY: Anchor Press, 1973. Arguably the most comprehensive and provocative history of African American Christianity from slavery through the Civil Rights movement.

6

Faith and Families

The Scientific Pursuit of Relational Spirituality

Annette Mahoney

Are religion and spirituality (R/S)[1] relevant to all types of partners and parents in the twenty-first century? Why do R/S often seem to be a source of strength in forming and maintaining family relationships? When can R/S create struggles for families? Are these questions worthy of scientific investigation? Regarding the last question, social scientists have begun to scratch the surface of the questions about for whom, why, and when R/S matter for the rapidly changing institution called family, but jaw-dropping gaps exist in peer-reviewed scientific research. Given the enormous amount of work to be done, expansion is needed for the network of family scholars from varying disciplines (sociology, psychology, marriage and family studies) who share the common goal to examine the roles of R/S, for better or worse, for families, a topic that is currently largely invisible within the social science community. The main aim of this chapter is to encourage more researchers to dive into the controversial middle of faith and family. To that end, I offer readers a user-friendly guide[2] to join the scientific pursuit of relational spirituality in the context of family life and to identify a research agenda when traveling down the many unexplored pathways where R/S and family life intersect.

The most fundamental issue that those who embark down these trails need to know is that their work will be relatively rare. Here is an anecdote to illustrate the remarkable blind spot that exists among academic researchers who study family life when it comes to R/S. I work at a state university that houses two major basic research centers on family life: the National Center for Marriage and Family Research and the Center for Family and Demographic Research. As a result, nationally renowned scholars routinely come to campus to give talks. For example, in the fall of 2014, I had the opportunity to meet with Phillip Cohen, who had recently published a major new sociological textbook on family for undergraduate and graduate courses.[3] I asked him why the textbook did not have a chapter on R/S. He explained that when he and his publisher reviewed similar books, none of them included a chapter on religion, with the clear implication that data-driven social scientists do not view R/S as sufficiently important topics to merit page space in a textbook on contemporary families.

Here are some data to anchor this anecdote. In preparing the introduction for a special section on R/S and marriage for the *Journal of Family Psychology*,[4] I entered the word *marriage* as a search term into the fields of Abstract or Keyword or Subject for the years 1980 to 2009. The PsycINFO search engine yielded 11,828 hits for empirical studies published in peer-reviewed journals in English, and the SocINDEX yielded 12,584 hits. By contrast, my colleagues and I were able to locate only 131 studies where the researchers had formulated and tested specific hypotheses on links between marital and R/S variables during this thirty-year time frame,[5] or around 1.1 percent of empirical studies on marriage. The scarcity of rigorous scientific research on R/S and parenting is even more striking. To prepare this chapter, I entered the term *parent* for the years 1980 to 2009 into PsycINFO and SocINDEX, with 49,976 and 21,196 hits, respectively. By contrast, our research group could locate only 162 peer-reviewed studies that examined specific hypotheses on R/S predicting parenting and family functioning across this time period.[6]

The relative dearth of focused scientific inquiry on ways that faith may shape family relationships stands in stark and puzzling contrast with the widespread prevalence of R/S practices and beliefs. In the

United States, for example, 92 percent of Americans report believing in a God or a universal spirit, and 65 percent pray daily to weekly outside religious services, with 68 percent believing that there is more than one true way to interpret the teachings of their religious tradition.[7] Further, 79 percent of American married mothers, 77 percent of single mothers, and 68 percent of cohabiting mothers report that religion is "somewhat" or "very important" to their daily lives, and 49 percent, 39 percent, and 32 percent, respectively, attend religious services at least two to three times per month.[8] These percentages suggest that many families often engage in both private spiritual beliefs or practices and publicly participate in a faith community to support their family lives. Conversely, religious groups offer families spiritual guidance about coupling and uncoupling, conceiving and childrearing, and caring for loved ones across the life span.

Fortunately, a window appears to be opening within the community of social scientists and practitioners to take a closer look at R/S in the context of family life. For example, Froma Walsh's popular textbook on families[9] used in marriage and family classes across multiple disciplines includes a chapter on R/S. In addition, the number of peer-reviewed studies published in social science journals that tested specific hypotheses about how R/S factors may be tied to marital or parental adjustment increased in the first decade of the twenty-first century compared to the prior twenty years.

I presume that the primary audience of this chapter consists of social scientists who are curious about and may want to expand rigorous empirical research on R/S and family life. There are rewards from engaging in this unusual line of work: (1) the intellectual stimulation that comes from grappling with the complex R/S issues involved in the search for family relationships, a quest that embodies some of life's most profound joys and heartbreaks; (2) the personal satisfaction of studying a topic relevant to many families around the globe; and (3) the professional challenge of using stringent scientific methods to uncover the helpful and harmful roles that faith can play for couples and parents. Perhaps the good news about the relative silence on R/S and family among social scientists is that these rewards are readily available because so many significant basic and applied research questions remain to be explored. The remainder of this chapter takes on three distinct tasks to help equip researchers with foundational knowledge to tackle the particular research questions of their choice.

First, I provide a necessarily short narrative history about the origins and development of social scientific research that has examined the influences of R/S on family relationships. Here I describe the basic contours of the research community and literature. Second, I introduce the Relational Spirituality Framework (RSF) that I created to organize the wide-ranging studies on the impact of R/S on the creation, maintenance, and transformation of family relationships. Third, I then highlight key research findings that pertain to each stage.

In each section, I point out one of three characteristics of this literature that pose a high risk that R/S will increasingly be viewed as irrelevant by mainstream family scientists and therefore pushed further to the edges of scientific exploration, including (1) a predominant focus on "traditional" families headed by married heterosexual parents, (2) heavy reliance on brief measures of involvement in organized religion, and (3) a nearly exclusive investigation of samples comprised of non-distressed families. Concurrently, I offer three parallel new directions for researchers to pursue so research on relational spirituality and family life grows rather than disappears completely over time. Specifically, I advocate for more study of (1) so-called nontraditional families, (2) specific measures to untangle the helpful and harmful roles that R/S factors can play for couples and parents, and (3) people experiencing significant relational distress where R/S may be especially problematic.

HISTORY OF RESEARCH

In this section, I sketch the history of research on R/S in marriage and parenting, with an emphasis on work published in peer-reviewed, scientific journals since 1980. In 1991, Jenkins published a comprehensive review of studies generated by social scientists on religion and families from the years 1930 to 1990.[10] This review indicates that the focus of family scientists throughout the twentieth century was on whether religious affiliation (e.g., Catholic, Protestant, Jewish, other, or none) and the frequency of religious attendance predicted rates of interreligious affiliation marriages, childbirth and divorce, marital satisfaction, and attitudes about marriage or parenting in Western counties. Another central concern was whether the marriages of spouses affiliated with the same religious tradition fared better than couples affiliated with different traditions in terms of lower divorce rates and greater overall marital satisfaction. In short, family sociologists with an interest in participation in well-established religious groups dominated the research literature during these six decades, but sociologists' interest in these issues appears to have waned by 1990. For example, unlike prior decades, the *Journal of Marriage and Family* (*JMF*), the premier journal where sociologists publish, declined to include a review paper on religion in *JMF*'s 1990 "Decade-in-Review" volume. This editorial decision implies that by the end of 1980s, the conventional wisdom among social scientists was that institutionalized religion was no longer of sufficient societal importance to families to merit page space in *JMF*.

Meanwhile, mainstream academic psychology displayed scant interest in R/S factors predicting family functioning throughout the twentieth century. For example, 1999 marks the first year to my knowledge that any journal sponsored by the American Psychological Association (APA) published a peer-reviewed study of R/S predicting marital adjustment[11] or parenting practices.[12] In 2001, APA's *Journal of Family Psychology* (*JFP*) then published the first special section on R/S and marriage/family life at the bequest of the outgoing senior editor Ross Parke. This special issue included a meta-analysis of 97 peer-reviewed studies published in social science journals from 1980 to 1999 that Mahoney and colleagues were able to locate that involved specific hypotheses on R/S variables predicting marital and family outcomes,[13] along with commentaries by leading family psychologists calling for more work on the topic of R/S and family life.

Academic social scientists have recently shown more interest in R/S as a persistent cultural reality for many couples and parents. For example, in 2009, *JMF* solicited a "Decade-in-Review" of research on R/S and family. I was invited to write this review, in which I located 184 peer-reviewed studies published from 2000 to 2009 that explicitly examined how R/S factors contribute to marital and family functioning.[14] In 2013, *JFP* put out another call for studies at the bequest of Nadine Kaslow, 2014 APA president and senior editor of *JFP*. In October 2014, *JFP* published a special section with five studies of ways that R/S factors enhance marriage, and in December 2014, *JFP* published another special section on the complex interplay of family and R/S factors in predicting family members' well-being. Hopefully, these developments will spur further interchanges between family psychology and the psychology of R/S.

With regard to who is conducting research, scholars from diverse disciplines have published at least one study that targets R/S factors as predictors of family outcomes. This group includes individuals in university-based psychology, sociology, social work, and marriage and family studies departments, as well as obstetrics and gynecology, pediatric, and nursing departments in medical centers. Thus, diverse research methods are evident in the literature that reflect the varying disciplinary backgrounds of researchers.

For example, family sociologists tend to conduct secondary analyses of telephone surveys with large community or nationally representative samples. Leading examples include work by John Bartkowski, Melinda Denton, Penny Edgell, Christopher Ellison, Sally Gallagher, Richard Petts, Mark Regnerus, Brad Wilcox, and Xiaohe Xu. By contrast, couples' and family psychologists tend to collect data from targeted community or college student samples using in-depth surveys, experimental designs, and/or observational techniques. Leading examples include the trio of Frank Fincham, Steven Beach, and Scott Stanley; Ev Worthington, Joshua Hook, Jennifer Ripley, and Elizabeth Hall; and researchers who work at or have graduated from Bowling Green State University, such as myself, Ken Pargament, Gina Brelsford, Elizabeth Krumrei, Krystal Hernandez, and Anna Hawley. Other researchers, particularly with training from marriage and family studies departments, have offered rich qualitative analyses of married heterosexuals who are highly involved in Christian, Muslim, or Jewish religious groups. Leading examples include David Dollahite, Loren Marks, and Nathan Lambert.[15]

It is important to emphasize that nearly all research on the role of R/S involves national or community samples, not subsamples of couples or parents seeking psychiatric or psychological interventions for marital or family problems, such as infertility, infidelity, or child abuse. For example, to my knowledge, no peer-reviewed studies have been published in journals that involve randomized clinical trials of the effectiveness or efficacy of therapists addressing R/S beliefs or practices when counseling distressed couples[16] or parents.[17] The notable exception is an initial randomized clinical trial that compared a religiously accommodative intervention designed for maritally distressed, predominantly conservative Christian couples (2014) to a parallel nonreligious version of the same marital intervention (HOPE), with no major differences found in outcomes.[18]

Nevertheless, an abundance of scholarly articles and book chapters have been written on integrating R/S into couples and family therapy, such as in Walsh's popular *Spiritual Resources in Family Therapy*.[19] These creative outputs rest on scholarship about diverse teachings on family life across religious denominations, broad psychological and sociological theories about R/S, inferences drawn from basic research on R/S for nondistressed couples or families, and clinical wisdom bolstered by case examples. Of course, even with such knowledge at hand, practitioners need to assess carefully with individual clients how faith may be part of the problem or solution in addressing dysfunctional relationships. Scientists also need to recognize that salutary findings about R/S within nondistressed samples do not necessarily generalize to distressed families where R/S may go awry more often. I revisit this issue later in this chapter.

I now sketch the contours of the state of science on faith and family life. For illustrative purposes, I summarize the characteristics of the 184 peer-reviewed studies that I located for the 2010 *JMF* review and describe topics examined in at least four studies (*n* in parentheses). A total of 80 studies were published on couples' unions between 1999 and 2009. Topics included mate selection and the likelihood of getting married (22), egalitarianism in male-female marriage (7), work-home balance (9), marital satisfaction (20), marital conflict (11), risk of divorce (6), risk of domestic violence (7), marital infidelity and sexuality (6), and coping with a prior history of divorce (4) or domestic violence (8). Another 104 studies covered parenting or family topics, including the likelihood of women giving birth (11) and men spending time with their offspring (9), pregnancy and infant care (10), parental discipline (8), warmth and monitoring (5), physical abuse toward children (4), and parenting style (8) and relational quality (8) with adolescents. Across all 184 studies, 26 percent involved unstructured interviews (i.e., qualitative data) and 74 percent of studies involved administering structured surveys with couples or parents (i.e., quantitative data). Notably, most quantitative studies (around 77 percent) relied on one or two general questions about R/S, such as how often participants report attending worship services or how important religion is to their daily life. As I will elaborate in subsequent sections, more in-depth measures are needed to expand and advance this research area.

Not surprisingly, research on faith and family life is limited by the same constraints that plague social science research generally.

Studies published in English have overwhelmingly involved samples drawn from Western societies, with around 91 percent drawn from the United States. Most of the 137 quantitative studies used national (52 percent) or community (34 percent) samples. Thus, consistent with U.S. norms, most participants self-identified as being affiliated with a Christian group or as being nonaffiliated, with wide variation in the frequency of religious attendance.[20] Clearly more work is needed by social scientists studying non-Western cultures, where many people identify with a R/S tradition, albeit not necessarily Christianity. Of the 47 qualitative studies, about half (51 percent) involved convenience samples of American married couples or families highly involved in various religious groups, again predominantly Christian, with other studies focusing on particular religious subgroups (e.g., Latter-Day Saints, Jews, Muslims). Methodologically, most quantitative studies (75 percent) have relied on cross-sectional rather than longitudinal or experimental designs. This makes causal inferences about the influence of R/S on couples or parents difficult to defend because critics can argue that many third-variable confounds, such as socioeconomic status, education, and personality variables, could explain away linkages.

Two other methodological issues involve the mono-method assessment of constructs. Specifically, studies on faith and family life (1) rely heavily on the self-report of a single family member, rather than on two or more members, to assess R/S predictors and relationship outcomes, and (2) direct observation of family interactions has been rare (i.e., two studies on marital dyads and eight on parent-youth dyads between 1999 and 2009). Hopefully, researchers will increasingly employ multiple reporters (e.g., both partners in a union, two parents, a parent and child) and assessment tools (e.g., self-report and observational data), as well as sophisticated longitudinal analyses, to advance the scientific credibility of findings on faith and family functioning, while reminding themselves, and journal editors, that the use of cross-sectional data and solo reporters from Western samples do not represent limitations unique to this area.

RSF: ORGANIZING AND ADVANCING RESEARCH

To organize and clarify linkages between R/S variables and couple and family outcomes, I developed the RSF (see Table 6.1).[21] In this

Table 6.1. Relational Spirituality Framework*

Relational Spirituality	Stages of Family Relationships: *Goals*		
	Discover: Form and Structure Relationship	Maintain: Preserve and Protect Relationship	Transform: Reform and/or Exit Relationships
Global R/S Factors: 1–2 items about the reporter — Overall importance of religion and/or attendance . . .	. . . increases likelihood of getting married, women wanting and having children when married, and married men spending time with offspring in nondistressed samples.	. . . increases marital satisfaction and positive parenting by married and single parents, and lowers risk of divorce, infidelity, domestic violence, and child physical abuse in nondistressed samples.	No studies focus on subsamples of intact distressed couples or parents. Some studies on individuals coping with prior divorce, romantic breakup, or domestic violence.
Specific Factors: Multiple items assess the reporter's religious (R)/spiritual (S) emotions, cognitions, and behaviors tied to the relationship. — **Tier 1:** Relationship with God/Higher Power(s) — Strength	? Does **Support from God** with dating, mating, or becoming a parent increase commitment and intentional decision making by heterosexual & LGBT individuals?	√ *Prayer for Partner's Well-Being* increases relationship quality for married and dating partners. ? Does **Support from God** motivate married or unmarried parents to use effective parenting?	√ *Support from God in Coping* predicts less distress after a divorce or romantic breakup. ? Does **Support from God** enhance positive coping with marital or parenting dysfunction?

(Continued)

Table 6.1. Relational Spirituality Framework* (Continued)

		Stages of Family Relationships: Goals		
Relational Spirituality		Discover: Form and Structure Relationship	Maintain: Preserve and Protect Relationship	Transform: Reform and/or Exit Relationships
Content of items and context of relationship determine whether the specific factor helps or harms the relationship or family member(s).	Strain	? Do **Struggles with God** over dating, mating, and becoming a parent increase ambivalence and poor planning by heterosexuals and LGBT individuals?	? Does **Support from/Struggles with God** motivate married and unmarried partners or parents to use ineffective relationship skills?	√ **Turning to God to Forgive** an ex-spouse predicts less forgiveness and more dyadic verbal hostility over time. ? Does **Prayer for Partner/Child** in distressed families intensify dysfunction?
Tier 2: Family relationship possesses spiritual properties	Strength	? Does **Sanctification of a Union** increase commitment and marital rates by same- and opposite-sex couples? ? Does **Sanctification of Parenting** increase commitment and intentional parenthood by married or single individuals?	√ **Sanctification of Marriage/Union** enhances relationship quality for married, same-sex, and cohabiting couples. √ **Sanctification of Sexuality in Marriage/Union** predicts greater sexual satisfaction. √ **Spiritual Intimacy/Disclosure** in family dyads relates to better relational quality for couples and parent-adult relationships.	? Does **Spiritual Intimacy or Sanctification** of marriage/union increase partners' adaptive efforts to repair a distressed marriage/union? ? Does **Sanctification of Parenting** increase distressed parents' motivation to change their parenting? (Or increase rigidity?)

	Strain	? Does viewing infertility as a **Desecration/Sacred Loss** predict greater relational and personal distress?	√ **Spiritual One-Upmanship/ Theistic Triangulation** is tied to greater verbal hostility and relational distress between spouses and parent-adult child dyads.	√ Viewing a romantic breakup, divorce, or parental divorce as a **Desecration/Sacred Loss** predicts greater personal distress. ? Does **Sanctification of a Union** increase excessive commitment to a destructive union?
Tier 3: Relationship with religious community	**Strength**	? Does **Support from a Religious Group** reinforce intentional decisions about marriage and parenthood?	? Does **Support from a Religious Group** increase virtuous behavior by married or unmarried partners or parents?	√ **Support from a Religious Group** is tied to women leaving & reconciling with abusive men, depending on the woman's goal.
	Strain	? Do **Struggles with a Religious Group** over dating, marriage, and parenthood increase ambivalence and poor planning?	? Does **Support from/Struggles with a Religious Group** increase ineffective relationship skills or distress by married or unmarried partners or parents?	? Does **Support from/ Struggles with a Religious Group** escalate blame and hostility by an abusive partner or parent?

* √ = Emerging findings; ? = Illustrative future research questions.

framework, spirituality refers to "the search for the sacred," and the two elements of this definition merit brief review.[22] In the RSF, the core of "the sacred" refers to human perceptions of the Divine, God/Higher Powers, or transcendent reality, but "the sacred" can extend to any aspect of life that individuals view as possessing supernatural character and significance.[23] Thus, for some people, family relationships may fall within the domain of the sacred. "The search" component includes three dynamic and recursive stages of the discovery, maintenance, and transformation of the sacred across the life span.[24] The term *relational spirituality* refers to spiritual emotions, cognitions, and behaviors that people may have as they strive to discover, maintain, and transform their relationships. Or, more elegantly stated, *relational spirituality* refers to when the search for the sacred is united, for better or worse, with the search for human relationships.

Given that this chapter focuses on family life, Table 6.1 illustrates the intersections of these co-occurring searches for couples and parents. Specifically, the columns across the top of the RSF sort the research literature into (1) *discovery*: forming and structuring a particular family relationship, (2) *maintenance*: preserving and protecting an established family relationship, and (3) *transformation*: coping with the reformation or termination of a distressed family relationship. Moving down, the rows of the RSF first divide the literature into two general approaches that researchers have taken to assess the role that R/S may play in shaping family relationships: *global* versus *specific* factors. Studies of global factors primarily reflect the assessment of a particular family member's engagement in organized religion, usually with one or two items, which is commonplace in sociological studies that rely on omnibus surveys of large national or community samples. Occasionally, researchers combine two reporters' responses on global factors to assess the degree of (dis)similarity between two family members, such as (dis)similarity in religious attendance rates between wives and husbands or between parents (nearly always mothers) and their adolescents or college-age offspring. Major findings based on studies that used global factors are summarized across the top row.

Studies of specific R/S factors involve the assessment of a particular family member's spiritual emotions, cognitions, and behaviors tied to a given relationship, usually with multiple items, which is commonplace in psychological research that recruits a targeted community sample. The RSF further divides specific factors into three relationship tiers, including *Tier 1*: the respondent's relationship with God/Higher Power(s), *Tier 2*: the respondent's human relationship under investigation (e.g., dating, cohabiting, marital, or parental relationship), and *Tier 3*: the respondent's relationship with a religious community.

Tier 1 in the RSF allows for the possibility that individuals draw on a felt connection to a theistic God/Higher Power(s) or nontheistic, supernatural phenomenon to inform their search for human relationships, with or without disclosing these processes to other family members. Tier 2 allows for the possibility both that individuals may privately perceive a given human relationship as possessing spiritual properties and that people may engage in overt, observable activities that infuse spirituality into a given relationship. Tier 3 allows for the possibility that individuals form connections to religious groups that affect the role that spiritual factors play in a relationship. Within each tier, specific spiritual constructs can be identified that would theoretically be expected to be a source of *strength* or *strain* for a relationship or individual. Whether a factor functions as a soothing resource or painful struggle depends on the content of the spiritual factor and the context of the relationship. For example, researchers have found that married and unmarried partners in generally happy unions who pray for the well-being of their partner are more likely to act in ways that maintain the relationship, such as being more forgiving.[25] However, in a relational context where individuals are embroiled in a dysfunctional union, prayer for one's partner may escalate maladaptive responses, such as excessive tolerance of wrongdoing. Table 6.1 offers examples of specific spiritual factors within each square that may function as a strength or struggle. Selected initial findings published in peer-reviewed journals are indicated by a checkmark ($\sqrt{}$), with a question mark (?) located next to factors that still need investigation.[26]

At this juncture, I address how the RSF deals with debates among social scientists about differentiating the domains of religion (R) and spirituality (S). Overarching definitions of R and S appear to be increasingly polarized in the scientific literature dominated by researchers working in Western societies. R tends to be portrayed as public engagement in a given religious tradition; adherence to orthodox beliefs, dogmas, or rituals; and external pressure to conform to social norms promoted by a religious group.[27] In family research, for example, attendance at worship services and endorsement of theologically conservative beliefs, such as a literalistic interpretation of the Bible, are typically labeled as "religiousness" or "religiosity." By contrast, S tends to be framed as personal belief in supernatural entities or phenomena, a private quest for enlightenment or virtues, and internal motivation to seek out a sense of purpose. However, the RSF resists polarizing R and S for at least three reasons.[28]

First, R remains the primary social institution that attempts to promote spirituality in peoples' daily lives, and in many societies, people continue to seek out resources for their spiritual journeys from one or more established religious traditions, such as enhancing their sense of connection to God/Higher Power(s) or a religious community. Second, religious traditions encompass diverse positions on family, social, political, and existential issues, and wide variation exists within and between religious denominations on controversial moral issues. Thus, as indicated in Tier 3 of the RSF, people can selectively seek out spiritual support from leaders or members within religious subgroups that reinforce their search for adult unions and parent-child relationships. For example, opposite- and same-sex couples can find religious groups who affirm the sanctity of their unions and encourage spiritual (and nonspiritual) pathways to sustain their bond.[29] RSF highlights that the goodness of fit between people and their religious group of choice helps determine whether they gain access to spiritual (or nonspiritual) resources or encounter spiritual struggles across the three tiers of RSF as they pursue family goals. Third, individuals can turn to secular groups to support their family values and reject the notion that seeking a sense of identity, meaning, or virtues is inherently "being spiritual," perhaps finding the phrase superfluous at best and insulting at worst.

KEY FINDINGS AND FUTURE DIRECTIONS FOR RELATIONAL SPIRITUALITY

Discovery Stage: For Whom Does R/S Matter?

In this section, I summarize empirical findings from studies using global R/S factors suggesting that people draw on their faith to motivate them to form and structure "traditional" family units comprising married heterosexual couples and biological offspring. I then discuss the conceptual lens of religious familism and why a broader perspective is needed to generate more research on the role of R/S in contemporary family life, at least within Western societies.

Forming and structuring heterosexual marriages. Research suggests that R/S global factors help to shape heterosexuals' decisions about whom to marry. Cross-culturally, men and women rank similarity in religious affiliation (e.g., "none," Catholic, Protestant) as an important factor when selecting a potential mate.[30] Individuals appear to decide early in courtship whether general (non)religious compatibility matters, with one study finding that the percentage of couples who have the same religious affiliation does not change across the stages of dating, being sexually intimate, cohabiting, or marrying.[31] In deciding to commit formally to a romantic partner, heterosexuals from all denominations who highly value religion are more likely marry in their early twenties rather than delaying marriage. Further, those who view religion as more important and who more often attend religious services are less likely to cohabit with a partner before or instead of getting married.

Empirical findings on how R/S factors affect the structure, or egalitarianism, of heterosexual marriages defy easy stereotypes. Muslims and conservative Christian Protestants living in the United States hold far more diverse and flexible *attitudes* about feminism, women's participation in paid work, and familial hierarchy than implied by conservative religious teachings that encourage patriarchal relations between men and women.[32] Even more telling are studies focused on *behavioral* indices of egalitarianism between couples that find almost no differences in how married heterosexuals who belong to socially liberal versus conservative religious groups manage decision making or divide general household labor.[33] However, R/S factors are tied to how married Americans structure their roles as co-parents. Specifically, after the transition to parenthood, greater religious attendance, biblical conservatism, and the sanctification of parent-infant relationships are associated with married heterosexuals adopting a traditional division of child care where mothers take a dominant position over fathers.[34]

Forming and structuring biological parent-child relationships. For centuries, religions have encouraged married heterosexuals to have biological children. Collectively, studies on maternal fertility suggest women's faith shapes their desire and decision making about when and whether to become a birth mother as follows.[35] Women who view religion as more important report a greater intention to bear children, regardless of how often they attend services or their particular religious affiliation. This finding also applies to women who do and do not hold socially conservative attitudes toward feminism or family life emphasized by socially conservative religious groups. Further, women who report that religion is important to them are more likely to have a child rather than remain childless into middle age. Unmarried pregnant teens who are more religiously engaged are also more likely to choose to give birth as single parents rather than terminate an unplanned pregnancy.[36]

In addition, R/S factors are tied to women's decisions to be a mother in a married family unit.[37] For example, higher religious attendance increases the odds that unmarried, pregnant women will marry a man after giving birth. Women who view religion as important in their lives are also more likely to give birth after age twenty-four, and less likely to have unplanned births, especially during adolescence, suggesting they intentionally try to delay motherhood until they are married.

Peer-reviewed research appears unavailable on R/S factors tied to male fertility rates (e.g., biological parentage rates by men). Researchers have sought to verify if married men involved in con- servative Protestant churches spend more time than other fathers forming a bond with their offspring rather than being distant or absent fathers. Studies have not supported this hypothesis.[38] On the other hand, across religious denominations, the more married men attend religious services, the more leisure time they spend with their children. This finding implies that more frequent attendance at a place of worship helps to motivate men to invest more time with biological offspring, although such studies reveal little about the quality of their fathering.[39]

Limitations with "religious familism." Taken together, these studies focus on the role that R/S factors play in peoples' decisions to form families comprising married heterosexual couples with children. Such research questions reflect a prominent conceptual lens underlying sociology literature called religious familism.[40] This model assumes that global religious factors reflect participants' acceptance that formation of family bonds should be governed by socially conservative positions emphasized by mainline and especially conservative branches of Christianity. For example, within evangelical circles, marriage is taught to be an explicit expression of lifelong commitment of one man and one woman that provides the only sanctioned structure for sexual intercourse and childbearing, resulting in nonmarital sex, cohabitation, same-sex marriage, single parenthood, divorce, and stepfamilies being morally undesirable.[41]

The lens of religious familism is also consistent with socially conservative teachings in Islam and Judaism that uphold the biological nuclear family as the ideal family structure.[42] For example, within Conservative and Orthodox Judaism, heterosexual marriage followed by procreation mirrors the very nature of God.[43] In Islam, heterosexual marriage is considered to be inherently spiritual and a religious obligation to complete one's faith.[44] Because marriage is considered the only legitimate way for men and women to be alone together within Islam, alternative family forms, such as cohabitation and same-sex unions, are ruled out as viable options.[45] In sum, three major monotheistic world religions (Judaism, Christianity, Islam) have traditionally argued that a family headed by a married heterosexual pair is the proper context to bear and raise human beings.[46] Religious familism, in turn, is a complementary model that focuses social scientists' attention on hypotheses that reflect such religious teachings.[47]

Future research: Extending R/S questions to diverse families. The risk of social scientists adopting religious familism to generate scientific research questions is that this model implies that the only people for whom R/S matter are individuals striving to marry an opposite-sex partner and be a co-parent of biological children with that spouse. The potentially incorrect assumption is that R/S are irrelevant to partners and parents who pursue the formation of adult unions and parent-child relationships that fall outside a mid-twentieth-century, middle-class, Western model of "the good family."[48] To the extent that researchers accept this premise, they are unlikely to ask whether R/S factors enhance peoples' motivation to create traditional and nontraditional families.[49] The RSF offers a broader conceptual lens for three reasons.

First, theological justifications have emerged in the past forty to fifty years within progressive branches of Christianity and Judaism that reject "natural law" rooted in biological ties as the optimal principles to guide the establishment of marital and family relationships.[50] For example, an increasing number of Protestant groups affirm same-sex marriage and honor same-sex covenants as vehicles of God's creation and grace in a similar fashion as opposite-sex marriage.[51] Ruether[52] provides an insightful description of recent shifts in ideologies about the family in progressive segments of the Christian community set within her analysis of the ever-changing history of diverse Christian perspectives on family life since the first century.

Second, and far more importantly, R/S factors may function similarly for diverse partners and parents regardless of statistically significant differences in the average rate of R/S factors based on religious affiliation, ethnicity, nationality, or family structure. For instance, in a recent national U.S. survey, religious attendance appeared to be similarly helpful to married and single mothers,[53] even though the latter group tends to be less involved in organized religion.

Third, many people selectively ignore teachings promoted by religious traditions as they seek out close relationships. For example, over half of Americans now in their mid to late thirties who were highly involved in organized religion as teens engaged in sex by the time they were eighteen. Specifically, 53 percent of teens who reported in 1995 that they attended religious services weekly had premarital sexual intercourse by the end of high school.[54] Further, 56 percent who said religion was "very important" as teens engaged in premarital sex, with 6.3 percent of the women and 4.2 percent of the men saying they engaged in consensual sexual relations with same-sex peers.[55] Contemporary young adults also appear to integrate R/S into their relationships in a manner at odds with orthodox religious teachings about sex. For example, Midwestern college students at a state university commonly viewed sexual intercourse in their loving but nonmarital relationship as possessing sacred qualities (e.g., holy, sacred, blessed), and the more they viewed premarital sex in this light, the more (not less) partners and sex they had had in the past.[56]

The fourth issue is the sharp rise in nontraditional forms of coupling and childbearing. For example, national surveys from 2011 to 2013 show that 65 percent of American women ages nineteen to forty-four reported having cohabited with at least one partner outside marriage at some point in their lives.[57] No studies, however, appear to exist on R/S factors that may shape women's or men's intentional decisions to enter stable cohabiting unions rather than remain single and then transition (or not) to a first marriage or remarriage after divorce. Similarly, no controlled research appears to exist as to what R/S factors motivate lesbian, gay, bisexual, or transgender (LGBT) partners' desire or decisions to get married, although one study has found that gay and lesbian individuals who view religion as important more often engage in ritualized commitment ceremonies and legal procedures (e.g., wills, mortgages) with same-sex partners to solidify their unions.[58]

Nontraditional family units are also on the rise, at least in Western culture. In the United States, for example, around 41 percent of American children are currently born outside marriage, up from just 5 percent in 1960.[59] Less than half (46 percent) of U.S. youth live with two married heterosexual parents in their first marriage, compared to 73 percent of children in 1960. Instead, 34 percent of children live with an unmarried parent, up from 9 percent in 1960, with most living with a single mother; only 4 percent of children are estimated to reside with two cohabiting parents. To keep up with these changes in family structure, studies could be done on the role that R/S factors play in premeditated decisions to take on a primary parent role. This would include becoming a single, step-, or foster parent; adopting children; adopting caretaker responsibility for relatives' offspring (e.g., grandchildren); and using assisted reproductive technology and donor eggs or sperm to conceive children. Yet I have located only one study that focused on adoption and that has examined associations between R/S factors and intentionally creating a nontraditional family unit.[60] Here, a greater importance of religion emerged as a strong factor tied to adoption by white U.S. women out of a host of other motivations and fertility issues.

To the extent that social scientists restrict their research questions to hypotheses that presume R/S is only relevant to married heterosexual parents, R/S are likely to be increasingly viewed as irrelevant and thus understudied. Alternatively, as illustrated in Table 6.1, social scientists could assume that specific R/S factors may increase commitment and intentional decision making across the growing diversity of contemporary families.[61] Studies could be aimed to identify specific ways that individuals turn to their felt relationship to God/Higher Power(s), the perceived sanctity of family bonds, or their religious communities to guide choices about when and with whom to form a committed adult union and/ or become a parent.

For example, do individuals with any sexual orientation turn to spiritual resources to cope with frustration when dating rather than settle for an unsuitable partner or give up the quest entirely? Is spirituality a source of strength or struggle as heterosexual and same-sex couples decide the pace and order of sexual intercourse, cohabitation, marriage, or remarriage? Do partnered and single individuals invest more effort in pursuing parenthood, whether via conventional or unconventional routes, if they believe that God/Higher Power(s) or their religious community validates their chosen ends and means? In short, do heterosexual and LGBT partners as well as single, cohabiting, married, remarried, divorced, and multigenerational parents turn to faith to create their family relationships? At the present, we need far more data to know.

Maintenance Stage: Why Do R/S Matter?

Although cultural conflicts exist over what constitutes ideal family structures, within and outside religious groups, diverse faith traditions teach that members of families should treat each other in ways that strengthen the stability and quality of relationships that they create.[62] For example, endorsement of relational virtues, such as being loving, unselfish, and ethical toward others, cuts across religions. Numerous studies have linked global R/S factors to better marital functioning and more positive parenting by married and single parents, indirectly suggesting that spiritual factors facilitate better relational functioning. In this section, I summarize these findings. However, such linkages tend to be small in size and interpreted to reflect psychosocial processes that have little or nothing to do with the substance of R/S emotions, cognitions, or behaviors. To convincingly demonstrate that R/S offer people resources to sustain established relationships, researchers have begun to examine specific spiritual constructs that tap into unique elements of R/S. In this section, I highlight three examples—prayer for partner, sanctification, and spiritual disclosure/intimacy—and refer readers elsewhere for additional examples.[63]

Global R/S factors and better marriages. Comprehensive reviews[64] indicate that higher religious attendance has been tied repeatedly to stable and well-functioning marriages, as follows. In cross-sectional and longitudinal studies, more frequent public worship, particularly by wives or by couples who attend the same denomination together, has been tied to a lower risk of divorce. People who often attend religious services are also less likely than infrequent attenders to perpetrate, or to be the victim of, domestic violence in marital, cohabiting, or dating relationships. By contrast, merely being a conservative Protestant, biblically conservative, or in an interfaith marriage has not been linked to interpartner aggression. Higher religious attendance is also tied to lower rates of extramarital sex. It is worth emphasizing that these laudatory findings on religious attendance are based on surveys of national and community samples and therefore are not restricted to people who worship with a particular religious group. In addition, type of religious affiliation (e.g., Catholic, mainline Protestant, evangelical Christian) has not been tied consistently to desirable marital outcomes in recent decades. Rather religious attendance may tap into R/S resources for marriage that cut across religious groups.

Global R/S factors and better parenting. Across religious denominations, R/S global factors have also been linked to positive parenting by married and single parents.[65] In national surveys, greater worship attendance has been tied to more parental warmth and lower risk of child physical abuse. In addition, greater importance of religion to parents or teens is associated with higher quality of parent-adolescent relationships. In numerous studies focused on predominantly single and female minorities living in poor, urban neighborhoods, R/S factors have been tied to more positive mothering in the absence of a biological father or ample economic resources. Specifically, religious attendance, overall importance of R/S, and quality of one's relationship with God have been linked to greater maternal satisfaction, authoritativeness, efficacy, and consistency, as well as lower parenting stress and risk of child maltreatment.

Problems with global R/S factors. Although findings reviewed above suggest that R/S may enhance generally healthy marriages and parenting, it is easy for skeptics to argue that a given global R/S factor is tied to *desirable* family outcomes for reasons that have little or nothing to do with the content of R/S beliefs, practices, or coping strategies. For example, the reason why religious attendance is correlated with lower divorce rates may be attributed to social coercion to remain married that people experience from being embedded in a social network that discourages marital dissolution, not because of spiritual beliefs about marriage that higher involvement in a religious group reinforces. High engagement in any social network that frowns on divorce may similarly lower divorce risk. Conversely, it is easy for critics of R/S to argue that a given global R/S factor is tied to *undesirable* family outcomes for reasons that have a great deal to do with the content of R/S teachings. For example, the well-established finding that parents affiliated with conservative Protestant denominations more often spank young children than other parents may fuel concerns that devout evangelical Christians are more physically abusive of their children.[66] Two in-depth studies, however, have pinpointed the exploitation of R/S for instrumental purposes (i.e., extrinsic religiousness) as a key predictor of risk of child physical abuse, not religious affiliation per se, orthodox religious beliefs, or the centrality of religion to one's identity (i.e., intrinsic religiousness).[67]

In short, single-item measures of religious involvement obscure the extent to which secular and spiritual mechanisms independently and interactively contribute to outcomes. Researchers who use global R/S measures, such as religious attendance, should make clear that desirable findings may tap into both spiritual and psychosocial processes. Alternatively, researchers could assess specific spiritual cognitions or behaviors that have no direct parallels in the secular world to help produce convincing evidence that faith can enhance relationships.

Specific Relational Spiritual Factors That May Facilitate Marriage and Parenting

Relationship with God/Higher Power(s). Tier 1 of the RSF highlights that individuals can privately turn to a felt relationship with God/ Higher Power(s) as a source of support to enact virtues that sustain their union with a partner or bolster parenting, even if the family relationship is not sanctioned by some religious groups. A compelling program of research by Fincham and colleagues shows that benevolent prayer for a partner facilitates relational quality in nondistressed couples.[68] In studies of dating college students, they found that privately praying for a romantic partner's well-being increased relationship satisfaction and decreased infidelity over time. Their experimental studies have also found that praying for a person with whom one has a romantic or close relationship increased the prayer's selfless concern, gratitude, and forgiveness of the other person.[69]

In addition, Beach and associates[70] conducted a randomized experiment with a community sample of married African Americans to see if prayer for a partner strengthens marriages. Couples were randomly assigned to one of three conditions: (1) a marital education program (Prevention and Relationship Enhancement Program, or PREP) previously found to protect marriages, (2) the same program supplemented by a module focused on private prayer for one's partner, and (3) self-help reading materials only. Over time, prayer for one's partner enhanced marital outcomes for wives beyond the beneficial effects of participating in PREP or self-help efforts. However, prayer did not function as an added resource for husbands' marital satisfaction. This research highlights that individuals may often turn to prayer, presumably to God/Higher Power, to help them to behave in a caring and responsible manner when trying to maintain a romantic or marital union. Additional studies are needed on the helpful role that prayer may play for parenting as well as other ways people may to turn to God/Higher Power(s) to cope effectively with major problems with partners or parenting.

Family relationship possessing spiritual qualities. Tier 2 of the RSF encompasses ways that people integrate R/S directly into their perceptions of a relationship or interactions with one another. For example, qualitative and quantitative studies have found that couples often view their union as having sacred qualities (e.g., part of a larger spiritual plan) or a manifestation of God (e.g., God plays a role in, is a reflection of God's will); these two cognitive processes have been coined, respectively, as nontheistic and theistic sanctification.[71] Greater belief in the sanctity of one's marriage has been repeatedly tied to greater marital satisfaction,[72] even after controlling for other marital resources (e.g., forgiveness and sacrifice),[73] as well as stable characteristics of the couple using rigorous fixed effects modeling.[74] Further, greater perceived sanctity of marriage predicts more observed warmth and collaborative communication skills by husbands and wives during videotaped conflictual interactions, after controlling for stable characteristics of the spouses, such as personality traits, education, or intelligence.[75]

These latter findings overcome criticisms that correlational results linking sanctification of marriage to marital well-being are merely due to mono-method bias or unmeasured third variables. Perceiving sexual relations with a partner as sacred also predicts greater sexual satisfaction among unmarried college students in nonmarital relationships cross-sectionally[76] and among newlyweds cross-sectionally[77] and longitudinally.[78] Overall, perceiving an intimate adult relation-ship as embodying divine qualities and/or God's presence appears to motivate partners to work harder to sustain their union and be happier with their bond.

Spiritual disclosure and intimacy. In addition to spiritual cognitions that individuals may hold about a relationship, Tier 2 of the RSF highlights that two people can engage in overt R/S behaviors together that imbue a given relationship with spirituality. Emerging research has examined ways that dyadic spiritual discussions could enhance relational quality. Brelsford and Mahoney[79] assessed the degree to which college students and parents candidly told each other about their R/S views, resources, and struggles, a process labeled spiritual disclosure. Notably, spiritual disclosure does not require two parties to strongly endorse a particular R/S worldview or agree with each other. Studies show that greater spiritual disclosure is tied to greater satisfaction within the mother-child and father-child relationship[80] and lower verbal hostility.[81]

Because R/S experiences can easily be disputed, people may avoid revealing such information to loved ones for fear of being dismissed, ridiculed, or misunderstood. Kusner and colleagues[82] thus created a measure of spiritual disclosure and ability to respond to a partner's spiritual disclosures in an empathic, nonjudgmental manner (i.e., spiritual support), labeling the combined processes spiritual intimacy. Greater spiritual intimacy by both spouses robustly predicted less observed negativity and more positivity exhibited by both husbands and wives when couples discussed their top three marital conflicts, even after controlling for unmeasured, stable characteristics of the spouses. Thus, family dyads who are able to share and affirm their respective spiritual journeys openly appear to enjoy more harmonious relationships and be more motivated to remain kind and inhibit hostility when they have conflicts.

Transformation Stage: Can R/S Be an Added Strain in Distressed Families?

Although basic research shows that R/S factors lower the risk of family difficulties in community and national samples, such findings cannot be generalized uncritically to clinically distressed couples or parents where maladaptive R/S processes may be more prevalent and likely to contribute to dysfunctional relational processes. By analogy, it is risky to generalize findings from research conducted on physically healthy people to those diagnosed with a serious medical illness or disease. More research is needed with distressed samples to untangle specific spiritual beliefs or behaviors that function as resources or added sources of strain when traditional and nontraditional partners and parents encounter family stressors. Religious leaders, medical staff members, and mental health practitioners would especially benefit from greater scientific insight into helpful and harmful manifestations of R/S to intervene effectively with distressed families.

Global R/S factors and family problems. Studies using global R/S factors bolster concerns that certain manifestations of faith can be problematic for families. Here are some salient examples from national U.S. samples. With regard to domestic violence, biblically conservative husbands married to biblically liberal wives were about four times more likely to engage in domestic violence than husbands married to wives with similar biblical views.[83] With regard to sexual infidelity, an extramarital affair was more likely to trigger a later divorce for couples who frequently attend religious services relative to other couples.[84] With regard to unplanned pregnancy, greater religious attendance by unmarried teens during pregnancy was linked to later higher levels of postbirth depression, particularly for girls affiliated with conservative religious groups.[85] Unmarried fathers living in poor, urban areas who are affiliated with conservative Protestant groups are much less likely to be involved than other unmarried fathers with their young children.[86] With regard to co-parenting, major disagreement between parents about religious beliefs or attendance increases the risk of child adjustment problems.[87] With regard to adolescence, in the minority of families where parents and teens diverge greatly in global R/S factors, there is more distance and dissatisfaction in their relationship.[88]

An underlying theme here is that faith-based conflicts can contribute to family distress. The base rate of major discord between couples or between parents and offspring on global R/S variables, however, is low. For example, Ellison and Anderson[89] found that only 7.5 percent of couples strongly disagree about the Bible, and

Stokes and Regnerus[90] found that only 11 percent of parents rated religion as much more important than did their teens. These data may lead researchers to conclude that R/S are largely irrelevant to understanding how faith can be part of the problem or solution when people encounter family difficulties. Ample research in the psychology of R/S, however, has found that some forms of R/S coping with natural disasters or medical illnesses, such as collaboratively turning to God for support, are prevalent and tend to reduce individual psychological distress, whereas greater spiritual struggles during times of stress, such as feeling angry at or abandoned by God, are relatively rare but robustly predictive of poorer mental and physical health outcomes.[91] By analogy, an important direction for researchers would be to uncover both prevalent and constructive as well as rare and destructive manifestations of R/S when people face significant family stressors.

R/S within distressed samples. As reviewed earlier, R/S often appear to function as a resource that motivates people to create and sustain harmonious relationships. Paradoxically, R/S may especially go awry when people face major obstacles in becoming and being a partner or parent. When people find that their most cherished and sought-after relationship goals conflict with their own or others' wishes for how to form and maintain intimate adult and parent-child bonds, they may encounter painful spiritual struggles internally, with others, or with God/Higher Power(s) that undermine their relationships or personal well-being, especially if such spiritual struggles are left unresolved. Alternatively, people may draw on R/S as a wellspring of resilience and personal growth when coping with family difficulties to the degree that their faith life is congruent with or can be reworked to fit their relationships goals.

Unfortunately, almost no controlled research exists on the roles that specific spiritual factors play within samples of distressed parents or intact couples, although some studies have been conducted on individuals coping with prior divorce, romantic breakup, or domestic violence. Salient situations where specific R/S beliefs or practices may function as an added strain when forming family relationships include coping with dating difficulties, an uncommitted partner, infertility, and unplanned pregnancy. Salient situations where faith may become an obstacle for those committed to maintaining an established adult union or parent-child relationship include coping with infidelity, domestic violence, child maltreatment, or serious dysfunction in marital dynamics or parenting processes.

Specific maladaptive spiritual processes. In the midst of serious family difficulties, people may engage in specific spiritual cognitions or behaviors that inadvertently undermine their own or the relationship's well-being. For example, Butler and Harper[92] describe ways that couples in marital therapy may privately pray for their partner to change and displace their marital woes onto God rather than effectively work to resolve problems with their spouse. In a study on spiritual one-upmanship, Brelsford and Mahoney[93] also found that college students and parents who triangulate God and faith to defend their position during conflicts reported more distance and conflict.

Studies on ways that individuals turn to R/S to cope with divorce and romantic breakups also illustrate the potential for faith to be an added source of strain when coping with relationship problems. For example, in a community sample of adults who had recently divorced, 75 percent viewed the marital dissolution as the loss or desecration of something sacred, and 50 percent believed that the event reflected the devil's influence.[94] Divorcees also commonly experienced spiritual struggles internally, with God and others, over the dissolution. Not surprisingly, the more all of these spiritual processes occurred, the more emotional distress the individual experienced. Furthermore, the more divorcees tried to turn to God to forgive their ex-spouse, the less forgiveness of and the more verbal hostility toward their ex-spouse they reported.[95] College students who similarly report viewing a romantic breakup as a sacred loss/desecration and encounter spiritual struggles likewise report higher postbreakup psychological distress.[96] Greater premarital sexual activity also led to such negative spiritual appraisals and emotional distress, particularly if the students more often attended services and saw religion as important.[97] Further, those who try to access spiritual resources are also most likely to report spiritual struggles when marriages and romantic unions end. Taken together, these studies highlight that practitioners need to be aware of and sensitive to ways that R/S can function as both a resource and added source of strain for people coping with major relational problems.

CONCLUSION

A promising but relatively small body of scientific research exists on the intersection of faith and family life. The scarcity of studies implies that most social scientists devoted to the study of family relationships view R/S as either irrelevant or too controversial to pursue. In this chapter, I summarized available empirical data using the RSF in hopes of encouraging more social scientists to conduct more research on global and specific R/S factors that may be relevant to contemporary family relationships.

Scientific evidence conducted primarily with U.S. samples suggests that faith tends to promote the formation and maintenance of traditional family ties. However, many unexamined issues exist across the fragmented literature, with theory and evidence also suggesting that faith could be a unique source of strength for all types of partners and parents seeking to create and sustain well-functioning relationships. Much empirical work remains to identify specific spiritual processes that could function as an added source of strain for subsamples of people who have become embroiled in or exited stressful family situations. I hope that social scientists will build more collaborative relationships with diverse families and people of faith to conduct more basic and applied research on R/S beliefs and practices that can help or harm family bonds during daily life and times of family distress.

NOTES

1. Debate exists among social scientists, particularly psychologists who specialize in the scientific study of religion and spirituality, about defining and differentiating the broad domains of religion (R) and spirituality (S). See, for example, Doug Oman, "Defining Religion and Spirituality," in *Handbook of the Psychology of Religion and Spirituality*, 2nd ed., eds. Raymond F. Paloutzian and Crystal L. Park (New York: Guilford Press, 2013), 23–47; and Kenneth I. Pargament, Annette Mahoney, Julie J. Exline, James W. Jones, and Edward P. Shafranske, "Envisioning an Integrative Paradigm for the Psychology of Religion and Spirituality: An Introduction to the *APA Handbook of Psychology, Religion, and Spirituality*," in *APA Handbook of Psychology, Religion, and Spirituality, Vol. 1*, eds. Kenneth I. Pargament, Julie J. Exline, and James W. Jones (Washington, DC: American Psychological Association, 2013), 3–19. Such distinctions are essentially moot within empirical research on religion

and spirituality in family relationships because most studies rely heavily on single-item questions to assess these two overlapping, complex, and multifaceted domains. Thus, for purposes of this chapter, I will use the term R/S when referring to the broad domain of religion and spirituality.

2. I intend for the tone and style of this chapter to be more engaging and less technical than the exhaustive reviews I authored on ninety-seven peer-reviewed empirical studies published on R/S and family life in peer-reviewed journals from 1980 to 1999 (Annette Mahoney, Kenneth I. Pargament, Nalini Tarakeshwar, and Aaron B. Swank, "Religion in the Home in the 1980s and 1990s: A Meta-Analytic Review and Conceptual Analysis of Religion, Marriage, and Parenting," *Journal of Family Psychology* 15 [2001]: 559–96) and another 184 studies published between 2000 and 2009 (Annette Mahoney, "Religion in Families, 1999–2009: A Relational Spirituality Framework," *Journal of Marriage and Family* 72 [2010]: 805–27). I rely heavily on those two reviews to make statements about findings in the literature based on global R/S variables rather than attempt to cite all relevant studies separately. Readers may consult these two reviews for citations and more detailed discussion. For a list of all studies located for the 2010 review, readers are referred to: http://www.bgsu.edu/arts-and-sciences/psychology/people/amahone.html.

3. Philip N. Cohen, *The Family: Diversity, Inequality, and Social Change* (New York: W.W. Norton and Company, 2014).

4. Annette Mahoney and Annmarie Cano, "Introduction to the Special Section on Religion and Spirituality in Family Life: Pathways between Relational Spirituality, Family Relationships and Personal Well-Being," *Journal of Family Psychology* 28 (2014): 735–38.

5. Mahoney et al., "Religion in the Home in the 1980s and 1990s"; and Mahoney, "Religion in Families, 1999–2009." These reviews omitted articles where a R/S measure (e.g., religious affiliation, frequency of attendance) was included in statistical models as a background or control variable, but the authors did not highlight related findings via title, abstract, or keywords. Also, some studies may have been unintentionally missed where authors featured R/S variables. Readers are encouraged to contact me with citations of such studies, as I plan to post lists of studies on Bowling Green State University's website devoted to the intersection of the psychology of R/S and relationships. See http://www.bgsu.edu/arts-and-sciences/psychology/graduate-program/clinical/the-psychology-of-spirituality-and-family.html.

6. This chapter, like the two reviews I published, focuses on studies where researchers conceptualized R/S variables as predictors of relationship outcomes, such as marital adjustment or parenting practices.

This chapter does not address the available research on family factors that predict offspring's R/S identity (i.e., intergenerational transmission of R/S) nor the ways that R/S variables may facilitate a family member's psychological adjustment (e.g., depression, anxiety, burnout) when caring for other family members or coping with a relative's illness or death.

7. Pew Forum on Religion and Public Life, *U.S. Religious Landscape Survey: Religious Affiliation: Diverse and Dynamic* (Washington, DC: Pew Research Center, 2008).

8. Centers for Disease Control and Prevention, "2011–2013 NSFG: Public Use Data Files, Codebooks, and Documentation," National Survey of Family Growth (January 29, 2015), accessed at http://www.cdc.gov/nchs/nsfg/nsfg_2011_2013_puf.htm.

9. Froma Walsh, ed., *Spiritual Resources in Family Therapy*, 2nd ed. (New York: Guilford Press, 2009).

10. Kip W. Jenkins, "Religion and Families," in *Family Research: A Sixty-Year Review, 1930–1990, Vol. 1*, ed. Stephen J. Bahr (New York: Lexington Books/Macmillan, 1991), 235–88.

11. Annette Mahoney, Kenneth I. Pargament, Tracey Jewell, Aaron B. Swank, Eric Scott, Erin Emery, and Mark Rye, "Marriage and the Spiritual Realm: The Role of Proximal and Distal Religious Constructs in Marital Functioning," *Journal of Family Psychology* 13 (1999): 321–38.

12. Elizabeth Thompson Gershoff, Pamela C. Miller, and George W. Holden, "Parenting Influences from the Pulpit: Religious Affiliation as a Determinant of Parental Corporal Punishment," *Journal of Family Psychology* 13 (1999): 307–20.

13. Mahoney et al., "Religion in the Home in the 1980s and 1990s."

14. Mahoney, "Religion in Families, 1999–2009." Due to page constraints, this review was printed in the August 2010, issue of *JMF* rather than the April 2010, "Decade-in-Review" issue.

15. See our website (http://www.bgsu.edu/arts-and-sciences/psychology/graduate-program/clinical/the-psychology-of-spirituality-and-family/about/other-research-teams.html) for a complete listing of all studies and authors that we located from 1980 to 2009.

16. Joshua N. Hook, Everett L. Worthington, Jr., Don E. Davis, and David C. Atkins, "Religion and Couple Therapy: Description and Preliminary Outcome Data," *Psychology of Religion and Spirituality* 6 (2014): 94–101.

17. Annette Mahoney, Michelle LeRoy, Katherine Kusner, Emily Padgett, and Lisa Grimes, "Addressing Parental Spirituality as Part of the Problem and Solution in Family Psychotherapy," in *Spiritual Interventions in Child and Adolescent Psychotherapy*, eds. Donald F. Walker and William L. Hathaway (Washington, DC: American Psychological Association, 2013), 65–88.

18. Jennifer S. Ripley, Cynthia Leon, Everett L. Worthington Jr, Jack W. Berry, Edward B. Davis, Amy Smith, Audrey Atkinson, and Tabitha Sierra, "Efficacy of religion-accommodative strategic hope-focused theory applied to couples therapy," *Couple & Family Psychology: Research and Practice 3* (2014): 83–98. doi:10.1037/cfp0000019

19. Walsh, *Spiritual Resources in Family Therapy.*

20. About 77 percent of Americans report a Christian affiliation, 16 percent no religious affiliation, and 7 percent a non-Christian affiliation (see Pew Forum on Religion and Public Life, *U.S. Religious Landscape Survey*). Rates of attendance at worship services and self-reported importance of religion vary widely across community and national samples.

21. Mahoney, "Religion in Families, 1999–2009"; and Annette Mahoney, "The Spirituality of Us: Relational Spirituality in the Context of Family Relationships," in *APA Handbook of Psychology, Religion, and Spirituality, Vol. 1*, eds. Kenneth I. Pargament, Julie J. Exline, and James W. Jones (Washington, DC: American Psychological Association, 2013), 365–89.

22. Pargament et al., "Envisioning an Integrative Paradigm for the Psychology of Religion and Spirituality."

23. Kenneth I. Pargament and Annette Mahoney, "Spirituality: The Search for the Sacred," in *The Oxford Handbook of Positive Psychology*, 3rd ed., eds. C.R. Snyder, Shane J. Lopez, Lisa M. Edwards, and Susana C. Marques (New York: Oxford University Press, 2017, doi:10.1093/oxfordhb/9780199396511.013.51); and Annette Mahoney, Kenneth I. Pargament, and Krystal M. Hernandez, "Heaven on Earth: Beneficial Effects of Sanctification for Individual and Interpersonal Well-Being," in *Oxford Handbook of Happiness*, ed. Jane Henry (New York: Oxford University Press, 2013), 397–410.

24. Kenneth I. Pargament, *The Psychology of Religion and Coping: Theory, Research, Practice* (New York: Guilford Press, 1997).

25. Frank D. Fincham and Steven R. H. Beach, "Can Religion and Spirituality Enhance Prevention Programs for Couples?," in *APA Handbook of Psychology, Religion, and Spirituality, Vol. 2*, eds. Kenneth I. Pargament, Julie J. Exline, and James W. Jones (Washington, DC: American Psychological Association, 2013), 461–79.

26. For a more complete discussion of various spiritual constructs that have been studied, see Mahoney, "The Spirituality of Us."

27. Oman, "Defining Religion and Spirituality"; and Pargament et al., "Envisioning an Integrative Paradigm for the Psychology of Religion and Spirituality."

28. Mahoney, "The Spirituality of Us."

29. Jill Duba Onedera, ed., *The Role of Religion in Marriage and Family Counseling* (New York: Routledge, 2008).

30. Mahoney et al., "Religion in the Home in the 1980s and 1990s"; and Mahoney, "The Spirituality of Us."
31. Debra L. Blackwell and Daniel T. Lichter, "Homogamy among Dating, Cohabiting, and Married Couples," *Sociological Quarterly* 45 (2004): 719–37.
32. Penny Edgell, *Religion and Family in a Changing Society* (Princeton, NJ: Princeton University Press, 2005); and Sally K. Gallagher, *Evangelical Identity and Gendered Family Life* (Piscataway, NJ: Rutgers University Press, 2003).
33. Mahoney, "Religion in Families, 1999–2009."
34. Alfred DeMaris, Annette Mahoney, and Kenneth I. Pargament, "Doing the Scut Work of Infant Care: Does Religiousness Encourage Father Involvement?," *Journal of Marriage and Family* 73 (2011): 354–68.
35. Mahoney, "Religion in Families, 1999–2009."
36. For example, Amy Adamczyk, "The Effects of Religious Contextual Norms, Structural Constraints, and Personal Religiosity on Abortion Decisions," *Social Science Research* 37 (2008): 657–72.
37. Mahoney, "Religion in Families, 1999–2009."
38. Ibid.; and Christopher Wildeman, "Conservative Protestantism and Paternal Engagement in Fragile Families," *Sociological Forum* 23 (2008): 556–74.
39. Mahoney, "Religion in Families, 1999–2009."
40. Penny Edgell, "In Rhetoric and Practice: Defining 'the Good Family' in Local Congregations," in *Handbook of the Sociology of Religion*, ed. Michele Dillon (New York: Cambridge University Press, 2003), 164–78; Edgell, *Religion and Family in a Changing Society*; and Bradford W. Wilcox, "Family," in *Handbook of Religion and Social Institutions*, ed. Helen Rose Ebaugh (New York: Springer, 2006), 97–120.
41. Daniel W. Zink, "The Practice of Marriage and Family Counseling and Conservative Christianity," in *The Role of Religion in Marriage and Family Counseling*, ed. Jill Duba Onedera (New York: Routledge, 2008), 55–71.
42. Annette Mahoney and Elizabeth J. Krumrei, "Questions Left Unaddressed by Religious Familism: Is Spirituality Relevant to Nontraditional Families?," in *Oxford Handbook of Psychology and Spirituality*, ed. Lisa J. Miller (New York: Oxford University Press, 2012), 165–81.
43. Elliot N. Dorff, "The Practice of Marriage and Family Counseling and Judaism," in *The Role of Religion in Marriage and Family Counseling*, ed. Jill Duba Onedera (New York: Routledge, 2008), 135–51.
44. Belkeis Altareb, "The Practice of Marriage and Family Counseling and Islam," in *The Role of Religion in Marriage and Family Counseling*, ed. Jill Duba Onedera (New York: Routledge, 2008), 89–104.

45. Ibid.
46. Dorff, "The Practice of Marriage and Family Counseling and Judaism."
47. For a fuller discussion of religious familism, see Mahoney and Krumrei, "Questions Left Unaddressed by Religious Familism."
48. Edgell, "In Rhetoric and Practice."
49. Mahoney and Krumrei, "Questions Left Unaddressed by Religious Familism."
50. For example, Rosemary R. Ruether, *Christianity and the Making of the Modern Family: Ruling Ideologies, Diverse Realities* (Boston: Beacon Press, 2000); and Jack Wertheimer, "What Is a Jewish Family? The Radicalization of Rabbinic Discourse," in *American Religions and the Family: How Faith Traditions Cope with Modernization and Democracy*, eds. Don S. Browning and David A. Clairmont (New York: Columbia University Press, 2007), 151–67.
51. Carol J. Cook, "The Practice of Marriage and Family Counseling and Liberal Protestant Christianity," in *The Role of Religion in Marriage and Family Counseling*, ed. Jill Duba Onedera (New York: Routledge, 2008), 73–87.
52. Ruether, *Christianity and the Making of the Modern Family*.
53. W. Matthew Henderson, Jeremy E. Uecker, and Samuel Stroope. "The role of religion in parenting satisfaction and parenting stress among young parents," *The Sociological Quarterly* 57 (2016): 675–710. doi:10.1111/tsq.12147.
54. Mark D. Regnerus, *Forbidden Fruit: Sex and Religion in the Lives of American Teenagers* (New York: Oxford University Press, 2007), 121.
55. Ibid., 73.
56. Nichole A. Murray-Swank, Kenneth I. Pargament, and Annette Mahoney, "At the Crossroads of Sexuality and Spirituality: The Sanctification of Sex by College Students," *International Journal of the Psychology of Religion* 15 (2005): 199–219.
57. Wendy D. Manning and Bart Stykes, "Twenty-Five Years of Change in Cohabitation in the U.S., 1987–2013," NCFMR Family Profiles FP-15-01 (2015), accessed at http://www.bgsu.edu/content/dam/BGSU/college-of-arts-and-sciences/NCFMR/documents/FP/FP-15-01-twenty-five-yrs-cohab-us.pdf.
58. For example, Sharon S. Rostosky, Melanie D. Otis, Ellen D. B. Riggle, Sondra Kelly, and Carolyn Brodnicki, "An Exploratory Study of Religiosity and Same-Sex Couple Relationships," *Journal of GLBT Family Studies* 4 (2008): 17–36.
59. Pew Forum on Religion and Public Life, *U.S. Religious Landscape Survey*.
60. Leslie Doty Hollingsworth, "Who Seeks to Adopt a Child?: Findings from the National Survey of Family Growth (1995)," *Adoption Quarterly* 3 (2000): 1–23.

61. Mahoney and Krumrei, "Questions Left Unaddressed by Religious Familism"; and Mahoney, "The Spirituality of Us."

62. Onedera, *The Role of Religion in Marriage and Family Counseling.*

63. Mahoney, "The Spirituality of Us."

64. Mahoney et al., "Religion in the Home in the 1980s and 1990s"; and Mahoney, "Religion in Families, 1999–2009."

65. Ibid.

66. Christopher W. Dyslin and Cynthia J. Thomsen, "Religiosity and Risk of Perpetrating Child Physical Abuse: An Empirical Investigation," *Journal of Psychology and Theology* 33 (2005): 291–98.

67. Ibid.; and Christina M. Rodriguez and Ryan C. Henderson, "Who Spares the Rod?: Religious Orientation, Social Conformity, and Child Abuse Potential," *Child Abuse and Neglect* 34 (2010): 84–94.

68. Frank D. Fincham, Steven R. H. Beach, N. Lambert, T. Stillman, and S. Braithwaite, "Spiritual Behaviors and Relationship Satisfaction: A Critical Analysis of the Role of Prayer," *Journal of Social and Clinical Psychology* 27 (2008): 362–88.

69. Fincham and Beach, "Can Religion and Spirituality Enhance Prevention Programs for Couples?"

70. Steven R. H. Beach, Tera R. Hurt, Frank D. Fincham, Kameron J. Franklin, Lily M. McNair, and Scott M. Stanley, "Enhancing Marital Enrichment through Spirituality: Efficacy Data for Prayer Focused Relationship Enhancement," *Psychology of Religion and Spirituality* 3 (2011): 201–16.

71. Mahoney et al., "Heaven on Earth."

72. For example, Allen K. Sabey, Amy J. Rauer, and Jakob F. Jensen, "Compassionate Love as a Mechanism Linking Sacred Qualities of Marriage to Older Couples' Marital Satisfaction," *Journal of Family Psychology* 28 (2014): 594–603.

73. Laura Stafford, Prabu David, and Sterling McPherson, "Sanctity of Marriage and Marital Quality," *Journal of Social and Personal Relationships* 31 (2014): 54–70.

74. For example, Daniel T. Lichter and Julie H. Carmalt, "Religion and Marital Quality among Low-Income Couples," *Social Science Research* 38 (2009): 168–87; and Katherine G. Kusner, Annette Mahoney, Kenneth I. Pargament, and Alfred DeMaris, "Sanctification of Marriage and Spiritual Intimacy Predicting Observed Marital Interactions across the Transition to Parenthood," *Journal of Family Psychology* 28 (2014): 604–14.

75. Kusner et al., "Sanctification of Marriage and Spiritual Intimacy Predicting Observed Marital Interactions across the Transition to Parenthood."

76. Murray-Swank et al., "At the Crossroads of Sexuality and Spirituality."

77. Krystal M. Hernandez, Annette Mahoney, and Kenneth I. Pargament, "Sanctification of Sexuality: Implications for Newlyweds' Marital and Sexual Quality," *Journal of Family Psychology* 25 (2011): 775–80.

78. K. M. Hernandez-Kane and A. Mahoney, "Sex through a sacred lens: Longitudinal effects of sanctification of marital sexuality," *Journal of Family Psychology*. Advance online publication (2018). doi:10.1037/fam0000392.

79. Gina M. Brelsford and Annette Mahoney, "Spiritual Disclosure between Older Adolescents and Their Mothers," *Journal of Family Psychology* 22 (2008): 62–70.

80. Two articles by Gina M. Brelsford: "Interpersonal Spirituality between College Students and Fathers," *Research in the Social Scientific Study of Religion* 21 (2010): 27–48; and "Sanctification and Spiritual Disclosure in Parent-Child Relationships: Implications for Family Relationship Quality," *Journal of Family Psychology* 27 (2013): 639–49. Also, Brelsford and Mahoney, "Spiritual Disclosure between Older Adolescents and Their Mothers."

81. Brelsford and Mahoney, "Spiritual Disclosure between Older Adolescents and Their Mothers."

82. Kusner et al., "Sanctification of Marriage and Spiritual Intimacy Predicting Observed Marital Interactions across the Transition to Parenthood."

83. Christopher G. Ellison, John P. Bartkowski, and Kristin L. Anderson, "Are There Religious Variations in Domestic Violence?," *Journal of Family Issues* 20 (1999): 87–113.

84. Alfred DeMaris, "Burning the Candle at Both Ends: Extramarital Sex as a Precursor of Marital Disruption," *Journal of Family Issues* 34 (2013): 1474–99.

85. Ann Marie Sorenson, Carl F. Grindstaff, and R. Jay Turner, "Religious Involvement among Unmarried Adolescent Mothers: A Source of Emotional Support?," *Sociology of Religion* 56 (1995): 71–81.

86. Wildeman, "Conservative Protestantism and Paternal Engagement in Fragile Families."

87. John P. Bartkowski, Xiaohe Xu, and Martin L. Levin, "Religion and Child Development: Evidence from the Early Childhood Longitudinal Study," *Social Science Research* 37 (2008): 18–36.

88. Charles E. Stokes and Mark D. Regnerus, "When Faith Divides Family: Religious Discord and Adolescent Reports of Parent–Child Relations," *Social Science Research* 38 (2009): 155–67.

89. Christopher G. Ellison and Kristin L. Anderson, "Religious Involvement and Domestic Violence among U.S. Couples," *Journal for the Scientific Study of Religion* 40 (2001): 269–86.

90. Stokes and Regnerus, "When Faith Divides Family."

91. Kenneth I. Pargament, *The Psychology of Religion and Coping: Theory, Research, Practice* (New York: Guilford Press, 1997).
92. Mark H. Butler and James M. Harper, "The Divine Triangle: God in the Marital System of Religious Couples," *Family Process* 33 (1994): 277–86.
93. Gina M. Brelsford and Annette Mahoney, "Relying on God to Resolve Conflict: Theistic Mediation and Triangulation in Relationships between College Students and Mothers," *Journal of Psychology and Christianity* 28 (2009): 291–301.
94. Elizabeth J. Krumrei, Annette Mahoney, and Kenneth I. Pargament, "Spiritual Stress and Coping Model of Divorce: A Longitudinal Study," *Journal of Family Psychology* 25 (2011): 973–85; and Elizabeth J. Krumrei, Annette Mahoney, and Kenneth I. Pargament, "Demonization of Divorce: Prevalence Rates and Links to Postdivorce Adjustment," *Family Relations* 60 (2011): 90–103.
95. Elizabeth J. Krumrei, Annette Mahoney, and Kenneth I. Pargament, "Turning to God to Forgive: More Than Meets the Eye," *Journal of Psychology and Christianity* 27 (2008): 302–10.
96. Heidi L. Warner, Annette Mahoney, and Elizabeth J. Krumrei, "When Parents Break Sacred Vows: The Role of Spiritual Appraisals, Coping, and Struggles in Young Adults' Adjustment to Parental Divorce," *Psychology of Religion and Spirituality* 1 (2009): 233–48.
97. Anna R. Hawley, Annette Mahoney, Kenneth I. Pargament, and Anne K. Gordon, "Sexuality and Spirituality as Predictors of Distress over a Romantic Breakup: Mediated and Moderated Pathways," *Spirituality in Clinical Practice* 1 (2014), online publication.

SUGGESTED READINGS

Browning, D. S., Green, M. C., & Witte, J., eds., *Sex, Marriage, and Family in World Religions*. New York: Columbia University Press, 2006. Provides in-depth and cross-cultural historical, theological, and sociological information about sex, marriage and family across multiple religious traditions.

Edgell, Penny. *Religion and Family in a Changing Society*. Princeton, NJ: Princeton University Press, 2005. This sociologist offers a thought-provoking and balanced analysis of ways that religious organizations in the United States are attempting to cope with the rapid changes that have occurred in family structure in the past fifty to sixty years and why men appear drawn to more religiously conservative congregations and women to nontraditional religious groups.

Mahoney, Annette. "Religion in Families, 1999–2009: A Relational Spirituality Framework." *Journal of Marriage and Family* 72 (2014): 805–27. This dense review summarizes scientific findings on R/S and marital or parent-child relationships based on 184 empirical studies published in peer-reviewed journal articles from 1999 to 2009.

Mahoney, Annette. "The Spirituality of Us: Relational Spirituality in the Context of Family Relationships." In *APA Handbook of Psychology, Religion, and Spirituality, Vol. 1*, eds. Kenneth I. Pargament, Julie J. Exline, and James W. Jones. Washington, DC: American Psychological Association, 2013, 365–89. This chapter summarizes empirical research on the role of R/S in family life and elaborates on theory and studies on numerous specific spiritual factors that may be helpful and harmful in the formation, maintenance, and transformation of couple and family relationships.

Onedera, Jill Duba, ed. *The Role of Religion in Marriage and Family Counseling*. New York: Routledge, 2008. This text summarizes for mental health professionals what different religious traditions currently teach believers about R/S beliefs and key family topics, including definitions of marriage; men's and women's family roles; child bearing; birth control; abortion; teenage pregnancy; finances; dissolving relationships, divorce, and annulment; managing the family after separation and/or divorce; death and dying; and homosexuality in couples and families.

Pargament, Kenneth I., *The Psychology of Religion and Coping: Theory, Research, Practice*. New York: Guilford Press, 1997. This classic and timeless book is foundational background reading to appreciate the helpful and harmful roles R/S can play in peoples' daily life.

Ruether, Rosemary R. *Christianity and the Making of the Modern Family: Ruling Ideologies, Diverse Realities*. Boston: Beacon Press, 2000. Beginning with pre-Christian Judaism and the Greco-Roman world, this theologian discusses evolving and contrasting Christian views on idealized forms of family up through the end of the twentieth century.

Walsh, Froma, ed. *Spiritual Resources in Family Therapy*, 2nd ed. New York: Guilford Press, 2009. Using an ecumenical and pluralistic view, this text offers fourteen family therapists' insights on how spirituality across diverse religious traditions can be a resource to facilitate change and growth in individual and family therapy work.

7

The Role of Religion in Advancing the Field of Criminology

Byron R. Johnson

As a graduate student in the early 1980s, I was interested in studying the relationship between religion and crime and, more specifically, the role of religion in crime reduction. Unfortunately, there were no lectures, much less courses, on this subject in my entire graduate school experience. When I shared my interest in studying the role of religion with a number of my professors, reactions would vary from bewilderment to sheer skepticism. This reaction was not unexpected. I knew that the prospect of religion having any meaningful relevance as a variable that might be linked to crime and delinquency would be quite foreign to most of them. On more than one occasion, professors suggested that if I pursued such a line of research, it would be difficult to have much of an academic career. The message was quite clear: The study of religion would be a dead end, and I should consider more traditional predictors and factors known to correlate with increasing or decreasing crime. Making matters worse, only a handful of empirical studies making the connection between religiosity and crime or deviance existed at that time. The sheer lack of research on religion and crime bolstered my professors' argument: if religion mattered, why was there not already a well-established literature?

I am thankful that I did not decide to forgo research on the relationship between religion and crime, and some three decades removed from my graduate school days, there is now a significant and growing body of empirical evidence suggesting: (1) measures of religiosity tend to relate inversely to crime and delinquency; (2) religious commitment is a protective factor from crime, delinquency, and drug use; (3) frequency of religious attendance is linked to prosocial behavior; (4) regular participation in faith-based programs is associated with recidivism reduction for offenders, prisoners, and former prisoners; (5) the addition of religion variables is helping to refine theoretical constructs and perspectives; and (6) the relationship between religion and crime continues to provide insights for crime prevention strategies that combine both sacred and secular approaches that are helping to improve the effectiveness of the criminal justice system.

To better understand the role of religion in addressing matters related to crime, delinquency, offender treatment, rehabilitation programs, and even the transition of prisoners back to society, I examine the relevant research literature in order to assess the influence of religion and religious measures on crime. In addition to summarizing the current state of knowledge regarding the relationship between religion and crime, I examine how religion, faith-based groups, and religious institutions are playing a more central role in efforts to reduce crime and promote prosocial behavior, and how these communities of faith are providing leadership in reform efforts that hold potential to make the criminal justice system safer and more effective.

I. RELIGION AND CRIME: A BRIEF LITERATURE REVIEW

Contemporary research on the religion–crime relationship is generally traced to Hirschi and Starks's often-cited article "Hellfire and Delinquency,"[1] published in 1969. The article caused a stir because the authors failed to find a significant inverse relationship between levels of religious commitment and measures of delinquency among youth. Subsequent replications both confirmed[2] and refuted[3] Hirschi and Stark's original finding. Stark, Kent, and Doyle later suggested that these opposing findings were the result of the moral makeup of the community being studied.[4] They found that areas with high church membership and attendance rates represented "moral communities," while areas with low church membership exemplified "secularized communities." Stark's moral communities hypothesis, therefore, predicted an inverse relationship between religiosity and delinquency in moral communities as well as the expectation that there will be little or no effect of religiosity on individuals in secularized communities. This important theoretical perspective provided a useful framework for understanding why some studies yielded an inverse relationship between religiousness and delinquency, and others did not.[5]

An increasing number of important delinquency studies as well as several systematic reviews have since helped to clarify the confusion surrounding the religion–crime relationship. In a systematic review of forty studies that focus on the relationship between religion and delinquency, Johnson and associates[6] found that most of these studies reported an inverse relationship between measures of religiosity and delinquency. Several studies found no relationship, and only one found a positive link between greater religiosity and increasing delinquency. Studies reporting inconclusive results tended to be less rigorous. Conversely, those studies with the most rigorous research design were more likely to find increasing religiosity linked to decreases in delinquency.

In a second meta-analysis, Baier and Wright[7] reviewed sixty studies within the religiosity–delinquency literature and reached much the same conclusion. They found that studies using larger and more representative datasets are more likely to find significant inverse effects (i.e., increasing religiosity and decreasing delinquency) than studies that utilize smaller, regional, or convenient samples. In a third systematic review, Johnson[8] reviewed studies examining religion and multiple outcome areas including several that are relevant for our current discussion (i.e., alcohol abuse, drug use/abuse, and crime/delinquency). Among the ninety-seven alcohol studies reviewed, only two studies found religiosity to be associated with deleterious outcomes. Another ten studies reported inconclusive findings, while eighty-five studies found an inverse relationship. This evidence indicated increasing religiosity was associated with a lowered likelihood of alcohol abuse. Johnson found a similar pattern among the fifty-four studies reviewed examining drug use or abuse. Fifty of the fifty-four studies found increasing religiosity was related to decreasing drug use or abuse, while only one study found a positive relationship. Finally, Johnson reviewed another forty-six studies within the religion–crime literature that examine the influence of religion and found the same trend: Increasing religiosity tends to be linked to decreasing criminal or delinquent behavior (thirty-seven studies), while increasing religiosity is positively related to delinquency in only one study.

In the most recent and comprehensive review of the religion–crime literature that covers studies published between 1944 and 2010, Johnson and Jang[9] examined the type of study (e.g., cross sectional, prospective cohort, retrospective, clinical trial, experimental, case control, descriptive, case report, or qualitative), the sampling method (e.g., random, probability, systematic sampling, convenience/purposive sample), the number of subjects in the sample, population (e.g., children, adolescents, high school students, college students, community-dwelling adults, elderly, church members, religious or clergy, gender, and race), location, religious variables included in the analysis (e.g., religious attendance, scripture study, self-reported religiosity, etc.), controls, and findings (e.g., no association, mixed evidence, beneficial outcome, or harmful outcome). In total, 109 studies were reviewed, and the results of this current review confirm that the vast majority of the studies report a beneficial relationship between measures of religion or religious commitment and various crime and delinquency measures or outcomes. Approximately 89 percent of the studies (97/109) find an inverse or beneficial relationship between religion and some measure of crime or delinquency (i.e., increasing religiosity is associated with lower crime/delinquency). Only eleven studies found no association or reported mixed findings, and only one study from this exhaustive literature review found that religion was associated with a harmful outcome.

Until recently, a lack of consensus has remained about the nature of the religion–crime relationship. Reviews of the research literature provide consistent evidence, however, that increasing religious commitment or involvement helps protect individuals from illegal behavior and deviant activities. Stated differently, in studies utilizing vastly different methods, samples, and research designs, increasing religiosity (religiousness, religious activities or participation) tends to be linked with decreases in various measures of crime or delinquency. These findings are particularly pronounced among the more methodologically and statistically sophisticated studies that rely on nationally representative samples. Although religion is a variable that tends to be associated with crime reduction, it remains largely overlooked by social scientists interested in the study of crime. But the tendency to overlook the study of religion within criminology may well be changing. In a recent paper, Francis Cullen, former president of both the American Society of Criminology and the Academy of Criminal Justice Sciences (the two largest professional associations in the world), expressed astonishment that (1) so many studies had been published examining the religion–crime relationship and (2) criminology textbooks completely overlooked this growing literature. Cullen proceeded to issue a call to criminologists to correct this oversight, and he raised the need for the development of a new subfield—the "criminology of religion and crime"—and offered a number of fruitful lines of inquiry for scholars to pursue.[10]

II. WHY RELIGION MATTERS IN REDUCING CRIME

Though consistent empirical evidence suggests religion matters in addressing crime, scholars have spent far less time considering how or why measures of religion, religious commitment, or religious institutions may be linked with crime and delinquency reduction. In this section, I briefly examine how religion variables may be protective for youth and adults, and how religion may be important in promoting prosocial behavior.

Religion as a Protective Factor

Research confirms that religious commitment and involvement help protect youth and adults from delinquent behavior and deviant activities.[11] Recent evidence also suggests that such effects persist even if there is not a strong prevailing social control against delinquent behavior in the surrounding community.[12] Stated differently, youth from "bad places" can still turn out to be "good kids" if religious beliefs and practices are regular and important in their lives. There is additional evidence that religious involvement may lower the risks of a broad range of delinquent behaviors, ranging from minor to serious forms of criminal behavior.[13] Research indicates that consistent religious involvement not only has a cumulative effect throughout adolescence in terms of reducing the likelihood of drug use, but it also significantly lessens the risk of later adult criminality.[14] Whereas criminologists have tended to focus on the effects of community disadvantage on predisposing youth to delinquent behavior, we are now beginning to understand the effects that religion or religious institutions may play in providing communities of "advantage" for youth. Stated differently, religiously committed youth may be more resilient to and protected from the negative consequences of living in impoverished communities if they are intentionally connected to houses of worship.

Studies confirm that individual religious commitment as well as religious congregations have the potential to help prevent high-risk urban youths from engaging in illegal activities.[15] For example, Johnson and colleagues[16] estimate a series of regression models and find that involvement of African American youth in congregations significantly buffers the effects of neighborhood disorder on crime and, in particular, serious crime. The authors conclude that African American churches are viable agencies of local social control that should not be overlooked. The role of these congregations and their networks of social support are even more critical in the lives of youth from communities of extreme poverty and disadvantage. Preliminary evidence suggests that youth who have continued religious involvement or participation throughout adolescence may be the beneficiary of a cumulative religiosity effect that lessens the risk of illicit drug use.[17] This finding suggests that youth who continue to attend and participate in religious activities are less likely to commit crime or delinquent acts. Indeed, Johnson[18] finds that church-attending youth from disadvantaged communities are less likely to use drugs than youth from suburban communities who attend church less frequently or not at all.

Religious involvement may provide networks of social support that help adolescents internalize values that encourage behavior and that emphasize concern for others' welfare. Such processes may contribute to the acquisition of positive attributes that give adolescents a greater sense of empathy toward others, which in turn makes them less likely to commit acts that harm others. Recent research confirms that religiosity can help youth to be resilient even while living in communities typified by poverty, crime, and other social ills commonly linked to deleterious outcomes. Frequent participation in religious activities may help adolescents learn values that give them a greater sense of empathy toward others. For individuals who become involved in deviant behavior, it is possible that participation in specific kinds of religious activity can help steer them to a course of less deviant behavior and, more important, away from potential career criminal paths.

Religion and Prosocial Behavior

Criminologists have studied factors thought to be linked to the causes of crime and delinquency for several centuries. Social scientists have much less often asked another equally important question: Why is it that most people do not commit crime? Social control theorists like Travis Hirschi[19] provided a unique and important perspective in arguing that there are very important reasons why people do not commit crime or delinquent behavior. Studying and emphasizing factors that essentially keep people from breaking the law, control theorists reason, ultimately advances our understanding of how to pursue crime prevention. Religion, therefore, is but one of many factors that control theorists might argue "bond" an individual to society and conventional or normative behavior. Indeed, it is easy to see how religion may play a central bonding role between each of Hirschi's four elements at the heart of social control theory: attachments, commitments, involvements, and beliefs.

Here is another equally important though understudied question: Why is it that people do good things (or what is sometimes referred to as prosocial behavior)? Less commonly acknowledged by researchers is the contribution of religious belief and practice in fostering positive or normative behavior. I would argue it is at least as important to understand why people turn into good citizens as to understand why they go bad. For example, scholars have discovered that at-risk youth from disadvantaged communities who exhibit higher levels of religiousness are not only less likely to commit crimes than their disadvantaged counterparts, they are also more likely to stay in school, make better grades, and find and retain steady employment.[20]

A number of recent studies document the relationship between increasing religiosity and higher levels of prosocial behavior. This body of research consistently finds that religiousness is a source for promoting or enhancing beneficial outcomes like well-being;[21] hope, meaning, and purpose;[22] self-esteem;[23] and even educational achievement.[24] Indeed, the more actively religious are more likely to give to charities (both religious and nonreligious), to provide social support,[25] and to volunteer time for civic purposes.[26]

Studies also suggest that involvement in or exposure to altruistic or prosocial activities and attitudes—something that many churches and other faith-based organizations encourage as intrinsic aspects of their mission—appears to reduce the risk of crime. A proper understanding of the mechanisms associated with prosocial behavior will assist in the development of future prevention and intervention strategies. Clearly, not enough scholarship has focused on the prosocial side of the equation. Criminologists need to be much more attentive in documenting the factors and conditions that motivate, cause, support, and sustain positive or prosocial behavior. Unraveling the role of religiousness, religiosity, religious institutions and congregations, and religious practices and beliefs in promoting prosocial behavior should be a priority for academic researchers.

The existing literature suggests that individual religious commitment or religiosity can have a significant buffering or protective effect that lessens the likelihood of criminal behavior. The research literature also documents that increasing measures of religiousness are associated with an array of prosocial outcomes. Thus, religiosity is increasingly recognized not only as important in understanding deleterious outcomes like crime but also prosocial outcomes that are considered normative and necessary for a productive and civil society.

III. THE ROLE OF RELIGION IN RETHINKING AMERICAN CORRECTIONAL PRACTICES

The absence of a comprehensive list or index of all faith-based programs operating in American prisons belies the fact that these programs exist in all prisons and correctional facilities in the United States. Religious programs for inmates are not only among the oldest but also among the most common forms of rehabilitative programs found in correctional facilities today.[27] The U.S. Department of Justice, which reports representative data on America's prison population, confirms this high prevalence of use.[28] After admission to prison, 69 percent of inmates report having working assignments, 45 percent report participating in some form of academic education, and 31 percent report attending vocational training. Among all other types of personal enhancement programs offered in prison, religious activities attracted the most participation: 32 percent of the sampled inmates reported involvement in religious activities such as Bible studies and church services, 20 percent reported taking part in self-improvement programs, and 17 percent reported that they had been involved in counseling. This national survey verifies that many inmates attend and participate in religious programs.

But what is new is the way in which the reach and nature of religious programs have changed in prisons over the last several decades. For many, the term *prison ministry* is likely synonymous with prison evangelism. Many congregations have prison ministries as part of an overall outreach strategy. But even more common than church-sponsored prison ministries are individual-led ministries. Rarely organized, these mom-and-pop ministries often operate in complete isolation from other congregation-based outreach efforts to prisoners. Regular observers of American prisons—rural or urban, large or small, minimum or maximum security—find that these prison ministries tend to be small and insular and are primarily aimed at preaching and evangelism. One might suspect that people driven to preach to prisoners would not really be very compassionate or have a more holistic vision for prisoner rehabilitation that prioritizes a host of nonspiritual or secular concerns related to needs like education, vocational training, life skills, and mentoring. Read the promotional material of some of these prison ministries and one will find plenty of assertions that would seem to reinforce this stereotype.

For several decades, though, prison ministries have done far more than simply preach to prisoners. Instead of just going into correctional facilities to participate in an evangelistic service or lead a Bible study, faith-motivated volunteers as well as faith-based organizations have increasingly developed and implemented much more pervasive and comprehensive programs for prisoners, ex-prisoners, and even the families of those incarcerated.

Kairos Prison Ministry International, one of the largest prison ministries in the world, seeks to address the spiritual needs of incarcerated men and women and their families. The Kairos Inside program currently operates in 350 prisons in thirty-one states and in eight countries outside the United States. More than 170,000 incarcerated men and women have been introduced to Kairos since its inception, and the current number of volunteers exceeds 20,000 per year. Recognizing that correctional environments can be stressful places for staff, Kairos volunteers also seek to encourage correctional employees. Though sharing the Christian faith is still central, Kairos volunteers provide all manner of assistance to prisoners, whether through education, life skills, or mentoring. Kairos volunteers actively mentor youthful offenders in an effort to prevent these same youth from ending up in the adult correctional system. Kairos Outside is a special weekend retreat designed to support the female loved ones of men and women who are incarcerated. It is a safe environment for women to interact with other women in similar situations and to support them in dealing with the many challenges facing families of the incarcerated. A similar story can be told for other national prison ministries such as Alpha for Prisons[29] and Horizon Prison Ministry.[30]

Perhaps the most innovative correctional program that I have encountered is the Prison Entrepreneurship Program (PEP), a Houston-based nonprofit organization that connects executives, MBA students, and leaders with convicted felons. PEP was founded on the proposition that if inmates who were committed to their own transformation were equipped to start and run legitimate companies, then they could succeed in business following release from prison. PEP sponsors entrepreneurship boot camps and reentry programs for inmates. It started with a "behind bars" business plan competition that drew on the entrepreneurial acumen of inmates. The initial experiment proved so successful that PEP was established in 2004. The mission of PEP is to stimulate positive life transformation for business executives and inmates, uniting them through entrepreneurial passion, education, and mentoring. Since the inception of PEP, over 700 inmates have graduated from the program. PEP graduates, on average, pay approximately $7,000 annually in taxes following release from prison. PEP is growing quickly and now recruits prisoners from more than sixty prisons throughout the Texas Department of Criminal Justice (TDCJ). PEP is at the cutting edge of rethinking how to reintegrate former offenders into society and is clearly one of the most promising correctional programs in the country.[31]

Data provided to the author by Prison Fellowship (PF), America's largest nonprofit organization offering religious programs in prisons, shows their systematic residential programs exist in nearly 30 percent of all U.S. prisons, and they operate occasional programs in 86 percent of prisons. At this point, more than half the states have some form of residential faith-based programs operating in their prison systems, and, by constitutional fiat, all U.S. prisons must allow for religious worship and free exercise of faith. Nationwide, literally hundreds of thousands of inmates participate in PF programs each year. Angel Tree, a program that unites offenders with their children while they are incarcerated, particularly around the holidays, currently exists in 81 percent of American state prisons.[32]

PF offers prisoners a variety of in-prison programs. Through one-to three-day seminars and weekly Bible studies, inmates are taught to set goals that prepare them for release. Weekly Bible studies usually last an hour, and one- to three-day seminars might be offered several times a year at a particular prison. The level of prisoner exposure to such religious programs is probably no more than fifty hours of Bible study and several days of intensive seminars annually—a relatively modest correctional intervention. Even so, evidence indicates regular participation in volunteer-led Bible studies is associated with reductions in recidivism.[33]

In the 1990s, PF began looking for a prison partner that would allow them to launch a new initiative replacing occasional volunteer efforts with a completely faith-based approach to prison programs. The ultimate goal would be to reform prisoners as well as the prison itself. The late Charles Colson, founder of PF, unsuccessfully pitched this idea to a number of governors before finding a partner in Texas governor George W. Bush in 1996. The collaboration between TDCJ and PF represented a first for American corrections. This partnership officially launched the InnerChange Freedom Initiative (IFI) in April 1997 at the Carol Vance Unit, a 378-bed prison in Richmond, Texas. IFI is responsible for inmate programs, and TDCJ is responsible for security and custody. PF and TDCJ formed a unique private-public partnership that would test the proposition that this sacred-secular collaboration could achieve the civic purpose of reducing recidivism and thereby increase public safety. The partnership established an approach that viewed religion and treatment as complementary.

Anchored in biblical teaching, life-skills education, and group accountability, IFI established a three-phase program involving prisoners in sixteen to twenty-four months of in-prison biblical programs and six to twelve months of aftercare while on parole. IFI focuses on rebuilding the inmate's spiritual and moral foundation as well as providing a wide variety of programs designed to meet criminogenic offenders. A heavy emphasis is placed on the following:

- Biblical education, GED, tutoring, substance abuse prevention, and life skills
- Work (jobs are similar to those of other prisoners in the general population)
- Support groups designed to increase one's personal faith
- Support groups for enriching relations with family members and crime victims
- Mentoring and peer groups
- Aftercare (assisting in reentry, housing, employment, and transportation).

Johnson and Larson[34] utilized a quasi-experimental research design and found that IFI program graduates had significantly lower rates of re-arrest than a matched group of inmates (17.3 percent versus 35 percent) and had significantly lower rates of reincarceration than the matched group (8 percent versus 20.3 percent). The fact that IFI graduates are significantly less likely to be either re-arrested or reincarcerated during the two-year period following release from prison represents initial evidence that program completion of this faith-based initiative is associated with lower rates of recidivism.

Modeled on PF's IFI in Texas, the Minnesota Department of Correction (DOC) established the InnerChange Freedom Initiative (InnerChange) in 2002, a faith-based prisoner reentry program located at the Minnesota Correctional Facility (MCF)–Lino Lakes on the edge of the Twin Cities. MCF–Lino Lakes is a medium security facility. InnerChange is privately funded, and the program depends heavily on volunteers from local churches and religious organizations for the delivery of many of the services provided. InnerChange programs cover areas related to substance abuse education, victim impact awareness, life skills development, cognitive skill development, educational attainment, community reentry, religious instruction, and moral development.

The Minnesota DOC completed an outcome evaluation of the InnerChange program.[35] The evaluation assessed the impact of InnerChange on recidivism among 732 offenders released from Minnesota prisons between 2003 and 2009. The average follow-up period for the 732 offenders was a little more than three years.

InnerChange participants had lower recidivism rates than the offenders in the comparison group. For example, 42 percent of the InnerChange participants had been re-arrested for a new offense by the end of December 2011 compared with 51 percent of the comparison group offenders. The results also show that 25 percent of the InnerChange participants were reconvicted for a new offense versus 34 percent in the comparison group. In addition, 9 percent of the InnerChange participants were reincarcerated for a new criminal offense versus 13 percent of the comparison group offenders. The results from the multivariate statistical analyses, which controlled for time at risk and other rival causal factors, revealed that participating in InnerChange significantly lowered the risk of recidivism by 26 percent for re-arrest, 35 percent for reconviction, and 40 percent for new offenses leading to reincarceration.

According to Duwe and King,[36] there are likely several reasons why InnerChange reduces recidivism. Though traditional Christian beliefs and doctrine promote living a prosocial and crime-free life, InnerChange also attempted to lessen the recidivism risk of those who participate by focusing on issues such as education, criminal thinking, and chemical dependency. InnerChange participants also receive a continuum of care that connects the delivery of programs in the institution to those found in the community. Finally, and perhaps most important, InnerChange expands offender social support networks by connecting participants to mentors and linking them with faith communities after their release from prison. The findings suggest that faith-based correctional programs can work if they incorporate elements of other correctional programs that are known to be effective.

A new study extends the research on the Minnesota InnerChange program by conducting a cost-benefit analysis of the program. Because IFI relies heavily on volunteers, and program costs are privately funded, the program exacts no additional costs to the State of Minnesota. As a result, this study focused on estimating the program's benefits by examining recidivism and postrelease employment. The findings show that during its first six years of operation in Minnesota, InnerChange produced an estimated benefit of $3 million, which amounts to nearly $8,300 per participant.[37]

Helping prisoners rewrite their life narrative can be a powerful and redemptive experience, giving ex-prisoners the hope and purpose

needed to start a new and positive life while at the same time helping them to come to grips with the antisocial life they have left
behind.[38] Preliminary evidence indicates that faith-based prerelease/
reentry prison programs can be effective in reducing recidivism.[39]
Most faith-based programs do not last very long, however, and
one can readily argue that, to have the biggest possible salutary
effect, prisoners need a more substantial or sustained faith-based
intervention. The most serious offenders tend to have longer prison
sentences and are often ineligible for consideration when it comes
to participation in programs.

Prison Seminaries

Two experimental programs are now ready to test the proposition
that a four-year prison seminary can be effective with even the hardest
of criminals serving very long sentences—even life sentences—within
maximum security prisons. The Darrington Unit (Rosharon, Texas)
resembles most other maximum security prisons around the country
except for the fact that it now offers a four-year seminary within
the prison. On August 29, 2011, thirty-nine prisoners were formally
installed as the first class of seminarians studying to become ministers
under a new program that operates within this prison. Referred to
as the Darrington Seminary, it is an extension of the Fort Worth–
based Southwestern Baptist Theological Seminary. The program is
carefully modeled after a similar initiative at the Louisiana State
Penitentiary, often referred to as Angola. Initiated by warden Burl
Cain, the Angola Bible College (which is an extension of the New
Orleans Baptist Theological Seminary) has received considerable
attention—especially from religious media outlets—since its inception in 1995. The unique aspect of these two seminaries is that they
focus on enrolling "lifers" as well as those with extremely long prison
sentences so that the men, once graduated, will have many years to
spend in sharing their faith and their moral convictions with others
inside the prison.

Angola has a notorious and well-documented history as one of
the most violent prisons in the United States. What an increasing
number of observers report in recent years, however, is a far less
violent Angola. Many have suggested that Angola has undergone a
total change in the prison culture during the last twenty years. Some
credit this change to the fact that the Angola seminary graduates

have remained inside the prison. Using this particular lifer-student approach, correctional leaders at Angola and Darrington are convinced they have the potential not only to rehabilitate prisoners but also to transform the prison environment itself.

Again, the difference between Angola and Darrington where faith-based programs are concerned is that these two seminaries accept only those inmates with extremely long sentences, so the inmates can be returned to service inside the prison system and therefore exert for many years an influence for moral change and spiritual renewal among the rest of the inmates. Another critical aspect of these two seminaries is their commitment to send their graduates out as field ministers to other prisons in their respective states. For example, Angola has been sending out a portion of their graduates to other Louisiana prisons as missionaries for a number of years, but a significant number of seminary graduates have remained inside the Angola prison. The Darrington Seminary now has approval from the highest levels of the TDCJ to follow this same approach.

The idea of placing a seminary within a maximum security prison is unprecedented within the field of corrections, but it is gaining traction among correctional leaders. In fact, The Urban Ministry Institute (TUMI) has launched more than twenty seminaries in the last several years within California's prison system. Prisons in almost a dozen other locations outside California have recently welcomed seminary programs. Indeed, serious discussions are now taking place with a variety of government leaders regarding the possibility of bringing these privately funded prison seminary programs to prisons across the country. If these discussions take root, we may well be observing a major shift within the American prison system in the next few years. Since these faith-based programs are privately funded and largely staffed by volunteers, they come at little or no cost to taxpayers. In a time of shrinking budgets and program cutbacks, correctional administrators are increasingly open to the idea of volunteer-led faith-based programs and even seminaries, especially if the evidence indicates that they can be effective in reducing recidivism.

A new American penitentiary movement is taking place, and a central tenet of faith-based programs helps explain its salience. On the one hand, church congregations, faith-based organizations, and volunteers largely fund faith-based programs through private donations, which appeals to conservatives' desire to shrink government;

on the other hand, faith-based programs also demonstrate a recommitment to having at least some level of rehabilitative programs in prisons despite the national trend to cut vocational and treatment prison programs. This commitment to prison programs satisfies the left's view that community building and social capital ultimately lower recidivism.[40]

By suggesting that program activities delivered by faith-based groups produce better results than similar programs run by the government, proponents of faith-based programs rely on claims of superior performance based on morality and caring—as well as the fact that volunteers often deliver these services at no cost to taxpayers. The argument frequently made on behalf of faith-based programs is twofold: that faith-based programs provide services at lower cost, but also that faith-based programs provide services that government cannot provide—through the loving kindness of volunteers motivated by love and not a government contract or a paycheck. The claim often made on behalf of faith-based programs is that they are both cheaper and better.[41]

The Need for More Research

Despite the widespread presence of faith-based programs in American prisons, research on faith-based programs remains limited. The field is in its infancy, beset by methodological and implementation challenges stemming from the broad diversity in scope and character of faith-based programs operating in American corrections. As the Urban Institute recently stated, "Basic but critical questions about the nature of faith-based programs and how they may improve offender outcomes, including recidivism and other reentry outcomes, remain largely unanswered."[42] Unfortunately, little research in the way of a deep-level examination of the specific elements of religiosity as they relate to desistance appears in the social science literature.[43]

In short, despite the fact that religious faith has long been a cultural proxy for criminal rehabilitation, social science research on the specific connections between religiosity and criminal desistance has been lacking. Social scientists have been reluctant to attempt to measure the impact of "faith" in correctional programs—for some very good reasons. First, federal agencies and private foundations have rarely funded or prioritized research on faith-based programs within the field of corrections. This oversight has been a disincentive to scholars looking to conduct research in this area. Second, in the United States, Constitutional strictures surrounding the First Amendment require voluntariness and a complete lack of coercion when governing participation in custodial "faith-based" programs, so the obvious problem of selection bias complicates all efforts to compare performance of volunteers for faith-based programs with that of people who did not participate. In other words, randomly assigning individuals into an experimental group (e.g., faith-based program) in order to be compared to a control group (those receiving no intervention) is problematic.

To address this gap in research, a number of studies utilizing exploratory "unstructured life-history narratives" help to identify and investigate the subjective experiences of desisters, by way of "cognitive shifts," "identity changes," and attempts at "making good" described by successful ex-offenders.[44] As demonstrated in this research, religiously anchored "redemption narratives" provide desisters with an important spiritual "toolkit" necessary for coping with what criminologist John Braithwaite calls "shame management."[45] Offenders often characterize the resources provided by religiosity as more accessible and comprehensive than those available through the justice system. Indeed, religiously motivated desisters often describe themselves as empowered or "fired up" to meet the challenges associated with constructing prosocial identities after release.

For the reasons mentioned, some of the research on faith-based programs relies on qualitative narrative accounts. Religious spirituality has, in fact, been found to be a highly salient resource for many successful ex-offenders, especially under conditions of low emotional support and weak informal social control.[46] Phenomenological analyses of the desistance process reveal that religion and spirituality frequently help offenders construct stories of change that become vital to an altered sense of self.[47] More important, religiosity seems to help desisters undertake preliminary agentic moves that, while often not outwardly visible to family members or justice officials, are the beginnings of an evolving self-narrative that is prosocial and provides a redemptive path.[48]

Specifically, life-history narratives highlight agentic moves that draw on stories of change emphasizing the ways religious practice and spirituality provide emotional, cognitive, and linguistic resources employed by desisters in their daily lives.[49] As Giordano and associates put it:

> Thus, in addition to its relative accessibility, religion seems to have potential as a mechanism for desistance because many core concerns within religious communities and the Bible relate directly to offenders' problem areas (e.g., temptation and forgiveness). Even more importantly, religious teachings can provide a clear blueprint for how to proceed as a changed individual.[50]

CONCLUSION

This chapter provides evidence that religious influences are consequential in crime reduction. The studies reviewed document the importance of religious influences in protecting at-risk youth from harmful outcomes as well as promoting prosocial outcomes. The beneficial relationship between religion and crime reduction is not simply a function of religion's constraining function or what it discourages (e.g., opposing drug use or deviant behavior) but also what it encourages (e.g., promoting prosocial behavior).

Rebuilding the lives of ex-offenders has proven exceedingly difficult. With national data showing a near 70 percent recidivism rate within three years after release from prison (by re-arrest) and a greater than 50 percent reincarceration rate within five, America's correctional system has proven not to be the curative answer to the crime problem. Nearly 20 years of "prisoner reentry" research has shown disappointing results—and in the comparatively few cases where desistance actually does take hold, desisters report succeeding despite the system rather than because of it.[51] For those few who do succeed after release from prison, the aphorism "you rehabilitate yourself" is what successful desisters report.[52] Indeed, the high failure rate and sheer fiscal impact of American corrections draws resources away from related areas of concern like education and childcare that might lesson crime. While crime is often disproportionately concentrated in economically impoverished neighborhoods, religiosity may provide a framework empowering to ex-offenders, assisting them in negotiating structural and economic challenges while also helping them to recognize personal dysfunction that brought them to incarceration.[53] In short, desisters report that religiosity can provide a spiritual fortitude useful for long-term desistance even in the context of structural inequality.[54] Faith-based programs in American corrections are growing in prominence and are likely here to stay.

Unfortunately, religion measures are still not routinely included in many current research initiatives. Future research on crime and delinquency should include multiple measures of religious practices and beliefs. It is time for researchers and federal funding agencies to discontinue the pattern of overlooking this important line of policy-relevant research. New research will allow us to understand more fully the ways in which religion directly and indirectly affects crime and criminal justice. Churches, synagogues, mosques, inner-city blessing stations, and other houses of worship represent some of the few institutions that remain within close proximity of most adolescents, their families, and their peers.

As policy makers consider strategies to reduce crime and improve the effectiveness of correctional programs, it is essential to consider seriously and intentionally the role of religion and religious institutions in implementing, developing, and sustaining multifaceted approaches to crime. Public/private partnerships bringing together secular and sacred groups to address social problems like prisoner reentry will be incomplete unless religious communities are integrally involved in these deliberations.

NOTES

1. Travis Hirschi and Rodney Stark, "Hellfire and Delinquency," *Social Problems* 17 (1969): 202–13; and Steven R. Burkett and Mervin White, "Hellfire and Delinquency: Another Look," *Journal for the Scientific Study of Religion* 13 (1974): 455–62.
2. Steven Burkett and Mervin White, "Hellfire and Delinquency: Another Look," *Journal for the Scientific Study of Religion* 13(4) (1974): 455–62.
3. Stan L. Albrecht, Bruce A. Chadwick, and David S. Alcorn, "Religiosity and Deviance: Application of an Attitude-Behavior Contingent Consistency Model," *Journal for the Scientific Study of Religion* 16 (1977): 263–74; and Gary F. Jensen and Maynard L. Erickson, "The Religious Factor and Delinquency: Another Look at the Hellfire Hypothesis," in *The Religious Dimension: New Directions in Quantitative Research*, ed. Robert Wuthnow (New York: Academic Press, 1979), 157–77.
4. Rodney Stark, Lori Kent, and Daniel P. Doyle, "Religion and Delinquency: The Ecology of a 'Lost' Relationship," *Journal of Research in Crime and Delinquency* 19 (1982): 4–24.

5. Rodney Stark, "Religion as Context: Hellfire and Delinquency One More Time," *Sociology of Religion* 57 (1996): 163–73.
6. Byron R. Johnson, Spencer De Li, David B. Larson, and Michael McCullough, "A Systematic Review of the Religiosity and Delinquency Literature: A Research Note," *Journal of Contemporary Criminal Justice* 16 (2000): 32–52.
7. Colin J. Baier and Bradley R. E. Wright, "'If You Love Me, Keep My Commandments': A Meta-Analysis of the Effect of Religion on Crime," *Journal of Research in Crime and Delinquency* 38 (2001): 3–21.
8. Byron R. Johnson, "Assessing the Impact of Religious Programs and Prison Industry on Recidivism: An Exploratory Study," *Texas Journal of Corrections* 28 (2002): 7–11.
9. Byron R. Johnson and Sung Joon Jang, "Crime and Religion: Assessing the Role of the Faith Factor," in *Contemporary Issues in Criminological Theory and Research: The Role of Social Institutions*, eds. Richard Rosenfeld, Kenna Quinet, and Crystal Garcia (Belmont, CA: Wadsworth, 2012), 117–50.
10. Francis T. Cullen, "Toward a Criminology of Religion: Comment on Johnson and Jang," in *Contemporary Issues in Criminological Theory and Research*, ed. Rosenfeld, Quinet, and Garcia (Belmont, CA: Wadsworth, 2012), 151–61.
11. Baier and Wright, "'If You Love Me, Keep My Commandments'"; Johnson et al., "A Systematic Review of the Religiosity and Delinquency Literature"; Johnson and Jang, "Crime and Religion"; and three earlier studies by Sung Joon Jang and Byron R. Johnson: "Strain, Negative Emotions, and Deviant Coping Among African Americans: A Test of General Strain Theory and the Buffering Effects of Religiosity," *Journal of Quantitative Criminology* 19 (2003): 79–105; "Explaining Religious Effects on Distress among African Americans," *Journal for the Scientific Study of Religion* 43 (2004): 239–60; and "Gender, Religiosity, and Reactions Strain Among African Americans," *Sociological Quarterly* 46 (2005): 323–58.
12. Byron R. Johnson, David B. Larson, Spencer De Li, and Sung Joon Jang, "Escaping from the Crime of Inner Cities: Church Attendance and Religious Salience among Disadvantaged Youth," *Justice Quarterly* 17 (2000): 377–91.
13. T. David Evans, Francis T. Cullen, Velmer S. Burton, Jr., R. Gregory Dunaway, Gary L. Payne, and Sesha R. Kethineni, "Religion, Social Bonds, and Delinquency," *Deviant Behavior* 17 (1996): 43–70; Paul C. Higgins and Gary L. Albrecht, "Hellfire and Delinquency Revisited," *Social Forces* 55 (1977): 952–58; Mark D. Regnerus, "Linked Lives, Faith, and Behavior: Intergenerational Religious Influence on Adolescent

Delinquency," *Journal for the Scientific Study of Religion* 42 (2003): 189–203; and John M. Wallace and Tyrone A. Forman, "Religion's Role in Promoting Health and Reducing the Risk among American Youth," *Health Education and Behavior* 25 (1998): 721–41.

14. Sung Joon Jang and Byron R. Johnson, "Neighborhood Disorder, Individual Religiosity, and Adolescent Use of Illicit Drugs: A Test of Multilevel Hypotheses," *Criminology* 39 (2001): 109–44; and Sung Joon Jang, Christopher D. Bader, and Byron R. Johnson, "The Cumulative Effect of Religiosity in Crime Desistance," *Journal of Drug Issues* 38 (2008): 771–98.

15. Byron R. Johnson, Sung Joon Jang, Spencer De Li, and David B. Larson: "The 'Invisible Institution' and Black Youth Crime: The Church as an Agency of Local Social Control," *Journal of Youth and Adolescence* 29 (2000): 479–98; and Byron R. Johnson, Sung Joon Jang, David B. Larson, and Spencer De Li, "Does Adolescent Religious Commitment Matter? A Reexamination of the Effects of Religiosity on Delinquency," *Journal of Research in Crime and Delinquency* 38 (2001): 22–44; and Jeffrey T. Ulmer, Scott A. Desmond, Sung Joon Jang, and Byron R. Johnson, "Teenage Religiosity and Changes in Marijuana Use During Transition to Adulthood," *Interdisciplinary Journal of Research on Religion* 6 (2010): 1–19.

16. Johnson et al., "The 'Invisible Institution' and Black Youth Crime."

17. Jang and Johnson, "Neighborhood Disorder, Individual Religiosity, and Adolescent Use of Illicit Drugs."

18. Johnson et al., "The 'Invisible Institution' and Black Youth Crime."

19. Travis Hirschi, *Causes of Delinquency* (Berkeley: University of California Press, 1969).

20. Richard B. Freeman, "Who Escapes? The Relation of Churchgoing and Other Background Factors to the Socioeconomic Performance of Black Male Youths from Inner-City Tracts," in *The Black Youth Employment Crisis*, eds. Richard B. Freeman and Harry J. Holzer (Chicago: University of Chicago Press, 1986), 353–76; and Johnson et al., "Escaping from the Crime of Inner Cities."

21. Harold G. Koenig, Dana E. King, and Verna Benner Carson, *Handbook of Religion and Health*, 2nd ed. (New York: Oxford University Press, 2012).

22. Sheena Sethi and Martin E. P. Seligman, "The Hope of Fundamentalists," *Psychological Science* 5 (1993): 58.

23. Christopher G. Ellison and Linda K. George, "Religious Involvement, Social Ties, and Social Support in a Southeastern Community," *Journal for the Scientific Study of Religion* 33 (1994): 46–61; Don E. Bradley, "Religious Involvement and Social Resources: Evidence from the Data Set

'Americans Changing Lives,'" *Journal for the Scientific Study of Religion* 34 (1995): 259–67; and Harold G. Koenig, Judith C. Hays, David B. Larson, Linda K. George, Harvey Jay Cohen, Michael E. McCullough, Keith G. Meador, and Dan G. Blazer, "Does Religious Attendance Prolong Survival? A Six-Year Follow-Up Study of 3,968 Older Adults," *Journal of Gerontology: Medical Sciences* 54 (1999): M370–M376.

24. Two studies by Mark D. Regnerus: "Shaping Schooling Success: Religious Socialization and Educational Outcomes in Metropolitan Public Schools," *Journal for the Scientific Study of Religion* 39 (2000): 363–70; and *Making the Grade: The Influence of Religion Upon the Academic Performance of Youth in Disadvantaged Communities*, CRRUCS Report (Philadelphia, PA: Center for Research on Religion and Urban Civil Society, 2001); Johnson et al., "Escaping from the Crime of Inner Cities"; and William H. Jeynes, *American Educational History: School, Society, and the Common Good* (Thousand Oaks, CA: Sage Publications, 2007).

25. Three studies by Neal Krause: "Exploring the Stress-Buffering Effects of Church-Based and Secular Social Support on Self-Rated Health in Late Life," *Journal of Gerontology: Social Sciences* 61 (2006): S35–S43; "Church-Based Social Support and Mortality," *Journal of Gerontology: Social Sciences* 61 (2006): S140–S146; and "The Social Milieu of the Church and Religious Coping Responses: A Longitudinal Investigation of Older Whites and Older Blacks," *International Journal for the Psychology of Religion* 20 (2010): 109–29.

26. Arthur C. Brooks, *Who Really Cares: The Surprising Truth about Compassionate Conservatism* (New York: Basic Books, 2006).

27. Byron R. Johnson, David B. Larson, and Timothy C. Pitts, "Religious Programs, Institutional Adjustment, and Recidivism among Inmates in Prison Fellowship Programs," *Justice Quarterly* 14 (1997): 145–66.

28. Allen Beck, Darrell Gilliard, Lawrence Greenfeld, Caroline Harrell, Thomas Hester, Louis Jankowski, Tracy L. Snell, James J. Stephan, and Danielle Morton, *Survey of Inmates in State Correctional Facilities, 1991*, Bureau of Justice Statistic NCJ-136949 (Washington, DC: U.S. Department of Justice, 1993).

29. Launched in London, England, in the late 1970s, the Alpha Course presents the basic principles of the Christian faith to new Christians. Over the last two decades, the course has expanded internationally, and Alpha USA has also launched Alpha for Prisons, which presently operates in 145 prisons within the United States. More recently, Alpha USA, through collaborative efforts with other faith-based and community organizations, has begun offering prisoner reentry services to the criminal justice system.

30. Founded in 2000, Horizon Prison Ministry works to restore prisoners and those formerly incarcerated to healthy, purposeful living through mentoring, education, skill training, and spiritual growth. Horizon attempts to bring the larger community into the process of restoring offenders back to society. The Horizon program extends over a twelve-month period. Inmates who volunteer to participate in Horizon are placed within a modified housing unit. The men come together as a community in a living and learning environment. Horizon has a focus on transition preparation, and men receive mentoring and guidance from Horizon volunteers and a group of resident encouragers. Preliminary evaluation research of the Horizon program shows promising results (see Jeanette M. Hercik, *Rediscovering Compassion: An Evaluation of Kairos Horizon Communities in Prison* [Fairfax, VA: Caliber Associates, 2004]).

31. Byron Johnson, William Wubbenhorst, and Curtis Schroeder, *Recidivism Reduction and Return on Investment: An Empirical Assessment of the Prison Entrepreneurship Program*, Baylor ISR Special Report (Waco, TX: Baylor Institute for Studies of Religion, 2013).

32. Byron R. Johnson and William Wubbenhorst, *Building Relationships with Prisoners, Their Families, and Churches: A Case Study of Angel Tree*, Baylor ISR Case Study (Waco, TX: Baylor Institute for Studies of Religion, 2012).

33. Johnson et al., "Religious Programs, Institutional Adjustment, and Recidivism among Inmates in Prison Fellowship Programs"; and Byron R. Johnson, "Religious Programs and Recidivism among Former Inmates in Prison Fellowship Programs: A Long-Term Follow-Up Study," *Justice Quarterly* 21 (2004): 329–54.

34. Byron R. Johnson and David B. Larson, *The InnerChange Freedom Initiative: A Preliminary Evaluation of a Faith-Based Prison Program* [2002], Baylor ISR Report (Waco, TX: Baylor Institute for Studies of Religion, 2008).

35. Grant Duwe and Michelle King, "Can Faith-Based Correctional Programs Work? An Outcome Evaluation of the InnerChange Freedom Initiative in Minnesota," *International Journal of Offender Therapy and Comparative Criminology* 57 (2013): 813–41.

36. Ibid.

37. Grant Duwe and Byron R. Johnson, "Estimating the Benefits of a Faith-Based Correctional Program," *International Journal of Criminology and Sociology* 2 (2013): 227–39.

38. Byron R. Johnson, *More God, Less Crime: Why Faith Matters and How It Could Matter More* (West Conshocken, PA: Templeton Press, 2011); and Shadd Maruna, *Making Good: How Ex-Convicts Reform*

and Rebuild Their Lives (Washington, DC: American Psychological Association, 2001).

39. Ibid.; Johnson and Larson, *The InnerChange Freedom Initiative*; and Grant and King, "Can Faith-Based Correctional Programs Work?"

40. Jang, Bader, and Johnson, "The Cumulative Effect of Religiosity in Crime Desistance."

41. Winnifred Fallers Sullivan, *Prison Religion: Faith-Based Reform and the Constitution* (Princeton, NJ: Princeton University Press, 2009), 1.

42. Janeen Buck Willison, Diane Brazzell, and KiDeuk Kim, *Faith-Based Corrections and Reentry Programs: Advancing a Conceptual Framework for Research and Evaluation* (Washington, DC: Justice Policy Center, Urban Institute, 2010).

43. Johnson and Jang, "Crime and Religion."

44. Peggy C. Giordano, Stephen A. Cernkovich, and Jennifer Rudolph, "Gender, Crime, and Desistance: Toward a Theory of Cognitive Transformation," *American Journal of Sociology* 107 (2002): 990–1064; Michael C. Adorjan and Wing Hong Chui, "Making Sense of Going Straight: Personal Accounts of Male Ex-Prisoners in Hong Kong," *British Journal of Criminology* 52 (2012): 577–90; Maruna, *Making Good*; Shadd Maruna and Derek Ramsden, "Living to Tell the Tale: Redemption Narratives, Shame Management, and Offender Rehabilitation," in *Healing Plots: The Narrative Basis of Psychotherapy*, ed. Arnia Lieblich, Dan P. McAdams, and Ruthellen Josselson (Washington, DC: American Psychological Association, 2004), 129–49; Shadd Maruna, Louise Wilson, and Kathryn Curran, "Why God Is Often Found behind Bars: Prison Conversions and the Crisis of Self-Narrative," *Research in Human Development* 3 (2006): 161–84; Ray Paternoster and Shawn Bushway, "Desistance and the 'Feared Self': Toward an Identity Theory of Criminal Desistance," *Journal of Criminal Law and Criminology* 99 (2009): 1103–56; and Ryan D. Schroeder and John F. Frana, "Spirituality and Religion, Emotional Coping and Desistance : A Qualitative Study of Men Undergoing Change," *Sociological Spectrum* 29 (2009): 718–41.

45. Peggy C. Giordano, Monica A. Longmore, Ryan D. Schroeder, and Patrick M. Seffrin, "A Life-Course Perspective on Spirituality and Desistance from Crime," *Criminology* 46 (2008): 99–132, especially p. 116; and John Braithwaite, *Crime, Shame and Reintegration* (New York: Cambridge University Press, 1989).

46. Giordano et al., "Gender, Crime, and Desistance"; Kent R. Kerley, Todd L. Matthews, and Troy C. Blanchard, "Religiosity, Religious Participation, and Negative Prison Behaviors," *Journal for the Scientific Study of Religion* 44 (2005): 443–57; and Kent R. Kerley, Heith Copes, Richard

Tewksbury, and Dean A. Dabney, "Examining the Relationship between Religiosity and Self-Control as Predictors of Prison Deviance," *International Journal of Offender Therapy and Comparative Criminology* 55 (2011): 1251–71.

47. Giordano et al., "Gender, Crime, and Desistance," 1018; Maruna, *Making Good*; and Paternoster and Bushway, "Desistance and the 'Feared Self.'"

48. Maruna and Ramsden, "Living to Tell the Tale"; Giordano et al., "Gender, Crime, and Desistance"; and Schroeder and Frana, "Spirituality and Religion, Emotional Coping and Desistance."

49. Adorjan and Chui, "Making Sense of Going Straight"; Giordano et al., "Gender, Crime, and Desistance"; and Schroeder and Frana, "Spirituality and Religion, Emotional Coping and Desistance." For centrality of narratives, see also Norman K. Denzin, *The Alcoholic Self* (New York: Sage Publication, 1987).

50. Giordano et al., "A Life-Course Perspective on Spirituality and Desistance from Crime," quotation on p. 116.

51. Nicholas W. Bakken, Whitney D. Gunter, and Christy A. Visher, "Spirituality and Desistance from Substance Abuse among Reentering Offenders," *International Journal of Offender Therapy and Comparative Criminology* 58 (2014): 1321–39; and Michael Hallett, "Reentry to What? Theorizing Prisoner Reentry in the Jobless Future," *Critical Criminology* 20 (2012): 213–28.

52. Maruna, *Making Good*, 32.

53. See Jang and Johnson, "Gender, Religiosity, and Reactions Strain among African Americans"; and Johnson, *More God, Less Crime*.

54. Maruna et al., "Why God Is Often Found behind Bars"; and Schroeder and Frana, "Spirituality and Religion, Emotional Coping and Desistance."

SUGGESTED READINGS

Cullen, Francis T., and Jody L. Sundt. "Reaffirming Evidence-Based Corrections." *Criminology and Public Policy* 2 (2003): 353–58. Cullen and Sundt write a reaction essay to Knepper and essentially support the notion led by Johnson and DiIulio that we need more, not less, empirical research to drive policy.

Duwe, Grant, and Byron R. Johnson. "Estimating the Benefits of a Faith-Based Correctional Program." *International Journal of Criminology and Sociology* 2 (2013): 227–39. This article is important because it is one of only a few papers within criminal justice to essentially apply a cost-benefit analysis to the study of faith-based initiatives or recidivism.

Hallett, Michael, Joshua Hays, Byron Johnson, Sung Joon Jang, and Grant Duwe. *The Angola Prison Seminary: Effects of Faith-Based Ministry on*

Identity Transformation, Desistance, and Rehabilitation. New York, NY: Routledge, 2016.

Hirschi, Travis, and Rodney Stark. "Hellfire and Delinquency." *Social Problems* 17 (1969): 202–13. This article was the impetus for the emergence of religion and crime literature. Many replications of this study in different locations would follow over the next decade.

Johnson, Byron R. *More God, Less Crime: Why Religion Matters and How It Could Matter More.* West Conshohocken, PA: Templeton Press, 2011. This book provides an extensive review of the state of the religion–crime literature as well as providing insights into why religion matters for crime reduction.

Johnson, Byron R. "Religious Programs and Recidivism among Former Inmates in Prison Fellowship Programs: A Long-Term Follow-Up Study." *Justice Quarterly* 21 (2004): 329–54. One of the first publications finding that a faith-based intervention reduced recidivism over time. Johnson tracked former prisoners from several prisons in the state of New York.

Johnson, Byron R., and Sung Joon Jang. "Crime and Religion: Assessing the Role of the Faith Factor." In *Contemporary Issues in Criminological Theory and Research: The Role of Social Institutions,* eds. Richard Rosenfeld, Kenna Quinet, and Crystal Garcia. Belmont, CA: Wadsworth, 2012, 117–50. This chapter is the most extensive systematic review of the religion–crime research literature. Frank Cullen, past president of the American Society of Criminology, provided a public response to the paper in which he indicated that he was shocked to know that so many publications existed on the subject and yet criminology textbooks are silent about it.

Johnson, Byron R., Sung Joon Jang, David B. Larson, and Spencer De Li. "Does Adolescent Religious Commitment Matter? A Reexamination of the Effects of Religiosity on Delinquency." *Journal of Research in Crime and Delinquency* 38 (2001): 22–44. An early publication showing cross-lagged effects of religiosity on crime reduction among youth. Contemporaneous effects are common, but finding effects over time are far less common.

Johnson, Byron R., Sung Joon Jang, Spencer De Li, and David B. Larson. "The 'Invisible Institution' and Black Youth Crime: The Church as an Agency of Local Social Control." *Journal of Youth and Adolescence* 29 (2000): 479–98. This study found initial support for the importance of the African American church in reducing crime. Criminologists have rarely acknowledged the potential of Black congregations to be agents of social control.

Johnson, Byron R., David B. Larson, Spencer De Li, and Sung Joon Jang. "Escaping from the Crime of Inner Cities: Church Attendance and Religious Salience among Disadvantaged Youth." *Justice Quarterly* 17 (2000): 377–91. This study replicated and extended the important work of Harvard economist, Richard Freeman. The study was important because it focused on a very large sample of young Black males living in poverty tracts in Boston, Chicago, and Philadelphia.

Knepper, Paul. "Faith, Public Policy, and the Limits of Social Science." *Criminology and Public Policy* 2 (2003): 331–52. Knepper argues in opposition to the increasing significance of social science research on public policy and singles out "faith factor" research led criminologists by Byron Johnson and John DiIulio. Clearly, Knepper thinks Johnson and DiIulio have had far too much influence in crime-related policy circles.

Tittle, Charles R., and Michael R. Welch. "Religiosity and Deviance: Toward a Contingency Theory of Constraining Effects." *Social Forces* 61 (1983): 653–82. An important study that utilizes a contextual analysis of the religiosity–delinquency relationship. Tittle and Welch were among the first to help scholars to demonstrate that matters of measurement and methodology are critical when it comes to a more nuanced understanding of the relationship between religion and crime.

Ulmer, Jeffery T., Scott A. Desmond, Sung Joon Jang, and Byron R. Johnson. "Religious Involvement and Dynamics of Marijuana Use: Initiation, Persistence, and Desistence." *Deviant Behavior* 33 (2012): 448–68. An initial empirical study of the role of religiosity in desistance—a new and rapidly growing area in criminology. This study confirms that religion is important not only as an initial deterrent but also because it carries significant potential to help former drug users remain off drugs.

8

Religion and Social Gerontology

Linda K. George

There is no obvious reason that religion should be especially important in research on aging and older adults. Sociologists focus on religion's dual functions of providing social integration and social control, but they do not suggest that these functions operate differently by age. Similarly, psychologists focus on issues such as religion as a coping strategy and the associations between religious involvement and personality traits—but, again, there are few expectations for significant age differences. In reality we know relatively little about the extent to which age moderates the relationships between religion and variables of interest in the social, behavioral, and biological sciences. A substantial amount is known, however, about religious involvement and its consequences in late life.

The purpose of this chapter is to examine selectively what *is* known about religion in later life. It is organized in four sections, and it begins with an overview of the conceptual foundations of research on religion in later life—how and why it emerged as an important issue. The next section examines the prevalence and distribution of religious involvement during later life, life-course patterns of religious commitment, and time trends in the broader landscape of older adults' religious participation in American life. The third section explores the consequences of religious involvement during later life, including health, subjective well-being (SWB), end-of-life (EOL) decision making, and volunteering. The final section provides recommendations for new research with the potential to advance our understanding of the complex relationships between religion and aging.

CONCEPTUAL FOUNDATIONS

Although there is a substantial volume of research on religion and aging, this research is not based on specific theories about either religion or late life. Instead, what is known about religion and aging has emerged from broad interest in the well-being of older adults and how social factors, including religious involvement, enhance or threaten well-being. That does not mean, however, that research on religion and aging totally lacks conceptual foundations. This section provides a brief chronology of the ways that religion has been linked to well-being in later life.

Early Contributions: The Scholarship of David Moberg

Among the topics that received attention prior to the dramatic increases in aging research during the 1960s was religion and aging, due in large part to David Moberg's early papers on that topic. He published two papers in 1953 and a somewhat longer paper on the same topic in 1956.[1] All three papers examined the relationships between one or more dimensions of religious participation and personal adjustment in late life. Moberg's first paper examined the relationship between church membership and personal adjustment.[2] Although a significant positive correlation was observed between church membership and personal adjustment, the relationship became nonsignificant when a variety of control variables were taken into account. Moberg concluded that the bivariate relationship was spurious. His second paper examined several dimensions of religious participation and personal adjustment after controlling for demographic variables, socioeconomic status, and self-rated health.[3] Engaging in church activities, being a former church leader, and holding orthodox Christian beliefs were all associated with higher levels of personal adjustment. Moberg's 1956 paper was similar to the previous two; the major addition was examining the relationships between religious involvement earlier in the life course and personal adjustment in late life.[4] He again reported significant differences in personal adjustment between religious participants and nonparticipants, with religious participants reporting better adjustment.

By today's standards, the methods used in Moberg's early studies were unsophisticated and even primitive. The measure of personal adjustment was an activities and attitudes inventory that had been used in previous research, which differs substantially from current measures of well-being. The samples in these studies consisted of persons age sixty-five and older who lived in institutions in the Twin City metropolitan area. Thus, study participants were less healthy and probably had fewer significant others than older adults living independently in the community. Multivariate analytic techniques permitting examination of a relationship with potential confounding factors statistically controlled were decades away from use. Instead, Moberg matched religious and nonreligious participants on the control variables. Many participants' data could not be used because there was no match on the entire set of control variables. This reduced the size of the analytic sample substantially. Indeed, some comparisons were based on only nine pairs.

Despite the methodological limitations of Moberg's papers, their logic and interpretations were sophisticated and raised issues that remain salient more than sixty years later. His focus on personal adjustment as the optimal outcome in studies of religion's effects on the lives of older adults is highly compatible with the focus on religion and well-being, especially health, in recent and contemporary gerontological research. Moberg also understood the importance of studying multiple dimensions of religious involvement and reported that some, but not all, dimensions were robustly related to personal adjustment. More than half a century later, efforts to identify the dimensions of religious participation that are related to well-being continue. Although he was restricted to matching to control on potential confounders of the religion–personal adjustment relationship, the rationales Moberg provided for the variables to be controlled remain compelling.

Moberg also recognized the limitations of cross-sectional data, noting that the relationships observed could reflect a causal effect of religion on personal adjustment or the effects of personal adjustment on religious participation.[5] Debates about social causation and social selection remain important in research on religion and well-being. Moberg further recognized the importance of the life-course perspective two decades before that term entered the sociological lexicon. In his 1956 article, he examined the relationships between religious participation at various life stages (childhood/adolescence, young adulthood), as retrospectively reported, and personal adjustment in late life. Thus, Moberg's early research set the stage for the surge of research on religion and health that occurred decades later.

The Social Foundations of Well-Being in Late Life

Although studies of social factors in later life first appeared more than a century ago, social gerontology, as a recognized area of research, emerged in the 1940s, with the volume of empirical studies reaching a critical mass in the 1960s. At the outset, gerontological research had a crisis orientation. In part because of ageist stereotypes of late life as a time of loss and limitations and in part because of statistical data (e.g., larger proportions of older adults lived in poverty than any other age group), early aging research was based on the assumption that large proportions of older adults experienced financial strain, illness and disability, social isolation, fear of impending death, and hence poor quality of life. Consequently, the impetus for much early research was to identify the factors that were associated with sustained rather than reduced well-being.

A number of challenges to the crisis orientation emerged from research conducted in the 1960s and 1970s. First, although they were more disadvantaged than their younger counterparts in most objective resources (including education, income, and health), older adults were significantly more satisfied with their lives than middle-aged and young adults.[6] Substantial evidence, now spanning more than half a century, documents that older adults require fewer resources than young and middle-aged adults to generate high levels of life satisfaction.[7] Second, older adults report fewer stressful life events than younger age groups, although they are more likely to report the deaths of loved ones.[8] Third, although death anxiety can be experienced at all ages, it peaks in middle age, and older adults report low levels of death anxiety on average.[9] Fourth, the vast majority of older adults maintain satisfying relationships with family and friends; large proportions are also active in the broader community via volunteering and organizations. Religion is the most frequently reported organizational affiliation.

Well-being has been defined in multiple ways in aging research. The most common form of well-being examined has been life satisfaction and related constructs, now generally referred to as SWB. Mental and physical health, especially subjective perceptions of health, have also been used in many studies. Quite a few social factors predict these various measures of well-being in both cross-sectional and longitudinal studies.[10] Religious involvement is one of those factors.

Given the large number of factors related to well-being in late life, efforts to identify categories of predictors is understandable. In line with this development, religious participation is one of several social factors subsumed under the rubric of social integration. The concept of social integration is especially attractive to social scientists because it can be traced back to Émile Durkheim's pioneering research on suicide.[11] In his classic book, Durkheim demonstrated that, with the exception of very high levels, social integration was negatively related to rates of suicide. Social integration was operationalized as attachments to social structure, including marriage, parenthood, employment, and religious participation.

Given the underlying assumption that the more attachments the better, it became popular in the 1970s and 1980s for researchers to create social integration indices in which relevant social roles were summed to yield social integration scores.[12] Even when attachments to communities were not added together, religious participation was interpreted as comparable to other forms of attachment. In essence, religious involvement became commonly viewed as a form of civic engagement, similar in function to membership in secular organizations. In addition, it became the norm to use attendance at religious services as the appropriate measure of religion's contribution to social integration.

Viewing religious involvement as a form of social integration remains the norm today. And this is one reasonable way of conceptualizing the role of religion in individuals' lives, albeit not necessarily specific to older adults. The problem with this view is that it ignores a myriad of other ways that religion may affect the lives of older adults. One aspect of this problem is the nearly exclusive focus on religious service attendance, which is but one form of religious participation. Other forms include private prayer, reading or studying religious texts, intrinsic versus extrinsic motivations, use of religious coping strategies, and others. Any or all of these dimensions of religious involvement may be related to well-being in later life, but they do not "fit" the conceptual foundation of social integration. Another difficulty with viewing religious participation as solely a form of social integration is that it discourages attention to whether and how religion has distinctive effects on well-being or other outcomes of interest. Social integration becomes both the label and the explanation for religious effects when, in reality, religious involvement may be an indicator of other important processes such as identity formation and maintenance or the formation of world-views through which life is understood.

In summary, after nearly seventy years of research, gerontologists still do not have well-articulated theories about the role of religion in older adults' lives—or even about whether religion plays a distinctive role for older adults that does not apply or is less important to younger age groups. This conceptual ambiguity has not, however, prevented research on religion and aging from contributing a great deal of knowledge about the lives of older adults.

RELIGIOUS PARTICIPATION IN LATER LIFE

If religious participation is hypothesized to be a significant antecedent of well-being in later life, it is important to know the extent to which older adults are involved in religious activities and hold religious beliefs. It is also useful to know whether religious participation is relatively stable across adulthood or whether there are patterned changes over time. This section examines three issues with regard to religious participation in late life: age/cohort differences in religious participation, what can be learned from age-period-cohort (APC) analyses of religious participation, and within-person changes in religious participation across adulthood.

Age/Cohort Differences in Religious Participation

It is commonly assumed in both public and professional discourse that people tend to become more religious as they age. This makes sense, it is argued, in light of the frequent role losses, declining health, and approaching death characteristic of later life. This assumption is typically supported by studies that examine differences in religious participation across age groups at a specific point in time. Age and cohort are confounded, however, in comparisons of age groups at a single point in time. Thus, age differences cannot provide valid information about changes in religious participation across the life course. They can, however, provide descriptive information about the distribution of religious involvement at a given point in time, and this information is valuable for some purposes (e.g., estimating the proportion of older adults who might be served by faith-based programs).

The Religious Landscape Survey, a recent nationally representative survey of the U.S. adult population conducted by the Pew Foundation, details age differences in multiple dimensions of religious involvement.[13] Overall, the patterns suggest that older adults (i.e., age sixty-five and older) are more involved in religion than their younger counterparts. Specifically, older adults report the highest levels of attending religious services, believing in God, claiming that religion is important in their lives, and praying daily or more often. The oldest age groups are also the least likely to report having switched religions since childhood and having no religious affiliation.

Although age distributions of religious involvement are compatible with the hypothesis that people become more religious as they age, they do not provide evidence of an aging effect. Differences across age groups could reflect cohort effects instead.

APC Analyses of Religious Participation

Although there is no way to disentangle the effects of age, period, and cohort completely, recent advances in the field have generated a dramatic increase in the volume of APC research, including religious participation. A recent study by Schwadel[14] provides the most recent and comprehensive APC analysis of religious involvement. This study covers the period from 1972 to 2006 and examined multiple dimensions of religious participation. Three of the four dimensions of religious participation had significant age, period, and cohort effects.

The dimension with the most dramatic changes was religious service attendance. As long hypothesized, there was a large age effect—people in the cohorts sampled increased service attendance over time. There also was a sizable cohort effect, with younger cohorts attending religious services in much smaller proportions than their older counterparts. Period effects were modest but statistically significant, with attendance declining over time. In contrast, belief in an afterlife had the fewest changes. Age and period effects were minimal. The cohort effect was curvilinear, with both the oldest (born from 1887 to 1912) and youngest (born 1972 and later) cohorts reporting higher levels of belief than cohorts born between 1913 and 1971.

Results from Schwadel's study advance our understanding of religion and aging in at least two ways. First, estimating age, period, and cohort effects net of each other is important. The age differences in service attendance observed in cross-sectional studies, for example, are due to both age changes and cohort differences. Second, the results demonstrate that age, period, and cohort effects vary for different dimensions of religious involvement.

Life-Course Patterns of Religious Participation

APC analyses provide accurate estimates for the population as a whole; nonetheless, substantial variability surrounds these population averages. Examining life-course patterns of religious involvement, using individual-level panel studies with multiple times of measurement, provides information about some of the variability underlying population patterns. Data sources that include high-quality samples, cover large proportions of the life course, and include multiple times of measurement are rare. Consequently, the number of studies available is small, and their findings should be viewed as suggestive rather than definitive.

Three longitudinal studies examine patterns of religious participation over much of the adult life course. Hayward and Krause[15] examined changes in religious service attendance over thirty-four years, from 1971 to 2005. At baseline, sample members ranged in age from 15 to 102. Because of the wide age range, substantial mortality-related attrition occurred over time for older sample members, and the youngest sample members were last observed in middle age. Piecewise growth curve modeling revealed a modal pattern in which attendance declined in late adolescence, increased modestly after that, stabilized in middle-age, then increased in early old age and declined somewhat at the oldest ages. In a second study, time series analysis was used to examine changes in the extent to which religion influenced participants' daily lives over three times of measurement spanning twelve years.[16] At baseline, the sample ranged in age from early to late adulthood. A monotonic increase in the influence of religion on daily life was observed from late adolescence to early old age.

The most statistically sophisticated study to date used growth mixture modeling to identify discrete trajectories of religious involvement.[17] The data source for the study was the Terman data. The Terman data are from boys and girls born in the early to mid-1920s in the San Francisco Bay area who were unusually intelligent (IQ scores of 135 and higher). The lack of representativeness is the key weakness of these data. On the plus side, participants were interviewed up to nine times, from when they attended grade school through their mid-seventies. Religiosity ratings were based on information about religious service attendance and the perceived importance of religion in one's daily life. Three trajectories were identified. One trajectory took the form of increasing religiosity from adolescence until middle age, followed by stable levels of attendance, followed by declines in attendance during late life. This trajectory was reported by 40 percent of study participants; 41 percent reported a second trajectory, characterized by very low religious involvement in adolescence and early adulthood, followed by further declines thereafter. The third trajectory (16 percent) included individuals who had high levels of religious involvement in early adulthood and increases thereafter. The authors acknowledge that rates of religious participation were substantially lower at all times of measurement for this sample than comparable national estimates.

I found only one study that examined patterns of stability and change in religious involvement during later life. Wang and colleagues examined trajectories of religious service attendance and strength of religious beliefs.[18] Study participants were age seventy-two and older at baseline and were measured six times in twelve years. Growth curve modeling indicated that, on average, religious attendance declined over time, whereas the strength of religious beliefs remained stable.

Because of the scarcity of data, few conclusions can be reached about life-course patterns of religious participation. Based on research to date, it appears that trajectories vary across dimensions of religious involvement. It also appears that several distinct trajectories are required to characterize life-course patterns of religious participation. This conclusion is offered cautiously, however, because only one study used growth mixture modeling (and was thus able to generate multiple trajectories) and the data source in that study was nonrepresentative.

RELIGION AND WELL-BEING IN LATER LIFE

The vast majority of research about religion in later life focuses on the associations between religious involvement and well-being, broadly defined. Most of this research focuses on the relationships between religious participation and several health outcomes—mental health, physical health, disability, cognitive functioning, and mortality. Another body of research examines the link between religiosity and SWB, which includes life satisfaction, happiness, and perceived quality of life. Much smaller bodies of research examine the associations between religion and other outcomes, including EOL decisions and civic engagement and volunteering. Space limitations preclude extensive review of any of these relationships; instead the studies cited should be viewed as exemplars representing major themes.

Religious Participation and Health

It is not possible to review adequately the massive amount of research on the associations of religious participation and health.[19] Beyond the sheer volume of research, the research base appropriately includes multiple dimensions of religious experience and an even larger array of health outcomes, which precludes simple conclusions. Because of space limitations, I reference meta-analyses and recent studies to the extent possible—these papers include extensive citations of previous research.

Mental health. A very large number of studies examine the associations between religious participation and mental health outcomes, including symptoms of depression and anxiety; psychological distress; and, less frequently, psychiatric diagnoses. The overwhelming majority of studies report that religion has a significant inverse relationship with mental health problems.[20] Many of these studies are longitudinal and include a broad array of control variables. Multiple dimensions of religious involvement have been studied. The volume and the strength of the findings suggest that three are particularly important: attendance at religious services, intrinsic religious motivation, and positive religious coping—especially attendance. Overall, this body of research is compatible with the conclusion that some forms of religious involvement have a protective causal effect on mental health.

Many studies also report that religion buffers the effects of stress on mental health outcomes.[21] Multiple dimensions of religious involvement have been examined, with no clear pattern across studies.

Cognitive functioning. Although the research base is not large, several studies report that religious participation protects against cognitive decline in later life.[22] The volume of studies is too small to determine whether specific dimensions of religious experience protect against cognitive decline. Most studies are longitudinal, however, providing strong evidence of temporal order.

Physical health. The most commonly examined physical health outcome is self-rated health, which is known to correlate significantly with both more objective measures of physical health (e.g., number of chronic diseases) and mental health. Religious variables are almost always associated with higher levels of self-rated health.[23] A number of dimensions of religious experience have been significantly related to self-rated health, with no clear pattern as to whether specific dimensions are differentially important.

Functional limitations. An emerging area of research examines the relationships between religious involvement and physical functioning or disability. Research documents that religious service attendance is associated with fewer limitations in activities of daily living (ADLs), instrumental activities of daily living (IADLs), and mobility in later life.[24] In cross-sectional analyses, the temporal order of service attendance and functional limitations is unclear—that is, attendance may protect physical functioning or functional limitations may preclude attending religious services. Longitudinal analyses show, however, that service attendance is associated with slower declines in physical functioning.[25] Indeed, these analyses also demonstrated that the onset or worsening of disability had no significant effect on religious service attendance.

Mortality. Perhaps the strongest evidence that religious involvement affects health is the sizable body of research examining the effects of religious service attendance on mortality. Numerous studies report that regular service attendance has a substantial protective effect on mortality, with a wide range of potential confounding variables statistically controlled.[26] A meta-analysis of data from forty-two independent samples also showed a significant and quite large inverse relationship between religious involvement and mortality.[27] The protective effect of religion on survival has also been documented in non-Western countries in which religious practices are very different from those in the West.[28] These studies are especially important because temporal order is unassailable; religion may exert a causal effect on mortality, but mortality cannot affect religious participation.

Biomarkers and biological function. A rapidly growing body of research examines the relationships between religious involvement and biological function as measured by levels of immune function, coagulation, inflammation, and allostatic load (i.e., a summary measure of biological "wear and tear") among older adults. The logic of these investigations is that, in addition to its associations with health outcomes, religious participation may affect subclinical factors that place individuals at risk for morbidity and mortality. In the first study of this kind, Koenig and colleagues documented a significant relationship between regular service attendance and better immune function as measured by interleukin-6 (IL-6).[29] While the research base remains small, investigators consistently report that religious service attendance is associated with better immune function, decreased inflammation, and lower allostatic load,[30] although Maselko and colleagues observed lower allostatic load only among women.[31] All studies to date have been cross-sectional. This precludes conclusions about temporal order, although it seems unlikely that subclinical biological dysfunction would affect service attendance. In addition, the only dimension of religion investigated has been service attendance.

The search for mediators. Given strong and generally consistent evidence that religious involvement is associated with multiple health outcomes, attention quickly focused on the mechanisms or mediators that might explain those relationships. Three sets of potential mediating factors have received the most attention. First, investigators hypothesized that social support would partially or totally mediate the links between religion and health. That is, attending religious services might generate more sources or a larger volume of social support, which would in turn protect health. Second, most religions encourage care of the body—and some prescribe and proscribe health-related behaviors. Thus, health behaviors might mediate religion–health relationships. Third, religious participation may promote psychosocial resources such as self-esteem, and those resources might benefit health.

After more than thirty years of investigation, research evidence based on samples of older adults, as well as adults of all ages, documents that social support, health behaviors, and psychosocial resources are significant predictors of health outcomes independent of religious involvement, but they explain only modest amounts of the relationships between religious involvement and health.[32] This conclusion applies to multiple dimensions of religious participation.

More recent research has examined additional potential mediators. For example, some research has focused on relationships within study participants' congregations, including church-based social support and criticism from church peers.[33] Researchers have also examined the extent to which various virtues such as gratitude, optimism, and forgiveness mediate the effects of service attendance on health outcomes.[34] Results suggest that these virtues partially mediate these relationships, but, again, the mediating effects are quite modest.

An emerging trend is to examine whether biomarker and other biological data mediate the link between religious involvement and health. The rationale for these studies is that religious participation may promote health by protecting biological functioning. Although the research base is far too small to permit conclusions, evidence to date is not encouraging. Hybels and colleagues,[35] for example, report that indicators of immune function and inflammation significantly mediated the relationship between religious attendance and physical functioning, but these biological mediators explained only 8 percent of the relationship.

Can religion harm health? Overall, religious participation is associated with better health and longer survival. This does not preclude the possibility that some dimensions of religious involvement are associated with poorer health outcomes. One dimension of religious involvement that does not have uniformly positive relationships with health is religious coping—that is, the extent to which individuals use religious beliefs to cope with problems. Religious coping is interesting because there are positive and negative forms of religious coping. Individuals who use positive religious coping rely on beliefs that God or a Higher Power desires positive outcomes for them and helps to achieve them. Individuals who use negative religious coping believe that God or a Higher Power is indifferent to their problems, has abandoned them, or is punishing them for their sins. Evidence clearly documents that these two styles of religious coping have very different relationships with health. Positive religious coping is associated with better adjustment to stress. In contrast, negative religious coping is associated with higher levels of depression and anxiety, as documented in a meta-analysis of forty-nine studies.[36] Although the research base is smaller, some studies report that religious doubts also are associated with elevated levels of depression and anxiety symptoms, as well as general distress.[37]

Subjective Well-Being

Given the strong, consistent negative relationships between religious involvement and mental health problems, it is not surprising that religious participation is strongly and positively related to SWB in later life.[38] This relationship is generally observed across multiple indicators of SWB and multiple dimensions of religious involvement. There are exceptions, however. Using data from a nationally representative sample of Hungarians, for example, Thege and colleagues[39] report that regular service attendance predicted high life satisfaction. In contrast, purely personal religious involvement (private prayer, reading sacred texts) was associated with lower SWB than having no religious involvement.

Although research on religion and health/SWB typically measures dimensions of religious involvement as continuous variables (e.g., frequency of prayer, amount of intrinsic motivation), there also may be threshold effects. Measures of service attendance, for example, are often dichotomized, contrasting those who attend services once a week or more with those who attend services less than once a week. Coding service attendance dichotomously assumes that the threshold for observing strong effects on health or SWB is once a week. Similarly, Mochon and associates[40] observed a threshold effect in the relationship between strength of religious beliefs and SWB. Individuals with strong religious beliefs reported the highest levels of SWB. Contrary to expectations, however, persons with weak religious beliefs reported lower levels of SWB than did those who described themselves as atheist or agnostic.

EOL Decision Making

A substantial body of research has examined the relationships between religious participation and EOL planning. Investigators initially hypothesized that religious involvement would encourage EOL planning, especially decisions to stop aggressive treatment and the use of life-prolonging technology once recovery and adequate quality of life are not possible. This hypothesis rested on the knowledge that religious individuals are more likely than the nonreligious to believe that death is natural and appropriate, to believe that there is an afterlife, and to have significantly less death anxiety.[41]

Unexpectedly, research findings consistently indicate that religious persons are less likely than their nonreligious or less religious peers to have living wills, arrange for a durable power of attorney, and have a do not resuscitate (DNR) order and other forms of advance directives.[42] There also are significant denominational differences, with Catholics and, especially, conservative Protestants least likely to make advance directives. Subsequent research suggests that many religious individuals believe that the time of death should be God's decision rather than a matter of personal preference, a desire to limit personal suffering, or a way to lower medical costs.[43]

Civic Engagement and Volunteering

The links between religious involvement and volunteering appear to be strong, with some interesting patterns observed in recent research. It is well-established that religious participation is a strong and significant predictor of volunteering in late life.[44] Religious involvement is strongly related to church-based volunteering and significantly but less strongly associated with volunteering for secular organizations. In an especially persuasive longitudinal study, Johnston[45] documents that regular church attendance predicts church-based volunteering and that individuals expand their efforts over time to secular volunteering as well. He aptly describes religious organizations as "feeder systems" for volunteering and civic engagement more broadly. Lima and MacGregor[46] describe a different form of spillover from religiously motivated volunteering. Nonreligious individuals who are close friends with religious volunteers are significantly likely to volunteer for both church-based and secular causes than nonreligious persons without close religious friends.

An emerging theme in research on religion is the issue of whether and how participation in religious organizations differs from participation in other civic organizations. As one set of investigators asked: Is religion "just another club"?[47] Their research, based on a sample of adolescents, showed that religious attendance was associated with several indicators of psychological adjustment and that attendance at clubs was not. Their analysis has not been replicated using data from a sample of older adults. A similar study compared the main and stress-buffering effects of religious and secular participation on psychological distress using data from a sample of adults of all ages.[48] The results indicated that religious engagement buffered the effects of some stressors that were not buffered by civic engagement and that overall religious involvement had stronger buffering effects than secular civic engagement. A priority for future research is comparing the effects of religious participation with those of civic engagement in later life.

FINAL THOUGHTS AND FUTURE DIRECTIONS

Much is already known about the role of religion in the lives of older adults. Many findings to date merit replication in other samples to permit confident conclusions. Given appropriate data, more can be learned by the application of cutting-edge statistical techniques to longitudinal data that cover large segments of adulthood, the transition to late life, and the twenty-five or more years that most older adults survive. These are important priorities for future research, but they are logical increments to an already large and robust knowledge base. At a broader level, are there new directions that would be profitable for future research? Conversely, are there research questions that have been answered as completely and rigorously as current science allows and that should therefore be allowed to enter a period of dormancy? I would answer both questions in the affirmative.

The topic that I believe merits far less attention in the future than it has to date is efforts to identify mediators of the religion-health/SWB connection. I believe that the field has taken that issue to the point of diminishing returns. Dozens of studies have examined social support, health behaviors, and various psychosocial resources as mediators of the relationships between religious involvement and well-being as broadly defined. Initial studies found that these factors are important independent predictors of well-being, but their mediating effects are modest at best. Recent studies have similar results. Other potential mediators that were put to the test more recently have fared no better. Church-based social support is not a substantially more powerful mediator of the relationships between religious involvement and well-being than secular support. Nor is having close congregational friends; it has about the same explanatory power as other measures of social bonds.

Other recent studies attempt to explain the nearly ubiquitous association of religious service attendance and well-being by posing other dimensions of religious participation as mediators. For example, Sternthal and associates[49] find that individuals' sense of meaning derived from religious involvement significantly but very modestly mediates the relationships between service attendance and depression and anxiety symptoms. The data are cross-sectional, however; therefore, it is just as likely that deriving a sense of meaning from religious involvement leads to attending religious services more frequently. Overall, then, I do not view further efforts to identify mediators of the relationship between religion and well-being as worthwhile.

What interests me most as a priority for future research is increased knowledge about how religious involvement pervades life domains other than health and SWB in late life. The emerging research on religious involvement and both EOL decision making and volunteering are examples of that kind of research. Many other life domains are worth exploring. Some research examines relationships of religious variables with political attitudes, voting, and attitudes about contemporary public issues. Almost none of them, however, are based on samples of older adults or compare age groups. Relationships between religious participation and interpersonal relationships in late life would be other logical topics for future research. Substantial research has examined these relationships in adolescence, but little, if any, comparable research has been based on data from samples of older adults.

And what about consumer behavior and money management? Do the religiously involved and the uninvolved differ in their spending patterns, in their propensity to save or use credit, or the dispositions of their estates? For example, Keister[50] reports that religious beliefs and traditions are strongly related to wealth accumulation and the value that individuals place on financial security. Whether these patterns differ by age or cohort is unknown. A myriad of attitudes and behaviors not yet examined may be related to religious involvement in general or specific religious beliefs and practices.

One of the ways that religion penetrates the lives of its practitioners is as a tool for making meaning. Culture provides answers to many questions about life and socialization, which is dominant during childhood but continues throughout life, and inculcates those answers in the human psyche. But socialization does not provide the answers to all questions because the breadth and depth of socialization vary widely across individuals and because culture itself does not provide answers to all questions. Thus, although culture accounts for much, probably most, of the meaning that humans experience, individuals also encounter situations in which meaning is not obvious or in which they question the taken-for-granted meanings provided by culture.

Philosophers, psychologists, and other scholars have ruminated about meaning for centuries, recognizing that meaning is central to the human psyche. As Emmons succinctly states, "Without meaning and purpose, there is little reason to do what is necessary to live and to endure the inevitable suffering and trials that come with life."[51] Scientific attention to meaning waxes and wanes over time. Fortunately, meaning making reemerged as an important part of psychology in the past decade or so, with special attention to religion as a tool for meaning making.

Religion's contributions to meaning making have been examined in multiple contexts, including coping with stress,[52] setting and striving toward goals,[53] motivating behaviors consistent with values,[54] and guiding behavior at work.[55] Although the evidence is limited in volume, results indicate that religious and nonreligious people create meanings that differ in process and outcome.[56] Much more research is needed to better understand the ways in which religion affects meaning making. It is especially important that the field move beyond simple religious/nonreligious comparisons to better understand the ways that specific beliefs and practices shape the meaning-making process. Older adults are ideal subjects for research on meaning making because they have decades of experience in creating meaning and have lived long enough to have confronted what Emmons calls the "ultimate issues" of life, death, suffering, achievement, failure, and loss.

Finally, we need to know much more about the temporal dynamics of religious involvement. Research to date suggests that no single trajectory can adequately describe the vast variation in life-course patterns of religious involvement. Research is needed to identify the conditions under which individuals increase or decrease their commitments to religion—and whether those changes have implications for other areas of life or differ by age. We also need to know whether changes in one dimension of religious involvement lead to changes in other dimensions or if dimensions of religious participation operate independently of each other. For a large proportion of older adults, religion is an important commitment that affects their attitudes, behaviors, and well-being. The better we understand the ways that religion affects older adults, the better we will understand aging.

NOTES

1. The three papers by David O. Moberg: "Church Membership and Personal Adjustment in Old Age," *Journal of Gerontology* 8 (1953): 207–11; "The Christian Religion and Personal Adjustment in Old Age," *American Sociological Review* 18 (1953): 87–90; and "Religious Activities and Personal Adjustment in Old Age," *Journal of Social Psychology* 43 (1956): 261–67.
2. Moberg, "Church Membership and Personal Adjustment in Old Age."
3. Moberg, "The Christian Religion and Personal Adjustment in Old Age."
4. Moberg, "Religious Activities and Personal Adjustment in Old Age."
5. Moberg, "The Christian Religion and Personal Adjustment in Old Age," 89.
6. For example, Angus Campbell, Philip E, Converse, and Willard L. Rodgers, *The Quality of American Life: Perceptions, Evaluations, and Satisfactions* (New York: Russell Sage Foundation, 1976).
7. Linda K. George, "Still Happy after All These Years: Research Frontiers on Subjective Well-Being in Later Life," *Journal of Gerontology: Social Sciences* 65B (2010): 331–39.
8. Dana C. Hughes, Dan G. Blazer, and Linda K. George, "Age Differences in Life Events: A Multivariate Controlled Analysis," *International Journal of Aging and Human Development* 27 (1988): 207–20.
9. Kenneth E. Vail, Zachary K. Rothschild, Dave R. Weise, Sheldon Solomon, Tom Pyszczynski, and Jeff Greenberg, "A Terror Management

Analysis of the Psychological Functions of Religion," *Personality and Social Psychology Review* 14 (2010): 84–94.

10. For a review, see George, "Still Happy after All These Years."

11. Émile Durkheim, *Suicide: A Study in Sociology* [1897] (New York: Free Press, 1966).

12. For example, see Lisa F. Berkman and S. Leonard Syme, "Social Networks, Host Resistance, and Mortality: A Nine-Year Follow-Up Study of Alameda County Residents," *American Journal of Epidemiology* 109 (1979): 186–204.

13. Pew Foundation, "Religion among the Millennials: Introduction and Overview" (February 17, 2010), accessed at http://www.pewforum .org/2010/02/17/religion-among-the-millennials/ on January 24, 2015; and "'Nones' on the Rise" (October 9, 2012), accessed at http:// www.pewforum.org/2012/10/09/nones-on-the-rise-demographics/ on December 24, 2015.

14. Phillip Schwadel, "Age, Period, and Cohort Effects on Religious Activities and Beliefs," *Social Science Research* 40 (2011): 181–192.

15. R. David Hayward and Neal Krause, "Patterns of Change in Religious Service Attendance across the Life Course: Evidence from a 34-Year Longitudinal Study," *Social Science Research* 42 (2013): 1480–89.

16. Amy Argue, David R. Johnson, and Lynn K. White, "Age and Religiosity: Evidence from a Three-Wave Panel Analysis," *Journal for the Scientific Study of Religion* 38 (1999): 423–35.

17. Michael E. McCullough, Craig K. Enders, Sharon L. Brion, and Andrea R. Jain, "The Varieties of Religious Development in Adulthood: A Longitudinal Investigation of Religion and Rational Choice," *Journal of Personality and Social Psychology* 89 (2005): 78–89.

18. Kuan-Yuan Wang, Kyle Kercher, Jui-Yen Huang, and Karl Kosloski, "Aging and Religious Participation in Late Life," *Journal of Religion and Health* 53 (2014): 1514–28.

19. For the most comprehensive review to date, see Harold G. Koenig, Dana King, and Verna Benner Carson, *Handbook of Religion and Health*, 2nd ed. (New York: Oxford University Press, 2012).

20. See meta-analyses by Gene G. Ano and Erin B. Vasconcelles, "Religious Coping and Psychological Adjustment to Stress: A Meta-Analysis," *Journal of Clinical Psychology* 61 (2005): 461–80; Charles H. Hackney and Glenn S. Sanders, "Religiosity and Mental Health: A Meta-Analysis of Recent Studies," *Journal for the Scientific Study of Religion* 42 (2003): 43–55; and Timothy B. Smith, Michael E. McCullough, and Justin Poll, "Religiousness and Depression: Evidence for a Main Effect and the Moderating Influence of Stressful Life Events," *Psychological Bulletin* 129 (2003): 614–36.

21. For example, see the meta-analysis by Smith et al., "Religiousness and Depression."

22. For example, see Terrence D. Hill, Amy M. Burdette, Jacqueline L. Angel, and Ronald J. Angel, "Religious Attendance and Cognitive Functioning among Older Mexican Americans," *Journal of Gerontology: Psychological Sciences* 61B (2006): P3–P9; and Peter H. Van Ness and Stanislav V. Kasl, "Religion and Cognitive Dysfunction in an Elderly Cohort," *Journal of Gerontology: Social Sciences* 58B (2003): S21–S29.

23. For example, see Tim Huijts and Gerbert Kraaykamp, "Religious Involvement, Religious Context, and Self-Assessed Health in Europe," *Journal of Health and Social Behavior* 52 (2011): 91–106; and Neal Krause and R. David Hayward, "Religious Involvement, Practical Wisdom, and Self-Rated Health," *Journal of Aging and Health* 26 (2014): 540–58.

24. For example, see George Fitchett, Maureen R. Benjamins, Kimberly A. Skarupski, and Carlos F. Mendes de Leon, "Worship Attendance and the Disability Process in Community-Dwelling Older Adults," *Journal of Gerontology: Social Sciences* 68 (2013): 235–45; and Celia F. Hybels, Linda K. George, Dan G. Blazer, Carl F. Pieper, Harvey J. Cohen, and Harold G. Koenig, "Inflammation and Coagulation as Mediators in the Relationships between Religious Attendance and Functional Limitations in Older Adults," *Journal of Aging and Health* 26 (2014): 679–97.

25. For example, see Fitchett et al., "Worship Attendance and the Disability Process in Community-Dwelling Older Adults"; and Ellen L. Idler and Stanislav V. Kasl, "Religion among Disabled and Nondisabled Persons II: Attendance at Religious Services as a Predictor of the Course of Disability," *Journal of Gerontology: Social Sciences* 52B (1997): S306–S316.

26. For example, see Harold G. Koenig, Judith C. Hays, David B. Larson, Linda K. George, Harvey J. Cohen, Michael E. McCullough, Keith G. Meador, and Dan G. Blazer, "Does Religious Attendance Prolong Survival?: A Six-Year Follow-Up Study of 3,968 Older Adults," *Journal of Gerontology: Medical Sciences* 54A (1999): M370–M376; Marc A. Musick, James S. House, and David R. Williams, "Attendance at Religious Services and Mortality in a National Sample," *Journal of Health and Social Behavior* 45 (2004): 198–213; and Douglas Oman and Dwayne Reed, "Religion and Mortality among the Community Dwelling Elderly," *American Journal of Public Health* 88 (1998): 1469–75.

27. Michael E. McCullough, William T. Hoyt, David B. Larson, Harold G. Koenig, and Carl Thoresen, "Religious Involvement and Mortality: A Meta-Analytic Review," *Health Psychology* 19 (2000): 211–22.

28. For example, see Yi Zeng, Danan Gu, and Linda K. George, "Association of Religious Participation with Mortality among Chinese Old Adults," *Research on Aging* 33 (2011): 51–83.

29. Harold G. Koenig, Harvey J. Cohen, Linda K. George, Judith C. Hays, David B. Larson, and Dan G. Blazer, "Attendance at Religious Services, Interleukin-6, and Other Biological Parameters of Immune Function in Older Adults," *International Journal of Psychiatry in Medicine* 27 (1997): 233–50.

30. For example, see Terrence D. Hill, Sunshine M. Rote, Christopher G. Ellison, and Amy M. Burdette, "Religious Attendance and Biological Functioning: A Multiple Specification Approach," *Journal of Aging and Health* 26 (2014): 766–85; Hybels et al., "Inflammation and Coagulation as Mediators in the Relationships between Religious Attendance and Functional Limitations in Older Adults"; and Joanna Maselko, Laura Kubzansky, Ichiro Kawachi, Teresa Seeman, and Lisa Berkman, "Religious Service Attendance and Allostatic Load among High Functioning Elderly," *Psychosomatic Medicine* 69 (2007): 464–72.

31. Maselko et al., "Religious Service Attendance and Allostatic Load among High Functioning Elderly."

32. For example, see Terrence D. Hill, Jacqueline L. Angel, Christopher G. Ellison, and Ronald J. Angel, "Religious Attendance and Mortality: An 8-Year Follow-Up of Older Mexican Americans," *Journal of Gerontology: Social Sciences* 60B (2005): S102–S109; and Koenig et al., "Does Religious Attendance Prolong Survival?"

33. For example, see R. David Hayward and Neal Krause, "Trajectories of Disability in Older Adulthood and Social Support from a Religious Congregation: A Growth Curve Analysis," *Journal of Behavioral Medicine* 36 (2013): 354–60; and Michelle J. Sternthal, David R. Williams, Marc A. Musick, and Anna C. Buck, "Depression, Anxiety, and Religious Life: A Search for Mediators," *Journal of Health and Social Behavior* 51 (2010): 343–59.

34. For example, see Neal Krause and R. David Hayward, "Hostility, Religious Involvement, Gratitude, and Self-Rated Health in Late Life," *Research on Aging* 36 (2014): 731–52; and Asani H. Seawell, Loren L. Toussaint, and Alyssa Cheadle, "Prospective Association between Unforgiveness and Physical Health and Positive Mediating Mechanisms in a Nationally Representative Sample of Older Adults," *Psychology and Health* 29 (2014): 375–89.

35. Hybels et al., "Inflammation and Coagulation as Mediators in the Relationships between Religious Attendance and Functional Limitations in Older Adults."

36. Ano and Vasconcelles, "Religious Coping and Psychological Adjustment to Stress."

37. Neal Krause and Keith M. Wulff, "Religious Doubt and Health: Exploring the Potential Dark Side of Religion," *Sociology of Religion* 65 (2004): 35–65.

38. For example, see Steven E. Barkan and Susan F. Greenwood, "Religious Attendance and Subjective Well-Being among Older Americans: Evidence from the General Social Survey," *Review of Religious Research* 45 (2003): 116–29; and James R. Peacock and Margaret M. Poloma, "Religiosity and Life Satisfaction across the Life Course," *Social Indicators Research* 48 (1999): 319–43.

39. Barna K. Thege, Janos Pilling, Andras Szekely, and Maria S. Kopp, "Relationship between Religiosity and Health: Evidence from a Post-Communist Country," *International Journal of Behavioral Medicine* 20 (2013): 477–86.

40. Daniel Mochon, Michael I. Norton, and Dan Ariely, "Who Benefits from Religion?," *Social Indicators Research* 101 (2011): 1–15.

41. See the review by Vail et al., "A Terror Management Analysis of the Psychological Functions of Religion."

42. For example, see Kathy Black, Sandra L. Reynolds, and Hana Osman, "Factors Associated with Advance Care Planning among Older Adults in Southwest Florida," *Journal of Applied Gerontology* 27 (2008): 93–109; and Shane Sharp, Deborah Carr, and Cameron Macdonald, "Religion and End-of-Life Treatment Preferences: Assessing the Effects of Religious Denomination and Beliefs," *Social Forces* 91 (2012): 275–98.

43. Melissa M. Garrido, Ellen L. Idler, Howard Leventhal, and Deborah Carr, "Pathways from Religion to Advance Care Planning: Beliefs about Control over Length of Life and End-of-Life Values," *The Gerontologist* 53 (2013): 801–16; and Laraine Winter, Marie P. Dennis, and Barbara Parker, "Preferences for Life-Prolonging Medical Treatments and Deference to the Will of God," *Journal of Religion and Health* 48 (2009): 418–30.

44. For example, see Caterina Grano, Fabio Lucidi, Arnoldo Zelli, and Cristiano Violani, "Motives and Determinants of Volunteering in Older Adults: An Integrated Model," *International Journal of Aging and Human Development* 67 (2008): 305–26; and Pamela D. Pilkington, Tim D. Windsor, and Dimity A. Crisp, "Volunteering and Subjective Well-Being in Midlife and Older Adults," *Journal of Gerontology: Social Sciences* 67B (2012): 249–60.

45. Joseph B. Johnston, "Religion and Volunteering over the Adult Life Course," *Journal for the Scientific Study of Religion* 52 (2013): 733–52.

46. Chaeyoon Lim and Carol Ann MacGregor, "Religion and Volunteering in Context: Disentangling the Contextual Effects of Religion on Voluntary Behavior," *American Sociological Review* 77 (2012): 747–79.

47. Marie Good, Teena Willoughby, and Jan Fritjers, "Just Another Club?: The Distinctiveness of the Relation between Religious Service Attendance and Adolescent Psychosocial Adjustment," *Journal of Youth and Adolescence* 38 (2009): 1153–71.

48. Gabriel A. Acevedo, Christopher G. Ellison, and Xiaohe Xu, "Is It Really Religion?: Comparing the Main and Stress-buffering Effects of Religious and Secular Civic Engagement on Psychological Distress," *Society and Mental Health* 4 (2014): 111–28.
49. Sternthal et al., "Depression, Anxiety, and Religious Life."
50. Lisa A. Keister, *Faith and Money: How Religious Belief Contributes to Wealth and Poverty* (New York: Cambridge University Press, 2011).
51. Robert A. Emmons, "Striving for the Sacred: Personal Goals, Life Meaning, and Religion," *Journal of Social Issues* 61 (2005): 731–45, quotation on p. 735.
52. For example, see Crystal L. Park, "Religion as a Meaning-Making Framework in Coping with Life Stress," *Journal of Social Issues* 61 (2005): 707–29.
53. Emmons, "Striving for the Sacred."
54. Sonia Roccas, "Religion and Value Systems," *Journal of Social Issues* 61 (2005): 747–59.
55. Marjolein Lips-Wiersma, "The Influence of Spiritual 'Meaning-Making' on Career Behavior," *Journal of Management Development* 21 (2002): 497–520.
56. For example, see Roccas, "Religion and Value Systems."

SUGGESTED READINGS

Ellison, Christopher G., Jason D. Boardman, David R. Williams, and James S. Jackson. "Religious Involvement, Stress, and Mental Health: Findings from the 1995 Detroit Area Study." *Social Forces* 80 (2001): 215–49. Although a large body of research relies implicitly on stress process theory, this article is unique in the explicit linkages drawn between stress process theory and religion. The findings are based on a sample of adults of all ages (rather than focusing on older adults), but the careful attention to theory explication and testing makes it an important contribution.

Hayward, R. David, and Neal Krause. "Trajectories of Disability in Older Adulthood and Social Support from a Religious Congregation: A Growth Curve Analysis." *Journal of Behavioral Medicine* 36 (2013): 354–60. Trajectory analysis is just beginning in research on religion, health, and aging. This article provides an excellent illustration of how religious involvement is associated with long-term patterns of change and stability in physical functioning.

Idler, Ellen L., ed. *Religion as a Social Determinant of Public Health*. New York: Oxford University Press, 2014. This unique volume examines the relationships between religious practices and institutions on the one hand and public health efforts on the other hand. Although both religious and public health programs often focus on the disadvantaged, the relationships between them have not always been positive. Examples of successful collaborations between religious and public health organizations are provided, however—examples that document the potential for simultaneously doing good and improving health.

Idler, Ellen L., Marc A. Musick, Christopher G. Ellison, Linda K. George, Neal Krause, Marcia G. Ory, Lynda H. Powell, Lynn G. Underwood, and David R. Williams. "Measuring Multiple Dimensions of Religion and Spirituality for Health Research: Conceptual Background and Findings from the 1998 General Social Survey." *Research on Aging* 25 (2003): 327–65. This article examines measurement of the most commonly used measures of dimensions of religious involvement in survey research. The conceptual rationales for selection of dimensions and the specific measures are carefully explicated, and survey results provide descriptive information about the measures from a nationally representative sample of American adults. Although the title of the article indicates that these measures are recommended for health research, they are, in fact, useful for a variety of research topics.

Koenig, Harold G., Dana King, and Verna Benner Carson. *Handbook of Religion and Health*, 2nd ed. New York: Oxford University Press, 2012. This handbook is the most comprehensive source available on the relationships between religious involvement and health, broadly defined. Like the first edition, this updated volume is a landmark publication. Although it does not focus exclusively on older adults, research on religion, health, and aging is covered in depth.

Krause, Neal M. *Aging in the Church: How Social Relationships Affect Health*. West Conshohocken, PA: Templeton Foundation Press, 2008. This volume is unique in several ways: by its focus specifically on church-based social relationships; in its balanced attention devoted to theory, measurement, and substance; and in its focus on the virtues (e.g., forgiveness, hope) that may underlie supportive church-based support. Attention is also paid to dysfunctional relationships that sometimes occur in congregations (e.g., criticism). The research reported here is based on a sample of middle-aged and older adults who attend religious services.

Levin, Jeff, Linda M. Chatters, and Robert J. Taylor. "Theory in Religion, Aging, and Health: An Overview." *Journal of Religion and Health* 50 (2011): 389–406. This article examines the role of theory in research on religion, health, and aging—a relatively neglected topic in this burgeoning research field. The most important contribution of this article is the attention to the extent to and the ways in which theory is implicit in much of the research on religion, health, and aging that appears to lack or be minimally guided by theory.

Musick, Marc A., James S. House, and David R. Williams. "Attendance at Religious Services and Mortality in a National Sample." *Journal of Health and Social Behavior* 45 (2004): 198–213. This is one of a sizable number of investigations demonstrating the protective effects of religious service attendance on mortality. The strengths of this article are that the sample is nationally representative and that the most commonly hypothesized mediators of the relationship between service attendance and mortality are tested.

Sharp, Shane, Deborah Carr, and Cameron Macdonald. "Religion and End-of-Life Treatment Preferences: Assessing the Effects of Religious Denomination, Beliefs, and Practices." *Social Forces* 91 (2012): 275–98. This article provides an excellent analysis of the associations between multiple dimensions of religious involvement and EOL treatment preferences. There is a lot of good research on this topic, but this article is the most comprehensive in terms of coverage of multiple forms of religious participation.

Snowdon, David. *Aging with Grace: What the Nun Study Teaches Us about Leading Longer, Healthier, and More Meaningful Lives.* New York: Bantam Books, 2001. This highly readable book summarizes a groundbreaking study, now called simply the Nun Study, that began in 1986 and continued for nearly two decades. Study participants include 678 Catholic nuns who were age 74 to 106 when first interviewed. Snowdon selected this population because of their unusually long lives and the near absence of dementia at even the most advanced ages. He became convinced, based on multiple forms of measurement, that the determinants of the nuns' health and longevity were rooted in multiple facets of their lives, all of which stemmed from their unassailable faith and their commitment to serving God and others.

9

Research on Religion and Education

William H. Jeynes

BACKGROUND

For centuries it was ingrained in Western society that religious faith was beneficial.[1] Hence, it was just assumed that Christian faith, in particular, yielded a bountiful supply of benefits.[2] Given that the Bible encouraged faithfulness, self-discipline, a strong work ethic, and other traits, it was assumed by people broadly across society that following the truths of the Bible would yield the benefits of which Jesus spoke.[3]

As time passed, however, historians and sociologists in particular thought it was sagacious to develop a greater understanding about why Christianity was positively related to scholastic and economic outcomes. Max Weber became the principal sociologist contributing to the maturation of this theory in the academic world.[4] Weber's myriad writings on the "Protestant ethic" contributed significantly to this development. Subsequent research supports the notion of a Christian ethic that pervades a variety of expressions of Christianity.[5] An impressive amount of research over the last 140 years has repeatedly confirmed the place of Christianity and family values in contributing to the overall welfare of society, including its economic prosperity. In addition, the Christian faith is a source of strong support for the two-biological-parent family.[6]

Probably the principal focus of study regarding the effects of religion, and Christianity especially, on education was historical in nature. The reason for this historical orientation was the fact that there appeared to be a concurrent development of the West's system of colleges and universities, which were definitively Christian, and the cultural and economic development of Europe and later what would become the United States. Weber's notion of what today might be called a "Christian ethic" was apparent in the founding of many of Europe's early universities, including Oxford (1096), Paris (1150), and Cambridge (1209).[7] That educational emphasis carried over to the New World with the founding of Harvard in 1636.[8] President John Adams, albeit speaking with some degree of hyperbole, shared that illiteracy in New England in the late 1700s and early 1800s was "as rare as a comet." Census figures from southern New England in 1840 indicate that the literacy rate in that area was 99.8 percent.[9] Historians believe that for 200 years New England was likely the most literate place on earth.[10]

There is no question that the study of religion and education grew in part because of the great effects on society that followed. When one studies the nations that enjoyed the highest standard of living and the most advanced cultures in the arts, the sciences, literature, and culture since about 1050 or 1100 A.D., it appears that the nations with the highest percentage of Christians domi-nate.[11] There is an unmistakable pattern that where Christianity flourished, cultural advancement and economic prosperity has followed. Lapin, for example, notes that 90 percent of the scien-tific discoveries over the last 1,000 years were in nations in which Christianity was the primary religion.[12] This relationship was most thoroughly developed, at least in the academic community, by Weber. Weber especially focuses on the Protestant economic dominance that emerged in the early 1500s, but after Martin Luther posted his ninety-five theses, Weber also avers that the momentum for this dominance developed centuries before in the Middle Ages.[13]

Weber pointed specifically to a number of qualities inherent in Christian practices that produced prosperity either through strengthening the family or through other means:[14]

> *A sense of calling*: Weber was convinced that the Christian sense of calling caused certain people to work harder than others, especially if they were fulfilling this calling in the context of a family.[15]

> *Morality*: As Samuel Huntington observes, Christianity "in America generally involves a belief in the fundamental opposition of good and evil, right and wrong.[16]

> *Work ethic*: Although people often associate the work ethic with Weber, in Weber's view the work ethic was often a result of love, both for God and other humans. That love, Weber believed, was antithetical to materialism because it continued to work to encourage people to work to help others, even after their own needs were satisfied.[17]

Events in the 1960s Causing a Renewed Academic Interest in Religion and Education

A plethora of measures indicated that the period beginning in 1963 ushered in a period of substantial educational moral decline, in the United States in particular. SAT scores plummeted for seventeen consecutive years, when previously these scores had never declined in even two consecutive years.[18] The decline took place from 1963 to 1980, and social scientists quickly noted that U.S. divorce rates, which had been in slight decline from 1948 to 1962, also surged for seventeen consecutive years from 1963 to 1980.[19] Illegal drug use surged during the same period, and it too appeared to peak in 1980.[20] Juvenile crime and premarital sex also skyrocketed by about fivefold during the same period, and premarital births increased sevenfold.[21]

The fact that the U.S. Supreme Court removed Bible reading and voluntary prayer from the public schools in 1962 and 1963 caused many politicians, civilians, and academics to wonder about the intricate connection between faith and the academic achievement and behavior of children and young adults.[22] These concerns multiplied when the Educational Testing Service conducted a quantitative study to determine the reasons behind the seventeen consecutive years of decline in SAT scores and concluded that American society's increasing departure from Christian values was one of the reasons behind the decline.[23] These concerns translated into a renewed interest in studying the relationship between faith and education.[24]

The Growth of Research on Faith-Based Schools

For many years, most research on the interplay between religion and educations focused on faith-based schools. This emphasis preceded the relationship between personal Christian faith, or religious beliefs in general, and school outcome largely for two reasons.

First, research is often generated by national public policy needs and dictates. In the 1960s, when the study of faith-based schools became quite prominent, a growing number of people thought it was important to better understand the contributions of these schools. This was thought important in order to help guide education policy regarding not only private school education but also what public educators might learn from their example.[25]

Second, until recently, American society generally assumed that Christian commitment was associated with positive social and academic outcomes.[26] Therefore, there did not seem to be a particularly pressing need to study the effects of religious commitment.[27]

The examination of the relationship between faith-based schools, nearly all of which are Christian, and school outcomes is the oldest component of the debate on the influence of religion on education.[28] Initially, in the 1960s, under the leadership of scholars such as James Coleman, social scientists focused specifically on the effects of Catholic schools.[29] However, after the removal of prayer and Bible reading from the public schools in 1963, the number of non-Catholic Christian schools soared from 1,000 to 13,000 during the period from 1965 to 1985.[30] The growth was especially apparent in the Northeast, the industrial portions of the Midwest, and California, where the contrast between the practices of Christian and public schools was particularly sharp.[31] The rising interest in Christian schools in the 1960s was directly related to the conclusion by many that the United States was paying a price for the increasing secularization, and perhaps anti-Christian tone, that its public schools and institutions were now initiating.[32] Many of the nation's leading minds believed that, in this environment, it was advisable to better understand the effects of faith and attempt to quantify them.[33]

The results that emerged from these studies on Christian schools were clear—that is, there was a faith-based advantage. Research by Anthony Bryk and his colleagues at the University of Chicago generated similar results to those found by Coleman.[34] What made the results of these studies all the more puissant is that, based on the findings of Coleman and others, a rising number of social scientists called for school choice programs to include private schools and believed that public schools could learn from certain components of the faith-based paradigm. Based on their findings, Bryk and his colleagues even inaugurated reforms in Chicago public schools.

Out of the ostensible faith-based advantage arose an interest in quantifying the effects of religious commitment. The first studies of this phenomenon used small and geographically limited samples, which propelled the field forward, but they were also subject to criticism by secularists that larger samples and more sophisticated data analysis were necessary to reach more concrete solutions about the influence of personal religious faith.[35] Great advances were made when nationwide data analysis using the National Education Longitudinal Study (NELS) showed a clear advantage for highly religious youth.[36] Further, meta-analyses of all studies of the effects of religious commitment on children's behavioral and academic outcomes[37] have found that individual religious commitment is consistently associated with positive behavioral and academic results, which over time affect the economy.[38] This being so, an increasing number of social scientists believe that, in order to improve the moral fabric of the country, Americans need to have a deeper tolerance and respect for faith.[39]

In the decades that followed the declining juvenile achievement and behavior of 1963 to 1980, social scientists and historians have commented on America's moral and academic decline. Although social scientists have advocated many possible approaches to these problems, and legislators have often acted on these recommendations, the problems stubbornly persist.[40] Over the last two decades, in particular, an increasing number of social scientists have begun to consider seriously the ameliorative effects that the practice of religious faith might have in increasing scholastic outcomes, reducing the achievement gap, and improving behavioral patterns that contribute to higher achievement.[41] But what has probably compelled numerous

Americans to acknowledge that public schools may need to open their minds to the benefits of faith has been the near-exponential growth in the number of shootings that have taken place in public schools and in other public settings.[42] Much of the interest that people at large and scholars have in faith today is based on the notion that religion may provide many of the answers for America's struggling youth, both academically and morally. On closer examination, religion may provide many of the answers that society seeks.

SUMMARY OF NOTABLE THEORY AND RESEARCH

The Relationship between Attending Religious Schools and Academic Outcomes

In all the types of studies that examine the relationship between faith and scholastic outcomes, the greatest attention from scholars has been on religious schooling.[43] This is probably because the results of these studies are easiest to apply to public policy. Over the last half-century, social scientists have engaged in considerable debate about the relationship between faith-based schools and educational outcomes.[44]

A variety of researchers have examined religious schools from a number of different angles that have often been determined by either the researchers' academic disciplines or their reasons for conducting the analyses. Sociologists such as James Coleman have focused on social capital and cultural strengths that faith-based schools provide. Bryk and his colleagues concurred with Coleman, which pushed the debate to the next logical step of asking whether there were certain moral dynamics and self-disciplinary practices extant in religious schools that can be partially applied to public education.[45] Public policy educators such as John Chubb have examined leadership style. Economists have tended to examine the effects of faith-based schools on future national output.[46]

In the last twenty-five years, the examination of faith-based schools has become more complex based on the likelihood that these school leaders may have a greater cognizance of the factors that are conducive to high levels of academic achievement. Chubb is one of those who has declared that, due to the religious school advantage, the United States would benefit if a larger percentage of its schools were faith-based.[47] Chubb and Moe ask a rhetorical question:

Why would educators and world leaders almost universally believe that the United States has the best system of university education system in the world and yet concurrently these same experts concur in their views that the American public system of elementary and secondary schooling is mediocre at best?[48] Their assertions take on a lot of credence when one examines the primary international rankings of the world's universities, based in Europe and China, and also considers the results of international comparison tests. Among the university ranking systems, American universities tend to dominate the top twenty lists of best universities.[49] For example, there is a pretty strong recognition that if one states that he or she attended Harvard, then that person is essentially claiming attendance at the best university in the world. The only competition that schools such as Harvard, Princeton, and Yale have in these world-ranking systems comes from Cambridge and Oxford, in the United Kingdom. Equally impressive is the fact that universities such as the Massachusetts Institute of Technology (MIT), Columbia, Chicago, Stanford, Dartmouth, and Duke typically rank in the top six to fifteen of these world university rankings.[50]

Chubb and Moe answered their own rhetorical question by declaring that, in contrast to the competition that it is encouraged at the collegiate level, the government sector has a virtual monopoly over the K–12 system of education. They assert the presence of significant competition at the collegiate level and the dearth of it among K–12 schools are the primary explanations about why people around the world have such admiration for American universities. Even the 90 percent enrollment domination that public schools enjoy does not fully depict the severity of the problem. Chubb and Moe note that because school choice vouchers or tax breaks are generally not used in the United States, it makes sending one's children to faith-based schools much less affordable than would otherwise be the case. As a result, in reality, the playing field is not equal between public and faith-based schools; thus, the government's domination of elementary and secondary school education is even greater than the 90 percent figure suggests.

If this problem is not bad enough, the fact that faith-based and other schools generally have a far higher percentage of students that are achieving at high levels means that not only is fair competition largely only among public schools but also the competition does not include many of America's best. The faith-based school advantage is substantial enough so that it is affecting the debates on public policy, how to best involve parents in their children's schooling, school discipline, and a variety of other issues affecting school instruction.[51]

A recent meta-analysis comparing the effects of religious, traditional public, and public charter schools also indicated that faith-based schools in the United States have a larger comparative advantage than those found in Europe.[52] There are several possible explanations for this result, including the possibility that it reflects, among other things, that state K–12 schools in Europe are better than in the United States. However, another likely possibility is that faith-based schools in Europe are diluted in their faith-based distinctiveness versus those in the United States. The cause of this dilution, according to most experts, is a higher level of government entanglement with religious schools in Europe than in the United States.[53] For example, given that most European school systems either grant tax breaks to parents who choose to send their youth to faith-based schools or use tax dollars to help such schools or parents, the systems tend to be infused with a plethora of government regulations. Therefore, the advantages that normally accrue to students by attending religious schools are not as large.

Charles Glenn, in his book *The Ambiguous Embrace*, further posits the idea that school choice proponents in the United States need to be certain that they limit the degree of government entanglement in any school choice program. The reason he gives is that, even though such initiatives will likely level the playing field, the distinctive identity and advantages inherent in Christian, Jewish, and other paradigms could be compromised with further government involvement.[54]

Glenn's words of caution have tempered the views of some regarding the school choice debate. To be sure, the historical record and the current body of quantitative findings, especially from nationwide studies and meta-analyses, are clear: The faith-based advantage is real, and it exists across a wide range of academic and behavioral measures.[55] On the surface, therefore, as Chubb and Moe as well as Bryk as his colleagues suggest, school choice, both in terms of increasing attendance in religious schools as well as intensifying competition, would ostensibly seem to provide an answer.[56] Nevertheless, Glenn's caution coupled with recent meta-analysis results suggest that advocates of school choice should proceed gingerly. There is a real possibility that the faith-based advantage may contract to some degree if the government becomes more entwined in the operation of these schools.[57]

The religious community is split on how they perceive the essence of this caveat. Protestants have become increasingly less likely to accept this approach, believing that they have already seen increasing evidence of government encroachment into religious affairs. Catholics, on the other hand, often perceive these same realities, but they also believe that the current near-monopoly that the government has in K–12 schooling is so daunting that they really do not have much of a choice. It is insightful to note that this debate has caused issues of faith and freedom of religion to enter into the public square.[58]

Effects of Religious Commitment on Factors That Affect Education

One of the greatest challenges facing social scientists who examine religious commitment is attempting to best define its nature. Ideally, religious commitment should be defined as having both an internal and external component. Both the internal and external components should be satisfied in order for a person to be considered as highly religious. The internal component depends on the extent to which one considers him- or herself highly religious. The external aspect depends on whether an individual has attended church, Bible study, youth group meeting, or other place of worship.

One of the first researchers to examine the relationship between religious commitment and school outcomes was Richard Koubek.[59] However, he used correlation as his means of analysis, which is highly simplistic. Over a decade later, William Sander heightened the interest that researchers had for study of faith-filled dedication when he found that non-Catholics benefitted scholastically from attending parochial schools more than did Catholic students.[60] The findings raised the likelihood that at least part of the Catholic school student advantage proceeds from the faith of many of those attending Catholic schools. This finding helped a new understanding of the influence of faith on scholastic outcomes that encompassed not only the school level but also the individual's religious dedication.[61]

The interest in examining the effects of religious commitment on academic achievement has widened so that social scientists from a number of different nations have examined this issue. For example,

AnneBert Dijkstra and Jules Peschar examined this relationship in Dutch children. They found that religious faith is associated with higher academic outcomes.[62]

Perhaps the most profound finding regarding religious commitment is that, using the NELS data, if African American and Latino children are highly religious and come from a two-biological-parent family, then the racial/ethnic achievement gap with children totally disappears.[63] These findings gained such attention that they were presented to the White House and three U.S. government departments, as well as at Harvard, Cambridge, Oxford, and Duke.

The study of the association between religious commitment and scholastic outcomes has become even more stimulating because it has become apparent from data that personal faith is not only related to academic outcomes but also to factors that have an impact on scholastic variables.[64] John Cochran found that religious devotion among teens was related to lower drug and alcohol use.[65] Other research indicates that the more severe the substance, the greater the likelihood that one's faith has a considerable impact on the likelihood that one will partake.[66]

One challenge in examining the relationship between faith and substance abuse is that ascertaining the direction of causality is more difficult than when assessing the relationship between religious commitment and scholastic outcomes. In the case of educational measures, it is not especially logical that improved school outcomes would cause someone to become more religious. However, there are many reasons why personal faith could cause academic outcomes to improve. On the other hand, the situation is somewhat different regarding substance abuse. Although one can see why Christian faith could cause one's alcohol and drug consumption to decline (because the Bible forbids drunkenness and losing control), exhibiting these behaviors could also cause someone to avoid going church.[67]

Social scientists have also increasingly examined the relationship between one's personal faith life and that person's attitudes toward premarital intercourse and the likelihood of engaging in that behavior.[68] The general trend of findings indicates that religious commitment was related to both attitudes and behavior regard premarital intercourse, although it may be more strongly related to attitudes than to behavior. This area of study is particularly interesting with reference to scholastic outcomes because there is no question that relations with the opposite sex can be a source of considerable distraction for youth, especially with regard to schoolwork and direction in life.[69]

The Bible as Literature

One of the most recent developments in religion and education research has been the examination of the relationship between Bible literacy and student academic achievement and behavioral outcomes. This type of analysis arose from the maturation of two realities.

First, it emerged from the thrust of research on the effects of religious commitment. Given that this research has been done primarily in nations with a substantial percentage of Christians, most of the religious commitment research is de facto primarily on the influence of the Christian faith in the lives of students. To whatever extent this is true, it would follow that at least part of this relationship was connected to the student's study of the Bible because the study of the Bible is one of the disciplines most emphasized in the church.[70] And given that the Bible is the most published book in world history and has been cited by a tremendous number of famous authors over the years, it seems that a knowledge of the Bible would add to one's understanding of substantial bodies of literature. For example, Shakespeare alone cites the Bible 1,300 times.[71]

Second, a large number of legal scholars have reexamined the 1962 and 1963 U.S. Supreme Court decisions and reached the conclusion that secularists and educators overreacted to the actual wording of the decisions and overlooked some of their key components. For example, many people overlooked one section of *Abington v. Schempp* (1963), which states:

> Nothing we have said here indicates that such study of the Bible or of religion, when presented objectively as part of a secular program of education, may not be effected consistently with the First Amendment.[72]

Even the American Civil Liberties Union acknowledges that teaching the Bible as literature is constitutional.[73] This awareness caused hundreds of school districts in forty-three states to adopt Bible-as-literature courses and ten states to either pass bills or resolutions allowing the Bible as literature to be taught as a course in the public schools.[74] Previously, any effort to study the relationship between personal Bible literacy and scholastic outcomes would have had limited applicability because the study of the Bible in schools was limited almost solely to faith-based schools. Now, as a result of closer examination of the U.S. Supreme Court cases on the Bible and prayer, the idea that public schools would forbid the study of what is likely the world's most influential published book seems archaic and anti-intellectual. To most fair-minded individuals, it would not only seem logical but also intuitive that, on average, people with a higher level of Bible literacy would excel more in school than those at lower levels. With the reexamination of the 1962 and 1963 U.S. Supreme Court cases in mind, revisiting the effects of Bible literacy on student outcomes takes on new relevance.

The results of recent studies on the effects of Bible literacy indicate a strong association between Bible literacy and higher academic achievement and not quite as potent a relationship between Bible literacy and student behavior. One can argue that part of this relationship manifests itself because there are certain traits that may burgeon in an individual as a result of studying the Bible, such as self-discipline, a work ethic, and a sense of purpose in life that are conducive to doing well in school. This component of the effects of Bible literacy are also at least partially reflected in the behavioral improvements that the studies showed had accrued in the lives of young people.[75] Nevertheless, it also seems logical that increased Bible literacy tends to facilitate greatly a student's comprehension of literature, American history, world history, art, music, and a variety of other subjects. Within this context, many leaders and social scientists who may not be religious themselves are beginning to gain a greater appreciation for the advantages of Bible literacy.

Reasons for the Religious Edge

As evidence has mounted that religious individuals and schools have an academic edge, social scientists have hypothesized about the reasons why.

First, and historically the most analyzed, is the religious work ethic. Traditionally, historians and sociologists have referred to this phenomenon as the Protestant work ethic. Recent research indicates that this ethic could be called more accurately a Christian ethic.[76] And this Christian work ethic transcends differences in nationality and race.[77]

Second, such an association between faith and achievement likely exists because there is a tendency for religious people to abstain from practices regarded as undisciplined and deleterious to academic achievement. A number of studies demonstrate that highly religious teens are less likely to become involved in drug and alcohol abuse.[78] Other studies indicate that religiously committed adolescents are less likely to engage in sexual behavior or become pregnant during this time in their lives.[79]

Third, research points to a relationship between personal faith and having an internal locus of control.[80] Upon cursory glance, this relationship may seem counterintuitive because believers perceive God as existing outside them. However, given that Christianity, the most widely practiced religion in the United States, teaches that God dwells in the hearts of believers, the propensity for religious people to have an internal locus of control would likely follow.

AN AGENDA FOR FUTURE RESEARCH

Two of the greatest needs for future research on the effects of religious schools and religious commitment on academic outcomes are (1) more studies to be undertaken overseas and (2) more sophisticated analyses.

There is no question that there has been an increase in the number of studies undertaken on faith topics overseas.[81] This trend is only natural because faith, particularly Christianity, is an international phenomenon, so it follows that more studies in different places would be initiated examining Christianity. It is also likely due to the academic community growing; this is having a two-pronged effect of producing more scholars interested in studying faith in foreign countries and larger numbers of researchers in the countries where further study is needed. It is nevertheless axiomatic that more work needs to be done on the international front for the following primary reasons.

First, it is essential that social scientists come to a greater understanding of the extent to which findings about faith apply across international boundaries. There is no question that most of the studies about faith have been undertaken in the United States and Western Europe. There are six inhabited continents in the world and the quality research on faith has been largely limited to two of those continents. To be sure, this is largely a result of almost all of the top-rated universities being from these parts of the world. Although this is likely to change in the coming decades and centuries, this is the contemporary reality.[82] It thus behooves scholars in these universities to become more interested in expressions of Christianity and other faiths overseas. It is not hyperbole to state that such a trend is absolutely essential if one is to bolster assertions that the benefits of commitment to Christianity, Judaism, or other beliefs transfer overseas.

Based on logic, the centuries-long observation that faith can change lives, and available data, one would expect positive findings.[83] There are many accounts of religious revivals in many areas of the globe eliminating the practices of cannibalism and child sacrifice, as well as ending tribal warfare and causing bars to close.[84] These phenomena have occurred throughout the world.[85] Famous religious revivals have also altered the course of history. The Revival of 1857 and those that preceded it under Charles Finney changed the attitudes of northerners in the United States toward slavery.[86] It is well documented through research that Christian conversions caused people to be willing to vote for Abraham Lincoln with the hope of abolishing slavery.[87] The first Great Awakening had a significant impact of leading the United States into independence.[88] The Civil Rights movement, led by Baptist minister Martin Luther King, Jr., was founded on Christ's principles of love and turning the other cheek.[89] Revival has had a considerable impact on Great Britain and has influenced other nations.[90]

More recently, a revival, known as the Brownsville Revival, took place in Pensacola, Florida. It has had such a dramatic impact that millions of people have attended services from all around the world, 200,000 became Christians as a result, and people have had to wait in line for an hour or two just to enter the church. A research study to assess the effects of revival compared along certain key dimensions a random sample of revival attendees versus two other randomly selected control groups.[91] These control groups were a randomly selected group of people from across the country, matched by the zip code of revival attendees, and a randomly selected group of people who were lined up to enter the church but had not yet attended the revival, and were also matched by the zip code of revival attendees.[92] By including two control groups, the study distinguished the effects of the revival itself versus any residual effects that might emerge simply from possessing the motivation to attend the revival.

The results of the study indicated that those attending the revival services showed a greater rate of improvement in behavior, such as reduced alcohol and drug consumption, and reported larger increases in the quality of family life and the quality of life as a whole than their counterparts in the control groups. However, attendance at revival services showed no direct relationship with academic outcomes.[93] Overall, these results indicate that should a teacher's students attend revival services, the instructor would likely see improvements in pupils' behaviors but not necessarily an improvement in grades. This is in contrast to the effects of Bible literacy, mentioned earlier. That is, on average, high levels of Bible literacy are related to student behavior but appear to be associated most strongly to academic outcomes.

As interesting as the results of the study were, such analyses need to be replicated overseas. There is little question, though, that these results would likely also emerge in studies done overseas. It seems intuitive that if people are exposed to teachings that emphasize love, joy, truth, family, and self-discipline, then, on average, they will likely experience changes for the better. The historical record also testifies to this relationship, as has been noted.[94] The secular world is skeptical, however, and certain principles that are acknowledged among people who appreciate the place of faith are convenient to deny if one is a secularist. One needs to understand that the thought of a righteous and just God, even if He is also infinitely loving and forgiving, makes those relatively unconcerned with treating other people well and with issues of character very uncomfortable.[95] If one is going to convince those secularists, one must speak their language, and among the secular intelligentsia, that language is data.

Discovering the extent to which faith-based variables are or are not generalizable to different countries and situations is vital because, in the past, many social science theories were assumed to be generalizable to the world at large, but in reality they were not.[96] Two of the most notable instances are Jean Piaget's theories and Sigmund Freud's assumptions. Piaget's theories of cognitive development are widely known for their simplicity and definitive structure.[97] Piaget was Swiss and based virtually his entire set of theories on the observation of his own children. Today, it would be considered unthinkable for theories with as insular a factual basis and with a nearly nonexistent sample to have such a pervasive presence in psychological theory.[98]

A number of Sigmund's Freud's theories are similar in this regard. Although Freud was able to discern limited elements of truth, as time goes on it seems evident that his beliefs likely speak more to his own psychological problems and personal struggles than they do for the general population.[99] The gradual divulging of Freud's excesses and unfounded conclusions should really be of no surprise given that his theories are based on the tenuous use of a limited and emotionally aberrant population.[100]

In addition to undertaking a greater number of international studies, it is also apparent that within the field of religion and education, more sophisticated quantitative analyses must be undertaken. Probably the specific approaches where there exists the greatest need are meta-analyses, the use of quantitative data, and longitudinal studies. Presently, the papers published on religion and education are pithy articles that people of faith appreciate and contain a great deal of truth. However, the community of believers needs to realize that secularists often search for truth differently and, although it is easy for faith-filled people to view the methods of unbelievers as devoid of any real comprehensive nature, one is wise to learn how to communicate to secular social scientists in their language.

Just as secular psychologists and educators made profound mistakes by presuming that Freud's and Piaget's methods were sufficient to establish well-founded truisms, people of faith must not assume that even if the results of local studies confirm biblical truths, common sense, and even mores of decency, skeptical secularists will be convinced. Consistent with these affirmations, it is absolutely essential that individuals interested in faith-based research design studies with this higher level of sophistication discussed here and communicate these principles not only to the faith community but also to the secular one. Localized studies that do not utilize sophisticated statistical methods but that work concurrently with the principles contained in the Bible, other spiritual writings, or other works that support common sense and decency may be sufficient to convince believers, but they might not convince doubters. A larger portion of faith-based research needs to use a higher level of methodological sophistication to reach those who do not currently believe.

The interest that social scientists have in research on religion and education is on the increase. This trend is likely to continue as Christianity continues to increase in the number of adherents worldwide, but also as academic, behavioral, and social problems become more formidable forces around the world. People tend to look to God when there is a need, and social scientists are likely to look to religious research when they perceive that need. Although that trend is likely to become more apparent, and concurrently much has been accomplished in research on religion and education, further progress is needed. As the demand for data on religion and education is increasing, so is the need for more sophisticated research both in Western settings and around the world. This likely confirms the prominent place that the human quest for uniting with God has had throughout history.

NOTES

1. Andreas J. Köstenberger, *God, Marriage, and Family: Rebuilding the Biblical Foundation* (Wheaton, IL: Crossway Books, 2004), 10–18.
2. Ibid.
3. Dinesh D'Souza, *What's So Great about Christianity* (Washington, DC: Regnery Publishing, 2007), 67–76; and William H. Jeynes, *A Call for Character Education and Prayer in the Schools* (Westport, CT: Praeger, 2010), 64–72.
4. Max Weber, *The Protestant Ethic and the Spirit of Capitalism* [1904–1905], trans. Talcott Parsons (New York: Charles Scribner's Sons, 1958), 13–31.
5. Gerald Lee Gutek, *New Perspectives on Philosophy and Education* (Columbus, OH: Prentice Hall, 2009), 252–55; William H. Jeynes, "A Meta-Analysis on the Effects and Contributions of Public, Public Charter, and Religious Schools on Student Outcomes," *Peabody Journal of Education* 87 (2012), 303–35, especially p. 326; and Rodney Stark, *How the West Won: The Neglected Story of the Triumph of Modernity* (Wilmington, DE: ISI Books, 2014), 129.
6. Andrew Root, *The Children of Divorce: The Loss of Family as the Loss of Being* (Grand Rapids, MI: Baker Academic, 2010), 87–118.
7. Gutek, *New Perspectives on Philosophy and Education*; Paul Johnson, *A History of the American People* (New York: Harper Collins, 1997), 53; and Stark, *How the West Won*, 279.
8. William H. Jeynes, *American Educational History: School, Society, and the Common Good* (Thousand Oaks, CA: Sage, 2007), 12; and Johnson, *A History of the American People*.
9. John Taylor Gatto, *The Underground History of American Schooling: A Schoolteacher's Intimate Investigation into the Problem of Modern Schooling* (New York: Oxford Village Press, 2001), 52.

10. Ibid.
11. Stark, *How the West Won*, 129, 134, 279.
12. Daniel Lapin, *America's Real War* (Portland, OR: Multnomah Press, 1999), 157.
13. Weber, *The Protestant Ethic and the Spirit of Capitalism*, 164.
14. Ibid.
15. Ibid.
16. Samuel Huntington, *Who Are We?: The Challenges to America's National Identity* (New York: Simon & Schuster, 2004), 69.
17. William H. Jeynes, *School Choice: A Balanced Approach* (Santa Barbara, CA: Praeger, 2014), 119.
18. Thomas D. Snyder and Sally A. Dillow, *Digest of Education Statistics 2012*, NCES 2014–2015 (Washington DC: U.S. Department of Education, 2013).
19. Jeynes, *American Educational History*, 368.
20. Rachel E. Dew, Stephanie S. Daniel, David B. Goldston, and Harold G. Koenig, "Religion, Spirituality, and Depression in Adolescent Psychiatric Outpatients," *Journal of Nervous and Mental Disease* 196 (2008): 247–51; and Drug Enforcement Administration, *Drugs of Abuse, 2011 Edition: A DEA Resource Guide* (Washington DC: U.S. Department of Justice, 2011).
21. Office of Adolescent Health, *United States Adolescent Health Facts*, U.S. Department of Health and Human Services (2014), accessed at http://www.hhs.gov/ash/oah/resources-and-publications/facts/us.html.
22. William H. Jeynes, *A Call to Character Education and Prayer in the Schools*, (Santa Barbara, CA: ABC-CLIO, 2011), 208–11.
23. Willard Wirtz, *On Further Examination: Report on the Advisory Panel on the Scholastic Aptitude Test Score Decline* (New York: College Entrance Examination Board, 1977), 42.
24. Tricia Andryszewski, *School Prayer: A History of the Debate* (Springfield, MA: Enslow, 1997), 8–21; and William H. Jeynes, "The Relationship between the Consumption of Various Drugs by Adolescents and Their Academic Achievement," *American Journal of Drug and Alcohol Abuse* 28 (2002): 15–35.
25. Anthony S. Bryk, Valerie E. Lee, and Peter B. Holland, *Catholic Schools and the Common Good* (Cambridge, MA: Harvard University Press, 1993), 56.
26. Jeynes, *American Educational History*, 337–39.
27. Two articles by William H. Jeynes: "The Effects of Religious Commitment on the Academic Achievement of Black and Hispanic Children," *Urban Education* 34 (1999): 458–79; and "The Effects of Black and Hispanic Twelfth Graders Living in Intact Families and Being Religious on Their Academic Achievement," *Urban Education* 38 (2003): 35–57.

28. Bryk et al., *Catholic Schools and the Common Good*, 56; and William Jeynes, "Assessing School Choice: A Balanced Perspective," *Cambridge Journal of Education* 30 (2000): 223–41.

29. James Samuel Coleman, Thomas Hoffer, and Sally Kilgore, *High School Achievement: Public, Catholic, and Private Schools Compared* (New York: Basic Books, 1982), 43–44.

30. David Barton, *America: To Pray or Not to Pray?* [1988] (Aledo, TX: WallBuilder Press, 1994), 9–12.

31. Jeynes, *A Call to Character Education and Prayer in the Schools*, 29.

32. Jeffrey T. Kuhner, "Tinseltown's War on Christianity," *Washington Times* (June 4, 2010): 1–1.

33. Two papers by William H. Jeynes: "The Effects of Religious Commitment on the Academic Achievement of Black and Hispanic Children," 459–64; and "A Meta-Analysis of the Effects of Attending Religious Schools and Religiosity on Black and Hispanic Academic Achievement," *Education and Urban Society* 35 (2002): 27–49, especially pp. 36–41.

34. Bryk et al., *Catholic Schools and the Common Good*, 263; and Coleman et al., *High School Achievement*, 137–50.

35. Annebert Dijkstra and Jules L. Peschar, "Religious Determinants of Academic Achievement in the Netherlands," *Comparative Education Review*, 40 (1996): 47–65; and Richard J. Koubek, "Correlation between Religious Commitment and Students' Achievement," *Psychological Reports* 54 (1984): 262.

36. Two papers by William H. Jeynes: "The Effects of Religious Commitment on the Academic Achievement of Black and Hispanic Children"; and "The Effects of Black and Hispanic Twelfth Graders Living in Intact Families and Being Religious on Their Academic Achievement."

37. Jeynes, "A Meta-Analysis of the Effects of Attending Religious Schools and Religiosity on Black and Hispanic Academic Achievement."

38. Three papers by William H. Jeynes: "The Effects of Religious Commitment on the Attitudes and Behavior of Teens Regarding Premarital Childbirth," *Journal of Health and Social Policy* 17 (2003): 1–17; "The Relationship between Urban Students Attending Religious Revival Services and Academic and Social Outcomes," *Education and Urban Society* 38 (2005): 3–20; and "Adolescent Religious Commitment and Their Consumption of Marijuana, Cocaine, and Alcohol," *Journal of Health and Social Policy* 21 (2006): 1–20.

39. Harold Koenig, *Faith and Mental Health: Religious Resources for Healing* (West Conshohocken, PA: Templeton Press, 2005), 258–60.

40. Allan Bloom, "Music," in *Music and Culture*, ed. Anna Tomasino (New York: Pearson Longman, 2005), 35–51; Joseph Lieberman, *The Shooting Game: The Making of School Shooters* (Santa Ana, CA: Seven Locks Press,

2006), 86–99; and Graeme Thomson, *I Shot a Man in Reno: A History of Death by Murder, Suicide, Fire, Flood, Drugs, Disease and General Misadventure, as Related in Popular Song* (New York: Continuum, 2008), 23–40.

41. Two papers by William H. Jeynes: "Adolescent Religious Commitment and Their Consumption of Marijuana, Cocaine, and Alcohol," 1–4; and "Religiosity, Religious Schools, and Their Relationship with the Achievement Gap: A Research Synthesis and Meta-Analysis," *Journal of Negro Education* 79 (2010): 263–79.

42. Beth Nimmo and Darrell Scott with Steve Rabey, *Rachel's Tears: The Spiritual Journey of Columbine Martyr Rachel Scott* (Nashville, TN: Thomas Nelson, 2000), 149–62.

43. John Chubb, "Transformational Leadership," *Independent School* 73 (2014): 9–11; Jeynes, "Assessing School Choice," 226–32; and Herbert J. Walberg, *School Choice: The Findings* (Washington, DC: Cato Institute, 2007), 61–78.

44. Coleman et al., *High School Achievement*, 4–14; and David R. Garcia, Rebecca Barber, and Alex Molnar, "Profiting from Public Education: Education Management Organizations and Student Achievement," *Teachers College Record* 111 (2009): 1352–79.

45. Bryk et al., *Catholic Schools and the Common Good*, 297; and James Coleman, "Social Capital in the Creation of Human Capital," *American Journal of Sociology* 94 (1988): S95–S120.

46. Chubb, "Transformational Leadership," 9–10; and John B. Horowitz and Lee Spector, "Is There a Difference between Private and Public Education on College Performance?," *Economics and Education Review* 24 (2005): 189–95.

47. Chubb, "Transformational Leadership"; and John E. Chubb and Terry M. Moe, *Politics, Markets, and America's Schools* (Washington, DC: Brookings Institution, 1990), 259.

48. Chubb and Moe, *Politics, Markets, and America's Schools*.

49. BBC News, "University Rankings Dominated by US, with Harvard Top" (September 15, 2010), accessed at http://www.bbc.com/news/education-11317176.

50. Ibid.

51. Two papers by William H. Jeynes: "The Relationship between Parental Involvement and Urban Secondary School Student Academic Achievement: A Meta-Analysis," *Urban Education* 42 (2007): 82–110; and "The Salience of the Subtle Aspects of Parental Involvement and Encouraging That Involvement: Implications for School-Based Programs," *Teachers College Record* 112 (2010): 747–74.

52. Jeynes, "A Meta-Analysis on the Effects and Contributions of Public, Public Charter, and Religious Schools on Student Outcomes," 318–22.

53. Charles L. Glenn, *The Ambiguous Embrace: Government and Faith-Based Schools and Social Agencies* (Princeton, NJ: Princeton University Press, 2000), 131–92; and Charles Glenn, *Contrasting Models of State and School: A Comparative Historical Study of Parental Choice and State Control* (New York: Continuum, 2011), 15–27.

54. Glenn, *The Ambiguous Embrace*, 289–95.

55. Horowitz and Spector, "Is There a Difference between Private and Public Education on College Performance?," 189–91; and William Jeynes. "Standardized Tests and Froebel's Original Kindergarten Model," *Teachers College Record* 108 (2006): 1937–59, especially pp. 1952–53.

56. Bryk et al., *Catholic Schools and the Common Good*, 338–43; Chubb, "Transformational Leadership," 9–10; and Chubb and Moe, *Politics, Markets, and America's Schools*, 215–25, 259.

57. Two books by Charles L. Glenn: *The Ambiguous Embrace*, 289–95; and *Contrasting Models of State and School*, 15–28. See also Jeynes, *School Choice*, 161.

58. Jeynes, *School Choice*, 161.

59. Koubek, "Correlation between Religious Commitment and Students' Achievement," 262.

60. William Sander, "Catholic Grade Schools and Academic Achievement," *Journal of Human Resources* 31 (1996): 540–48.

61. Jeynes, "Religiosity, Religious Schools, and their Relationship with the Achievement Gap"; and Sander, "Catholic Grade Schools and Academic Achievement."

62. Dijkstra and Peschar, "Religious Determinants of Academic Achievement in the Netherlands," 50–56.

63. Jeynes, "The Effects of Black and Hispanic Twelfth Graders Living in Intact Families and Being Religious on Their Academic Achievement," 46–54.

64. Jeynes, "The Relationship between the Consumption of Various Drugs by Adolescents and Their Academic Achievement," 17–22.

65. John K. Cochran, Leonard Beeghley, and E. Wilbur Bock, "The Influence of Religious Stability and Homogamy on the Relationship between Religiosity and Alcohol Use among Protestants," *Journal for the Scientific Study of Religion* 31 (1992): 441–56; and John K. Cochran, "The Variable Effects of Religiosity and Discrimination on Adolescent Self-Reported Alcohol Use by Beverage Type," *Journal of Drug Issues* 23 (1993): 479–91.

66. Jeynes, "Adolescent Religious Commitment and Their Consumption of Marijuana, Cocaine, and Alcohol," 12–17.

67. Cochran et al., "The Influence of Religious Stability and Homogamy on the Relationship between Religiosity and Alcohol Use among Protestants," 445–50; and Cochran, "The Variable Effects of Religiosity

and Discrimination on Adolescent Self-Reported Alcohol Use by Beverage Type," 482–86.

68. Jeynes, "The Effects of Religious Commitment on the Attitudes and Behavior of Teens Regarding Premarital Childbirth"; Jeremy E. Uecker and Charles E. Stokes, "Early Marriage in the United States," *Journal of Marriage & Family* 70 (2008): 835–46; and Kesha Morant Williams, Kyla DeFazio, and Regina May Goins, "Transitions: Negotiating Sexual Decision Making in the Lives of Students Attending a Christian University," *Sexuality and Culture* 18 (2014): 547–59.

69. John W. Santrock, *Adolescence: An Introduction*, 14th ed. (New York: McGraw Hill, 2012), 58–71.

70. J. I. Packer, *Knowing God* [1973] (Downers Grove, IL: InterVarsity Press, 1993), 11–29.

71. Jeynes, *A Call to Character Education and Prayer in the Schools*, 221.

72. *Abington School Dist. v. Schempp*, 374 U.S. 203 (1963), quotation on p. 225.

73. ACLU, "Statement on *The Bible in The Public Schools: A First Amendment Guide*," ACLU Program on Freedom of Religion and Belief, April 2007 (May 9, 2007), accessed at https://www.aclu.org/religion-belief/ statement-emthe-bible-public-schools-first-amendment-guideem.

74. Bible as Literature, "Where the Bible Is Being Taught in the U.S.A." (2011), accessed at http://bibleasliterature.org/where-the-bible-is-being-taught-in-the-usa.php.

75. William H. Jeynes, "The Relationship between Bible Literacy and Academic Achievement and School Behavior," *Education and Urban Society* 41 (2009): 419–36; and William Jeynes, "The Relationship between Bible Literacy and Academic and Behavioral Outcomes in Urban Areas: A Meta-Analysis," *Education and Urban Society* 42 (2010): 522–44.

76. Leland Ryken, "In Search of a Christian Work Ethic for the Corporate Worker," *Business and Professional Ethics Journal* 23 (2004): 153–70.

77. L. Kretzschmar, "Towards a Christian Ethic of Work in South Africa," *Acta Theologica* 32 (2012): 125–46.

78. Jeynes, "Adolescent Religious Commitment and Their Consumption of Marijuana, Cocaine, and Alcohol," 14–18; and Joseph J. Palamar and Dimitra Kamboukos, "An Examination of Sociodemographic Correlates of Ecstasy Use among High School Seniors in the United States," *Substance Use and Misuse* 49 (2014): 1774–83.

79. Eileen K. McMillen, Herbert W. Helm, Jr., and Duane C. McBride, "Religious Orientation and Sexual Attitudes and Behavior," *Journal of Research on Christian Education* 20 (2011): 195–206.

80. Laurence E. Jackson and Robert D. Coursey, "The Relationship of God Control and Internal Locus of Control to Intrinsic Religious Motivation, Coping, and Purpose in Life," *Journal for the Scientific Study of Religion* 27 (1988): 399–410.

81. Tim Heaton, Spencer James, and Yaw Oheneba-Sakyi, "Religion and Socioeconomic Attainment in Ghana," *Review of Religious Research* 51 (2009): 71–86; and Solmon Zwana, "Failure of Ecumenism: The Rise of Church Related Universities in Zimbabwe," *Exchange* 38 (2009): 292–311.
82. BBC News, "University Rankings Dominated by US, with Harvard Top."
83. Jeynes, "A Meta-Analysis on the Effects and Contributions of Public, Public Charter, and Religious Schools on Student Outcomes," 306–8; and Stark, *How the West Won*, 339–56.
84. Jeynes, *American Educational History*, 98–102; and Timothy L. Smith, *Revivalism and Social Reform: American Protestants on the Eve of the Civil War* [1957] (Baltimore: Johns Hopkins University Press, 1980), 180.
85. Stark, *How the West Won*, 116–35.
86. Mark C. Carnes. *Invisible Giants: Fifty Americans Who Shaped the Nation but Missed the History Books* (New York: Oxford University Press, 2002), 92–94; and Jodie Zdrok-Ptaszek, "Introduction," in *The Antislavery Movement*, ed. Jodie Zdrok-Ptaszek (San Diego, CA: Greenhaven Press, 2002), 10–24.
87. J. Edwin Orr, *The Event of the Century: The 1857–1858 Awakening*, ed. Richard Owen Roberts (Wheaton, IL: International Awakening Press, 1989), 20–38; and Smith, *Revivalism and Social Reform*, 200–3.
88. Johnson, *A History of the American People*, 109–17.
89. Martin Luther King, Jr., *The Autobiography of Martin Luther King, Jr.*, ed. Clayborne Carson (New York: Warner, 1997), 15–28.
90. David Matthews, *I Saw the Welsh Revival: An Account of the 1904 Revival in Wales* [1957] (Goshen, IN: Pioneer Books, 1992), 5–24.
91. Jeynes, "The Relationship between Urban Students Attending Religious Revival Services and Academic and Social Outcomes," 10–20.
92. Ibid.
93. Ibid.
94. Carnes. *Invisible Giants*, 89–94; Stark, *How the West Won*, 346–50; and Zdrok-Ptaszek, "Introduction," 10–24.
95. Stark, *How the West Won*, 1–2.
96. Edward Dolnick, *Madness on the Couch: Blaming the Victim in the Heyday of Psychoanalysis* (New York: Simon & Schuster, 1998), 19–33; Kieran Egan, *Getting It Wrong from the Beginning: Our Progressivist Inheritance from Herbert Spencer, John Dewey, and Jean Piaget* (New Haven, CT: Yale University Press, 2002), 11–26; and Joseph Price and Gordon B. Dahl, "Using Natural Experiments to Study the Impact of Media on the Family," *Family Relations* 61 (2012): 363–73.
97. Charis Psaltis. "Culture and Social Representations: A Continuing Dialogue in Search for Heterogeneity in Social Developmental Psychology," *Culture and Psychology* 18 (2012): 375–90.

98. Robbie Case, "Advantages and Limitations to the Neo-Piagetian Position," in *The Mind's Staircase: Exploring the Conceptual Underpinnings of Children's Thoughts and Knowledge*, ed. Robbie Case (Hillsdale, NJ: Lawrence Erlbaum, 1992), 37–51; and Psaltis, "Culture and Social Representations."

99. Dolnick, *Madness on the Couch*, 19–33; Egan, *Getting It Wrong from the Beginning*, 101–6; and Price and Dahl, "Using Natural Experiments to Study the Impact of Media on the Family," 363–73.

100. Dolnick, *Madness on the Couch*, 20–33; and Steven J. Kirsh, *Children, Adolescents and Media Violence* (Thousand Oaks, CA: Sage Publications, 2006), 46.

SUGGESTED READINGS

Andryszewski, Tricia. *School Prayer: A History of the Debate*. Springfield, MA: Enslow, 1997. This book gives a detailed overview of the legal issues involved in the debate regarding prayer in the schools.

Bryk, Anthony S., Valerie E. Lee, and Peter B. Holland. *Catholic Schools and the Common Good*. Cambridge, MA: Harvard University Press, 1993. Bryk and his colleagues do a fine job of delineating not only the effects of Catholic schools but also how the public school system might benefit from the religious school rubric.

Coleman, James. "Social Capital in the Creation of Human Capital." *American Journal of Sociology* 94 (1988): S95–S120. This is the finest presentation of the notion of social capital as it relates to schooling. Coleman presents this relationship concisely and cogently.

Coleman, James Samuel, Thomas Hoffer, and Sally Kilgore. *High School Achievement: Public, Catholic, and Private Schools Compared*. New York: Basic Books, 1982. This book is a classic summary of Coleman's findings regarding religious schools.

Jeynes, William H. *American Educational History: School, Society, and the Common Good*. Thousand Oaks, CA: Sage, 2007. This book has been purchased by universities in eighty nations around the world in part because it presents a very comprehensive history of American education and includes the place that faith played in its development and reform throughout time.

Jeynes, William H. "The Effects of Black and Hispanic Twelfth Graders Living in Intact Families and Being Religious on Their Academic Achievement," *Urban Education* 38 (2003): 35–57. This article includes much of the NELS analysis indicating that the achievement gap totally vanishes when one compares African American students who are highly religious and from two-parent-biological families with white students.

10

The Epidemiology of Religion

Jeff Levin

E pidemiology is most often defined as the study of the distribution and determinants of morbidity and mortality, or of the frequency of health-related outcomes generally, in human populations.[1]
A key word here is *population*: epidemiology is about describing
population-wide patterns and trends in particular outcomes (in popular jargon, effects) and identifying and analyzing their determinant
factors (causes), including, but not exclusively, etiologic factors. The
study subjects, if you will, are entire populations—typically, political
or geographical units: nations, states, regions, communities.

Epidemiology is one of the basic biomedical sciences taught
to medical students in their first two years of medical school, but
more typically it is referred to as the basic science of public health.
Departments or divisions of epidemiology are among the core units
of every graduate school of public health.[2] Like any scientific discipline, epidemiology is associated with a unique set of conceptual,
theoretical, and methodological models and tools.

Like other scientific disciplines, and like medicine, epidemiology
comprises specialties and subspecialties. These may be defined in
terms of disease outcomes or classes of disease (e.g., cardiovascular epidemiology, infectious disease epidemiology, psychiatric

epidemiology), special populations (e.g., geriatric epidemiology, reproductive epidemiology), or categories of determinants (e.g., environmental epidemiology, genetic epidemiology). One of the latter types of specialty fields is known as social epidemiology. This can be thought of as the field defined by the theories and methods of epidemiology crossed with the conceptual content, and often the methods and theories, of the social sciences. Social epidemiologists investigate how human behavior; psychological states and traits and personality features; and social-structural, demographic, and sociocultural factors have an impact on rates of health and disease outcomes in populations.[3] These areas of focus define, respectively, three subspecialties within the specialty of social epidemiology, known as behavioral epidemiology; psychosocial epidemiology; and, perhaps confusingly, social epidemiology. In recent years, this latter subspecialized type of social epidemiology has been rebranded as the social determinants of health.[4]

Social epidemiology (in the broader sense) is thus a kind of hybrid. It is not formally a social science discipline, of course, but because it is epidemiology conducted using social science concepts and methods, and drawing on social and behavioral theories, it is defensible to consider it as an applied social research field. Thus, it is included in the present book.

Since the 1980s, a principal area of focus within social, behavioral, and especially psychosocial epidemiology has been the research field often referred to as the epidemiology of religion.[5] This entails population health research on how domains and dimensions of religious identity or participation, broadly defined—religious affiliation, behaviors, beliefs, attitudes, affects, values, experiences, and so on—affect epidemiologic outcomes. The underlying question here is whether facets of the religious life of people serve to elevate significantly the probability of certain adverse health-related events or instead serve to prevent such events, at the population-wide level. As in all epidemiologic studies, empirical results thus tell us whether a particular determinant factor or independent variable (or, in epidemiologic parlance, exposure variable) is a risk factor or a protective factor, respectively. In a nutshell, this is and has been the programmatic focus of the epidemiology of religion.

An important caveat: For research on a putative association between religion and health to qualify as explicitly "epidemiologic," strictly speaking, implies the study of such relationships within defined populations and with an emphasis on calculating the impact of religion on frequency rates of outcomes or otherwise structurally modeling such relationships. Numerous outstanding psychological and clinical studies have reported findings linking religious and health variables in some ways,[6] but by itself that does not make such research epidemiologic, as the field is being defined here.

The remainder of this chapter takes on three distinct tasks. First, a narrative history of population health research on religion is provided. This includes describing the origins and development of the field, identifying key publications, and giving an overview of important researchers and research programs. Second, a summary overview is provided of empirical research findings. The religion-and-health field is much too large—by now, thousands of published studies—to go into great depth here, but an overall sense of the literature is provided, especially population studies of heart disease, hypertension and stroke, cancer, mortality, general health status, and psychiatric outcomes. Attention is also paid to theoretical efforts proposing "mechanisms" (i.e., mediators or explanatory variables) to account for or make sense of positive findings. Third, a research agenda is presented to guide empirical investigations in this field for the coming years. In addition, a section called Suggested Readings at the end of this chapter contains an annotated list of a dozen key publications to introduce interested readers to this field; it includes works by the present author.

HISTORY OF POPULATION HEALTH RESEARCH ON RELIGION

One of the few historical summaries of this field stated succinctly, "Scholarly writing on the interface of religion and health is not a new development."[7] Researchers and clinicians have thoughtfully considered how religious identity and practice, personal faith, and expressions of spirituality might elevate or diminish the risk of various psychiatric or physical maladies for nearly two hundred years. For example, Amariah Brigham, a founder of the American Psychiatric Association, published his thoughts on this subject in 1835, in his *Observations on the Influence of Religion upon the Health and Physical Welfare of Mankind.*[8] Other nineteenth-century medical pioneers, such as Benjamin Travers and John Shaw Billings, published clinical observations or rudimentary descriptive-epidemiologic tabulations of morbidity and mortality differentials across religious groups.[9] Perhaps the first empirical study conducted in psychosocial epidemiology was Émile Durkheim's famous investigation of denominational differences in suicide rates in Europe.[10] Even William Osler weighed in on the topic, in his essay entitled, "The Faith That Heals," published in 1910 in the *British Medical Journal*,[11] and *JAMA* followed suit in 1926 with a series of essays on religious healing.[12]

Over the next half century, empirical studies continued to be published providing statistical evidence of religious differences in or religious impacts on rates of morbidity or mortality due to numerous diseases or overall. But it was not until the mid-1980s that researchers began to take notice of these studies and make an effort to review them. Indeed, until that time, the existence of an epidemiologic literature on religion was almost unknown. Even investigators conducting analyses of religious variables rarely cited other such studies; it is possible that they did not know that such studies existed.

In 1987, two comprehensive literature reviews were published that for the first time succeeded in documenting the scope of research on this subject. Levin and Schiller, in *Journal of Religion and Health*, provided a complete accounting of published work, excluding psychiatric studies, dating to the nineteenth century and summarized by disease categories (e.g., heart disease, hypertension, cancer).[13] By contrast, Jarvis and Northcott, in *Social Science and Medicine*, reviewed epidemiologic findings on religion and morbidity and mortality by categories of religious affiliation.[14] To the surprise of many, including the authors of the reviews, the literature on this topic exceeded two hundred published studies, and featured studies published in most leading medical and epidemiologic journals: *New England Journal of Medicine, American Journal of Public Health, JAMA, The Lancet, Archives of Internal Medicine, Annals of Internal Medicine, American Heart Journal, American Journal of Epidemiology, Cancer, Milbank Quarterly*, and elsewhere. Until these reviews appeared, however, not much note was ever made of this literature, except for a rare mention or citation of one or two such studies, as if there were no others. This holds true even for the authors of most of the studies reporting religion–health findings.

As shown in these reviews, the history of epidemiologic research on religion has experienced several "epochs." In the early decades of the twentieth century, a series of studies identified lower morbidity and mortality rates due to cancers of the cervix and uterine corpus among Jewish women, attributed at the time to the protective effects of male circumcision.[15] Mid-century, a series of investigations compared rates of morbidity and mortality due to a variety of causes across Protestant, Catholic, and Jewish respondents, mostly on the East Coast of the United States and some with reference to occupational exposures.[16] By the 1960s, psychiatric epidemiologic studies began appearing that made similar denominational comparisons, beginning with the Midtown Manhattan Study.[17] Throughout the 1970s and 1980s, a large body of epidemiologic studies documented the favorable health profile of Latter-Day Saints in Utah and Seventh-day Adventists in California, including lower morbidity and mortality rates and greater longevity.[18] Among all these studies, the closest thing to a formal research program was the work of George Comstock and colleagues at Johns Hopkins, who published about a dozen papers validating a protective effect of certain religious indicators, such as frequent attendance at services, in relation to multiple outcomes, including overall mortality.[19]

By the mid-1980s, the existence of a large body of published research on religion and health was no longer a secret, and other investigators began to focus their efforts here. Early investigators included the team of social demographer Kyriakos Markides and epidemiologist Jeff Levin; physicians David Larson and Harold Koenig and their colleagues, including physician Keith Meador; the team of sociologist Robert Taylor and psychologist Linda Chatters; sociologist Diane Brown and colleagues; psychologist Kenneth Pargament; and sociologists Ellen Idler, David Williams, and Christopher Ellison. By 1990, many other researchers were added to the mix, and it was not long before this area of research became a self-identified field. A unique and pleasant characteristic of this field is the extent to which these pioneers and those who have followed have often come together in collaboration, in various combinations, regardless of academic discipline, for research papers, books, and conference events.

The 1990s saw the first National Institutes of Health (NIH)–funded research on religion and health, as well as publication of field-summary pieces in important academic handbooks, encyclopedias, reports, and review articles.[20] Prominent social and behavioral scientists continued to concentrate their work in this field, which elevated the sophistication of studies, resulted in an increase in funded research, and raised the prestige of publication outlets. Sociologists including Neal Krause, Linda George, and Kenneth Ferraro and psychologists including David Myers, Lisa Miller, Michael McCullough, Robert Emmons, Crystal Park, Doug Oman, and Amy Ai each have made significant and programmatic contributions. If one considers that modeling population health outcomes is the province of epidemiology, one can see that few formally credentialed epidemiologists have made a mark here, although many of the people mentioned above also have advanced training or expertise in epidemiology or public health and function expertly as de facto social or psychiatric epidemiologists. Where credentialed epidemiologists have weighed in, the results have been meaningful: for example, the sophisticated mortality studies of William Strawbridge and colleagues;[21] the insightful theoretical writing of Peter Van Ness;[22] and the recent methodologically sophisticated contributions of Tyler VanderWeele.[23]

Today, the norms for this field have evolved to match the standards of other prominent areas of research within chronic disease and psychiatric epidemiology and the medical social sciences. Published research makes increasing use of data from population censuses or surveys or from large-scale community surveys with randomly drawn or otherwise representative samples. There have been many national, regional, or multisite investigations and considerable longitudinal research of various designs. Most encouraging, even where the intent of an original data collection effort is not to focus on religion, multiple measures of religious identity and practice are now routinely included in population-based and clinical studies, especially in psychiatric epidemiology. This has resulted in published findings on religion and mental health, for example, from important data sources such as the Established Populations for Epidemiologic Studies of the Elderly (EPESE) and the Epidemiologic Catchment Area (ECA) study.[24] In addition, data from many of epidemiology's most famous community-based studies have been used to conduct significant analyses of the impact of religion on morbidity and mortality, including the Alameda County (California), Washington County (Maryland), Evans County (Georgia), and Tecumseh (Michigan) studies.[25]

OVERVIEW OF RESEARCH AND THEORY

Empirical Research Findings

In taking account of the volumes of empirical research that have been conducted on this subject (by now thousands of published studies), two basic questions arise. These might be called the "what" question—that is, how much research evidence is out there and for what categories of diseases or health-related outcomes?—and the "how" or "why" question—that is, what does this all mean and can we make sense of it in light of existing theories of the determinants of health or illness?

The first question ("what") can be addressed through a summary of the systematic review of published studies provided in both editions of Koenig and colleagues' *Handbook of Religion and Health* (see Table 10.1). This is the most encyclopedic resource within this

Table 10.1. Number of published studies and salutary findings on religion and health for selected health- and disease-related outcomes, excerpted from *Handbook of Religion and Health*, first and second editions

Health- or Disease-Related Outcome	First Edition (until 2000)		Second Edition (between 2000 and 2011)	
	Number of Studies	Number of Positive or Mixed Findings	Number of Studies	Number of Positive or Mixed Findings
Heart disease morbidity and mortality	39	31	25	16
Hypertension and cerebrovascular disease	43	35	44	20
Cancer morbidity and mortality	50	44	34	20
All-causes mortality	54	42	62	50
Self-rated health	21	12	49	32
Pain and somatic symptoms	27	13	91	37
Physical disability	12	9	52	21
Depression	120	92	339	225
Anxiety	79	48	235	122

field, and the respective editions capture the scope of this literature roughly up until the year 2000 (first edition) and between 2000 and 2011 (second edition).[26] The highlight of each edition of the *Handbook* is a lengthy table summarizing methodological details and results for every published study. The first edition reviews about 1,200 studies; the second edition, about 3,000. The respective summary tables are about 75 pages in the first edition, and over 350 pages in the second edition. For purposes of the present chapter, material pertinent to chronic disease epidemiology and psychiatric epidemiology have been excerpted; studies of psychological well-being, health behaviors, medical care utilization, religious coping, healing, pathophysiological and other biomarkers, and other non-epidemiologic subjects have been excluded.

Studies of *heart disease* morbidity and mortality have been a staple of epidemiologic research on religion since the 1950s. In Levin and Schiller's original review from 1987, significant results were obtained for a variety of cardiovascular outcomes or diagnoses: ateriosclerotic heart disease and arteriosclerotic and degenerative heart disease incidence and mortality, myocardial infarction incidence and mortality, coronary artery disease prevalence, angina pectoris incidence, rheumatic and hypertensive heart disease mortality, coronary heart disease incidence and prevalence, aortic calcification prevalence, chronic endocarditis mortality, and more. Some of these labels overlap with others, and nomenclature has shifted some over the subsequent decades, but the diversity of diagnoses within this category of the religion and health literature is replicated in the *Handbook*. Across both editions, sixty-four studies were identified, with forty-seven (73.4 percent) reporting at least some positive findings—that is, a protective effect for religiousness.

Likewise, studies of *hypertension and cerebrovascular disease* outcomes, both morbidity and mortality, have been present in this literature for many decades. These studies were included in the review by Levin and Schiller, who concluded that "high religiosity (whether frequent attendance or high self-rating) is associated with lower [blood] pressures."[27] Findings were considered provocative enough and published in sufficient numbers to encourage the spinning off of a separate systematic review of eighteen studies.[28] Currently, across both editions of the *Handbook*, eighty-seven studies have been identified, fifty-five (63.2 percent) with positive findings, validating the link observed earlier between religiousness and normotension.

The empirical study of religion in relation to *cancer* rates extends back to the nineteenth century. A protective effect for particular religious groups (e.g., Latter-Day Saints, Seventh-day Adventists, Jews) has been observed for many decades, especially for those site-specific cancers for which behavioral risk/protection has been observed or hypothesized. Examples include cervical and uterine cancer (in relation to circumcision), lung cancer (in relation to smoking), digestive tract cancers (in relation to vegetarian diet), and so on. Nearly 100 studies were identified in the Levin and Schiller review, and a contemporaneous review detailed rates of cancer morbidity and mortality overall and for many sites among studies of Mormons, Adventists, Amish, and Hutterites.[29] The *Handbook* editions, which include studies published up through a quarter century after these earlier reviews, seems to have underestimated the scope of research on religion and cancer. Both editions together include only eighty-four studies selected according to their systematic inclusionary criteria, but of these, sixty-four (76.2 percent) report positive findings, in line with the findings for heart disease.

Studies of religion and *mortality* have appeared for almost as long as there have been studies of religion and health. For most of the nineteenth and twentieth centuries, this meant investigations of religious differences in mortality rates by categories of religious affiliation, which included studies of both all-causes and cause-specific mortality. As summarized in both the Levin and Schiller and the Jarvis and Northcott reviews, these studies reported results in relation to a variety of measures, such as standardized and proportionate mortality ratios, and included studies of general populations, of particular religious denominations or sects, of clergy, and of dozens of specific causes and cancer sites.[30] Through the mid-1980s, at least sixty of these studies had appeared. Since that time, research has focused more on how measures of religious practice or strength of commitment have an impact on mortality, and large-scale general population studies have proliferated using methods such as Cox proportional hazards modeling. Focusing just on studies of all-causes mortality, in both *Handbook* editions 116 studies are cited, of which ninety-two (79.3 percent) report positive findings. Studies of cause-specific mortality are many and include some of the studies of heart disease, hypertension, and cancer noted above.

Research on religion and *morbidity and health status*, in the broadest sense, has been a staple of religion and health studies conducted by social scientists, especially in the field of gerontology. Single-item self-ratings of global or overall health status and single items and indices of functional health, activity limitation, or physical disability are common features of social research studies and are generally included in questionnaires when sociologists conduct population-based health surveys. This category of studies was summarized in the Levin and Schiller review and research on religion published using these endpoints has proliferated in the years since. In Table 10.1, information is reported separately for studies of self-rated health, pain and somatic symptoms, and physical disability, based on both editions of the *Handbook*. Overall, 252 studies are cited, with 124 (49.2 percent) reporting positive findings. The relative ambiguity of findings, compared to the other disease categories reported above, is due primarily to the studies of pain and disability. Among those published studies just of religion and self-rated health, the totals are seventy studies, forty-four (62.9 percent) with positive findings.

Finally, the largest growth area for empirical studies of religion and health has been within *psychiatric epidemiology*. This topic was not covered in the Levin and Schiller or Jarvis and Northcott reviews but was featured in the systematic reviews of Larson and colleagues. By the mid-1980s, according to Larson, a few dozen such studies had been published in leading psychiatric journals, but these represented only a fraction of the published academic literature on religion and mental health. For example, a bibliography on this subject published by the U.S. Department of Health and Human Services in 1980 contained 1,836 references, but most of these were not empirical studies; rather, they were books, reviews, essays, practice guidelines, psychological studies, and other types of publications.[31] Since that time, however, things have changed dramatically. Across both editions of the *Handbook*, focusing just on diagnoses of depression and anxiety, there were 773 studies, 487 (63.0 percent) with positive findings. The weight of evidence is much stronger for depression (69.1 percent of studies with positive results) than for anxiety (54.1 percent).

Besides these studies of mood disorders, there have been many investigations of religion and psychotic disorders, suicide, addictive behavior, personality disorders, and other mental health–related topics, and the second edition of the *Handbook* reports that the weight of evidence, on average, favors a salutary religious effect for these diagnoses except for psychoses. Religious ideations and behaviors are often features of the clinical expression of these illnesses; regardless, results of existing studies are inconsistent compared to the other psychiatric categories.

Across these selected disease categories, through 2000, the *Handbook* reports that there were 445 studies, 326 of which (or 73.3 percent) included statistically significant positive, or salutary, findings. Since 2000, the *Handbook* reports that there were 931 studies, 543 of which (58.3 percent) were significant and in a salutary direction. The grand totals are 1,376 studies, 869 (63.2 percent) reporting positive findings.[32] While the proportion of studies with at least some positive findings differed between the two editions of the *Handbook* and also among the different disease outcomes, for all disease categories through 2000 and for six of nine categories since 2000, most studies reported salutary results. The weight of evidence according to this review is that religiousness, however defined or assessed, seems to exhibit a generally protective or primary-preventive effect, on average, with respect to these chronic disease and psychiatric outcomes.

An earlier review, not intended as comprehensive or systematic, surveyed this literature in order to determine the generalizability of this positive link between religiousness and health status.[33] In other words, was this much observed salutary association a function in part of the population characteristics of the people being studied or of the particular religious variables that were being included in analyses? The answer, at the time, appeared to be a firm no. Salutary findings were observed—and remain so today—across categories of most of the important demographic variables and across numerous religious measures, and they are found across religions and denominations. Positive religion–health findings have been observed across age cohorts throughout the life course, in males and females, in married and unmarried people, across racial and ethnic groups and nationalities, across social classes, and in both rural and urban populations, regardless of study design, in each decade since the nineteenth century. A systematic review of just the gerontological and geriatric studies in this field, commissioned by the NIH in the late 1990s, found that three dozen different religious measures had been used and were found to be significantly associated with particular health outcomes.[34]

Theoretical Perspectives, Models, and Mechanisms

The second question ("how" or "why") is just as important as the first. Hundreds or thousands of published studies may exist for a given subject, and the weight of evidence may be statistically significant and in a common direction, as for the literature on religion and health. But unless such findings can be shown to make sense—to fit into the prevailing theories of the determinants of health or illness or what is known about the natural history of disease—then it is unlikely that medical scientists or clinicians or public health professionals will pay much attention, nor should they.

In this literature, considerable theoretical writing has appeared. This is no surprise: Since the 1980s epidemiologic studies of religion are mainly the work of social scientists, and within social science, in contrast to biomedical science, theory is a component of the research process for many substantive topics. This includes evaluating competing theoretical perspectives, testing explicit theoretical models, and positing theoretical mechanisms that may mediate, moderate, or otherwise account for observed exposure–outcome associations. This exemplifies how social epidemiology benefits from the culture of social research, which treats theory as an integral part of the research process. Elsewhere in epidemiology, theory is more marginal, although it is still present (e.g., providing benchmarks for evaluation of biological plausibility of observed associations). For religion and health, the primary use of theory has been to offer putative explanations for how and why characteristics, functions, or expressions of religious or spiritual identity and practice are or could be health-related.

It has been suggested that, in the social sciences, there are four distinct "tenses" of theory—four theoretical constructions or "uniquely inflected forms of theory arrayed along a kind of quasi-temporal line."[35] These include (1) what sociologists term grand theory and what psychologists refer to as schools or forces; (2) theoretical perspectives that govern impacts of social, psychological, or behavioral constructs in particular subject areas, referred to by sociologists as midrange theories; (3) theoretical models that posit explicit, testable associations among a system of constructs, including specifically defined outcome measures; and (4) "mechanisms," including mediators, moderators, and other variables or constructs that intervene in, have an impact on, or otherwise account for the variance in a specific exposure–outcome association. Ideally, or rather hypothetically, each type of theory evolves from the antecedent category of theory (e.g., grand theory begets midrange theories, which beget testable models, which posit specific mechanisms).

For the religion and health field, accordingly, some have tried to make sense of the accumulated findings from population-based studies. This has involved positing, testing, or in some other way evaluating theory according to its usage, as in "2," "3," and "4," above. Evaluations of theoretical perspectives are fewest, as this entails an overall judgment of a segment of the literature, such as within a particular population subgroup, and can be laborious. For example, an early review of the religion and health literature among older adults determined that the weight of findings mapped up more against the expectations of what gerontologists at the time referred to as multidimensional disengagement, as opposed to competing eschatological, deterioration, activity theory, disengagement, and social decrement or isolation perspectives.[36] In other words, public and private expressions of religiousness exhibit differential impacts on health status indicators as people age, due in part to the tendency of declines in function to limit behavior and result in compensation by heightened involvement in noninstitutional forms of religious life. Programmatic research since that time has modified these initial conclusions, but the reference to theoretical perspectives continues to provide a touchstone for study hypotheses, model building, and interpretation of findings.

The testing of theoretical models is commonplace within subsets of this literature, particularly within the research of several leading sociologists who specialize in use of structural-equation modeling applied to multifactorial systems of equations. The most noted proponent of this approach is Neal Krause, who has published dozens of empirical studies of religion and physical or mental health using data from large-scale national population surveys and positing effects for a variety of social, behavioral, and psychosocial mediators or exogenous constructs. Much of this work is cited in his masterful book, *Aging in the Church*,[37] which summarizes his published research since the early 1990s. Almost all of his religion and health studies provide a test of respective theoretical models, explicitly drawn according to structural-modeling conventions, with inclusion of latent constructs and posited directional arrows.

No one single study, naturally, is capable of positing and testing every possible mediator or pathway linking particular religious constructs with a specific health or disease outcome. Research studies, such as those by Krause, more typically carve out a discrete problem—for example, his analysis of national data on church support and health, which examined the impact of church attendance and congregational cohesiveness on self-ratings of health, with intervening paths connecting the primary exposure variables and the outcome variable via directional paths among measures of connectedness with God, spiritual and emotional support, and optimism.[38] An example of a more global version of a theoretical model, meant to apply generally to multiple outcomes and study settings, is found in the Jarvis and Northcott review, whereby religious affiliation leads to public and private religious participation, markers of religiosity, and involvement in religious communities, which in turn influence health-related attitudes and behaviors and social support; these in turn have an impact on health risks.[39] The ultimate example of a global theoretical model is by Koenig and colleagues, who famously laid out the multiple pathways of hypothesized religious determinants and correlates in a multifactorial etiologic model of geriatric depression.[40] This model mapped out religion's effects alongside and indirectly through nearly twenty other biological, behavioral, and biomedical variables, including genetic factors, personality, brain disease, psychiatric comorbidity, physical illness, stressful events, chronic pain, cognitive appraisal, social support, economic resources, and more.

It is in enumerating mechanisms that explain or make sense of religion–health associations that theory is most typically engaged in this field. The earliest comprehensive list was put forth in 1976 by Vaux,[41] who suggested three dozen health-related activities, grounded in religious beliefs or behaviors, that may account for observed associations between religion and health. These included preventive health behaviors (e.g., diet, vaccination, care of the body) and salutary attitudes regarding health-related ethical decisions (e.g., related to medical compliance, substance use, reproduction, care of others). Subsequently, other lists have appeared of the sorts of behaviors, beliefs, attitudes, and affects believed to account for why religious measures were significantly associated with health outcomes. These include the work of sociologists[42] and psychologists,[43] and they have been focused on either physical or mental health or both.

Among the mechanisms proposed throughout this work are health behaviors, social cohesiveness, cognitive coherence, social support, psychosocial resources, meaning in life, body sanctification, stress moderation, locus of control, self-regulation, personality, transcendence, and coping.

Among physicians, Koenig has most frequently addressed the issue of mechanisms. His most comprehensive take on providing a rationale for religious effects is found in a chapter in the second edition of his *Handbook*.[44] Here, he differentiates among psychological pathways, including positive psychological traits (e.g., forgiveness, altruism, gratefulness, well-being, quality of life, hope and optimism, meaning and purpose, self-esteem, personal control), negative emotions (e.g., loneliness, depression, suicide, anxiety—which, in another context, are also psychiatric outcomes themselves), and substance abuse; social pathways (e.g., social support, marital stability, social capital, and antisocial behaviors); and behavioral pathways (e.g., exercise, diet and cholesterol, weight, sexual activity, smoking, disease screening and compliance).

A noted approach to this issue by an epidemiologist is found in the work of the present author since the late 1980s.[45] His objective has been to outline biomedical, biobehavioral, and psychosocial correlates or functions or expressions of religiousness or spirituality that seem to best make sense of significant findings linking religious measures and population health outcomes. The model seeks to link respective religious dimensions, associated pathways to health (via particular religious functions or expressions), posited biobehavioral and psychosocial mediating factors, and underlying salutogenic processes. Among the constructs, variables, and biological and psychological processes that are specified are health-related behavior and lifestyles (through mitigating disease risks), heredity (through familial transmission), social support (through stress buffering, coping, and adaptation), psychodynamics of ritual (through expression of positive emotions) and belief (through identification with healthy beliefs, personality styles, or behavioral patterns), and psychodynamics of faith (through salutary cognitions and ideations such as optimism, hope, and positive expectation). The model even posits what are termed "superempirical" effects (e.g., activation of a healing bioenergy or attainment of altered states of consciousness) and supernatural effects (such as the result of divine healing).

Of course, not all of these hypothesized mechanisms have been validated or tested, and, in the case of the latter two, they may be untestable, at least by epidemiologists, social scientists, or medical researchers.

AN AGENDA FOR THE NEXT THIRTY YEARS

The past thirty years have seen epidemiologic research on religion evolve from a curiosity to a well-established field of study. There is no longer much justification for purely exploratory research, and, except for research among specialized populations of relatively small size (e.g., Jewish Americans), investigators are not solely at the mercy of whatever few religious variables happen to be present in available social or population health surveys. Researchers are encouraged to be more intentional about crafting thoughtful, conceptually coherent, and theoretically meaningful studies of relevant health or disease outcomes.

By now, innumerable review articles and essays have set forth research agendas for this field. In fact, so many such papers have appeared, dating back to the 1960s, that these agenda-setting pieces have been subject to their own review.[46] A common concern identified throughout these papers is the general laxity of the methodology of studies in this field. In recent years, this concern has been alleviated: Studies of religion and health are just as sophisticated as any in social epidemiology or the medical social sciences, using longitudinal designs and state-of-the-art analytic procedures. Other concerns, however, first expressed decades ago, still remain. These are related to the quality of *measures*, the homogeneity of *study populations*, and lacunae of *theory*. Addressing each of these issues holds the most promise for moving this field forward.

First, despite repeated calls dating back decades, the norm for religious assessment in this literature is single-item measures of discrete religious behaviors. For example: How often do you attend church? How often do you pray? Do you read the Bible? Granted, there is nothing intrinsically wrong with these questions or with the underlying constructs of public or private religious behavior. If these are what are being theorized as having an impact on physical or mental health, then they require assessment. But, too often, responses to such questions are used to infer grand statements of social fact regarding a broad and generic "religiosity" and its impact on human well-being. Even after decades of research on religion and health, and consistent efforts to call attention to this problem, these types of analyses and interpretations continue to predominate.

Other domains of religious expression merit consideration as potential influences on health. They may be more likely to produce substantive results than studies of, for example, frequency of religious service attendance, measures of which may be confounded in part by functional health scores in certain age cohorts (i.e., people with disabilities may be less able to go to services).[47] Over one hundred validated measures exist for numerous domains and dimensions of religiousness: beliefs and practices, attitudes, orientations, development, commitment and involvement, experiences, values, coping, spirituality and mysticism, conceptions of God, and more.[48] This multidimensional approach to religious assessment goes back half a century in both the sociology and psychology of religion,[49] but it remains less prevalent within the religion and health field. The work of an expert panel convened by the NIH in the mid-1990s did much to encourage movement in this direction,[50] and theoretical work has connected respective religious dimensions to particular health-related mechanisms,[51] but analyses of single-item measures of public religious behavior still prevail.

If religious assessment is not yet what it could be, health assessment has become considerably more sophisticated within this field, especially over the past decade. "Harder" outcome measures, including physiological and psychophysiological assessments and use of biomarkers, are being used more frequently, as are expanded psychiatric diagnoses beyond indices of depression and anxiety. The second edition of Koenig's *Handbook* lists over forty neuroscience studies and over seventy studies with immune or endocrine outcomes (including assessments of cell counts, cell functioning, cytokines, infection, viral load, cortisol, and epinephrine/norepinephrine). This is greatly encouraging and suggests that earlier efforts to identify psychoneuroimmunology as a cutting edge for this field are finally coming to fruition.[52]

Second, despite repeated calls for change going back decades, most of what is known about the relationship between religion and population health is based on study samples of Whites, Christians, and U.S. residents. To be fair, findings from excellent studies of ethnic-minority populations have begun to accumulate, but they are relatively fewer and are mainly the work of respective research teams who have been working programmatically, mostly in isolation.[53] Nonetheless, a need for greater diversity by racial or ethnic group, culture, nationality, and religion continues.

On the last point, religious diversity, there has been some progress in the new decade. Studies of the physical health and mental health impact of Jewish religious observance and Muslim religiousness and spirituality have begun to appear in sufficient quantity to generate their own comprehensive reviews.[54] The public availability of data on both religion and health from global population survey programs (e.g., the Gallup World Poll; the World Values Survey; the European Social Survey; the International Social Survey Programme; the Survey of Health, Ageing and Retirement in Europe) means that the capability exists to conduct studies of religion and health with national or international scope both within respective faith traditions and comparatively, across traditions. Naturally, one is limited by the variables available in any given data source, but this is a simple and inexpensive way to begin to combat the religious and cultural homogeneity that plagues this field. This approach has been used to great success in studies of the physical and mental health of Jews, in both Israel and the Jewish diaspora.[55]

Third, while the best work in this field makes an effort to engage theory, as noted earlier, these efforts focus on explaining or making sense of religion–health associations in terms of accepted biological, psychological, or sociological constructs known to have an impact on health. There is a different way to engage theory, and a different type of theory, that merits consideration: the theories and conceptual models that are used in biomedicine and public health to think through etiologic factors and potential intervention strategies, respectively, whether in a clinical or population health context. An example would be the concept of the natural history of disease.

Nearly all population-based research to date has focused on whether or how religious identity or practice function to protect against subsequent morbidity or mortality. General populations are studied, their religious characteristics assessed, and then they are followed in time to obtain counts of health-related events (or, alternatively, prevalence designs are used and associations between religious and health variables are statistically determined). Ideally, this enables us to gauge whether religion exhibits a primary preventive effect—whether it is associated with less of the adverse event. This tells us nothing about whether or not religiousness or spirituality or faith can "heal"—that is, whether religion is associated with recovery or remission from disease among clinical populations followed forward in time. As noted, this type of research, for the most part, has not been done, except for a subset of controversial trials of distant prayer, which for purposes of the present chapter are not pertinent because they are not population-based and do not use epidemiologic or social survey methods.[56] The key takeaway point is this: Those factors (religious or otherwise) that are etiologic for cases of disease or are determinants of rates of morbidity and mortality are not necessarily the same factors that are therapeutic among diseased cases or ill populations.[57]

A renewed clinical rather than primary preventive focus may produce significant yields for the epidemiology of religion. Large samples of hospitalized patients or populations or community-based outpatient samples could be used for longitudinal, disease-specific studies. A clinical-epidemiologic approach would enable religious risk or protection to be estimated not just for well populations and with respect to future health events but also for populations suffering from particular health challenges and in need of (spiritual) resources that may contribute to endpoints such as amelioration of symptoms, shorter hospital stays, and even cure. Coupled with more creative assessment of religious domains and greater diversity and inclusivity among study populations, this is where the future of this field lies.

NOTES

1. The definition proffered by the U.S. Centers for Disease Control and Prevention (CDC), for example, states that epidemiology is "the study of the distribution and determinants of health-related states or events in specified populations." From *Principles of Epidemiology in Public Health Practice: An Introduction to Applied Epidemiology and Biostatistics*, 3rd ed., CDC Self-Study Course SS1000 (Atlanta: U.S. Department of Health and Human Services, 2006), quotation on pp. 1–2.
2. See Council on Education for Public Health, *Accreditation Criteria: Schools of Public Health, Amended June 2011* (Silver Spring, MD: Author, 2011), 13.
3. For example, in Last's authoritative text, the chapter on social and behavioral determinants of health differentiates among "social factors,"

"psychosocial factors," and "life style." From John M. Last, *Public Health and Human Ecology* (East Norwalk, CT: Appleton & Lange, 1987), 211–42.

4. A representative early usage can be found in Michael Marmot and Richard G. Wilkinson, eds., *Social Determinants of Health* (Oxford, UK: Oxford University Press, 1999).

5. The phrase *epidemiology of religion* appeared in Jeffrey S. Levin and Harold Y. Vanderpool, "Is Frequent Religious Attendance *Really* Conducive to Better Health?: Toward an Epidemiology of Religion," *Social Science and Medicine* 24 (1987): 589–600.

6. An outstanding meta-analytic review of a mix of clinical, behavioral, and some population-based studies of depression, for example, is found in Timothy B. Smith, Michael E. McCullough, and Justin Poll, "Religiousness and Depression: Evidence for a Main Effect and the Moderating Influence of Stressful Life Events," *Psychological Bulletin* 129 (2003): 614–36.

7. Jeff Levin and Harold G. Koenig, "Faith Matters: Reflections on the Life and Work of Dr. David B. Larson," in *Faith, Medicine, and Science: A Festschrift in Honor of Dr. David B. Larson*, eds. Jeff Levin and Harold G. Koenig (New York: Haworth Pastoral Press, 2005), 3–25, quotation on p. 3.

8. Amariah Brigham, *Observations on the Influence of Religion upon the Health and Physical Welfare of Mankind* (Boston: Marsh, Capen & Lyon, 1835).

9. These and other early works are cited in Jeffrey S. Levin and Preston L. Schiller, "Is There a Religious Factor in Health?," *Journal of Religion and Health* 26 (1987): 9–36.

10. Émile Durkheim, *Suicide: A Study in Sociology* [1897], trans. John A. Spalding and George Simpson (Glencoe, IL: The Free Press, 1951).

11. William Osler, "The Faith That Heals" *British Medical* Journal 1, 2581 (1910): 1470–72.

12. Alice E. Paulsen, "Religious Healing: Preliminary Report," *JAMA* 86 (1926): 1519–22, 1617–23, 1692–97.

13. Levin and Schiller, "Is There a Religious Factor in Health?"

14. George K. Jarvis and Herbert C. Northcott, "Religious Differences in Morbidity and Mortality," *Social Science and Medicine* 25 (1987): 813–24.

15. See E. L. Kennaway, "The Racial and Social Incidence of Cancer of the Uterus," *British Journal of Cancer* 2, 3 (1948): 177–212. This is one of the very finest literature reviews ever published in epidemiology. It reviews decades of morbidity and mortality data and research, comparing rates by categories of religious affiliation (Jewish Muslim, Hindu, Parsi, Christian, etc.), and offering possible explanations for

findings based on ritual, socioeconomic, genetic, and behavioral characteristics of these populations.

16. See, for example, Brian McMahon and Ernest K. Koller, "Ethnic Differences in the Incidence of Leukemia," *Blood: The Journal of Hematology* 12 (1957): 1–10; and Brian McMahon, "The Ethnic Distribution of Cancer Mortality in New York City, 1955," *Acta Unio Internationalis Contra Cancrum* 16 (1960): 1716–24.

17. Ground zero for subsequent research on religion in psychiatric epidemiology is the chapter entitled, "Religious Origin," by Leo Srole and Thomas Langner in *Mental Health in the Metropolis: The Midtown Manhattan Study, Volume* 1, eds. Leo Srole, Thomas S. Langner, Stanley T. Michael, Marvin K. Opler, and Thomas A. C. Rennie, (New York: McGraw-Hill, 1962), 300–24.

18. An excellent Mormon study: John W. Gardner, Jill S. Sanborn, and Martha L. Slattery, "Behavioral Factors Explaining the Low Risk for Cervical Carcinoma in Utah Mormon Women," *Epidemiology* 6 (1995): 187–9. An important and much cited Adventist study: Roland L. Phillips, "Role of Life-Style and Dietary Habits in Risk of Cancer among Seventh-Day Adventists," *Cancer Research* 35 (1975): 3513–22.

19. The best known and most influential of the Comstock studies: George W. Comstock and Kay B. Partridge, "Church Attendance and Health," *Journal of Chronic Diseases* 25 (1972): 665–72; and George W. Comstock and James A. Tonascia, "Education and Mortality in Washington County, Maryland," *Journal of Health and Social Behavior* 18 (1977): 54–61.

20. Examples include: several chapters on physical and mental health in Melvin A. Kimble, Susan H. McFadden, James W. Ellor, and James J. Seeber, eds., *Aging, Spirituality, and Religion: A Handbook* (Minneapolis, MN: Fortress Press, 1995); Jeffrey S. Levin, "Religion," in *The Encyclopedia of Aging*, 2nd ed., ed. George L. Maddox (New York: Springer Publishing Company, 1995), 799–802; Susan H. McFadden, "Religion, Spirituality, and Aging," in *Handbook on the Psychology of Aging*, 4th ed., eds. James E. Birren and K. Warner Schaie (San Diego: Academic Press, 1996), 162–77; David B. Larson, James P. Swyers, and Michael E. McCullough, eds., *Scientific Research on Spirituality and Health: A Consensus Report* (Rockville, MD: National Institute for Healthcare Research, 1998); and Linda M. Chatters, "Religion and Health: Public Health Research and Practice," *Annual Review of Public Health* 21 (2000): 335–67.

21. See, for example, William J. Strawbridge, Richard D. Cohen, Sarah J. Shema, and George A. Kaplan, "Frequent Attendance at Religious Services and Mortality over 28 Years," *American Journal of Public Health* 87 (1997): 957–61.

22. See, for example, Peter H. Van Ness, "Theology and Epidemiology as Complementary Perspectives on Aging," *Journal of Religious Gerontology* 15, no. 3 (2003): 25–40.

23. See, for example, Tyler J. VanderWeele and Alexandra E. Shields, "Religiosity and Telomere Length: One Step Forward, One Step Back," *Social Science and Medicine* 163 (2016): 176–78.

24. For a representative study of religion using the EPESE data, see Harold G. Koenig, Judith C. Hays, Linda K. George, Dan G. Blazer, David B. Larson, and Lawrence R. Landerman, "Modeling the Cross-Sectional Relationships between Religion, Physical Health, Social Support, and Depressive Symptoms," *American Journal of Geriatric Psychiatry* 5 (1997): 131–44. For a representative study of religion using the ECA data, see Keith G. Meador, Harold G. Koenig, Dana C. Hughes, Dan G. Blazer, Linda K. George, and Joanne Turnbull, "Religious Affiliation and Major Depression," *Psychiatric Services* 43 (1992): 1204–8.

25. Representative analyses of religion from these four community studies: Strawbridge et al., "Frequent Attendance at Religious Services and Mortality over 28 Years"; Comstock and Partridge, "Church Attendance and Health"; Thomas W. Graham, Berton H. Kaplan, Joan C. Cornoni-Huntley, Sherman A. James, Caroline Becker, Curtis G. Hames, and Siegfried Heyden, "Frequency of Church Attendance and Blood Pressure Elevation," *Journal of Behavioral Medicine* 1 (1978): 37–43; and James House, Cynthia Robbins, and Helen L. Metzner, "The Association of Social Relationships and Activities with Mortality: Prospective Evidence from the Tecumseh Community Health Study," *American Journal of Epidemiology* 116 (1982): 123–40.

26. The two editions of the handbook are: Harold G. Koenig, Michael E. McCullough, and David B. Larson, *Handbook of Religion and Health* (New York: Oxford University Press, 2001); and Harold G. Koenig, Dana E. King, and Verna Benner Carson, *Handbook of Religion and Health*, 2nd ed. (New York: Oxford University Press, 2012).

27. Levin and Schiller, "Is There a Religious Factor in Health?," quotation on p. 16.

28. Jeffrey S. Levin and Harold Y. Vanderpool, "Is Religion Therapeutically Significant for Hypertension?," *Social Science and Medicine* 29 (1989): 69–78.

29. Henry Troyer, "Review of Cancer among 4 Religious Sects: Evidence That Life-Styles Are Distinctive Sets of Risk Factors," *Social Science and Medicine* 26 (1988): 1007–17.

30. At the time of the Levin and Schiller review, statistically significant religious findings had been found in relation to morbidity and/or mortality rates for numerous causes, including accidents/violence, asthma,

atherosclerosis, bronchitis/respiratory diseases, coronary artery disease, circulatory system diseases, central nervous system diseases, cerebrovascular disease, diabetes, digestive diseases, duodenal or peptic ulcer, emphysema, endocrine/metabolic disorders, genitourinary diseases, hypertension/stroke, infant mortality, infectious disease, kidney disease, liver disease, myocardial infarction, nonrheumatic chronic endocarditis, pneumonia/influenza, prostate hyperplasia, syphilis, tuberculosis, and diseases of undefined symptoms.

31. Florence A. Summerlin, comp., *Religion and Mental Health: A Bibliography*, DHHS Pub. No. (ADM) 80-964 (Washington, DC: U.S. Government Printing Office, 1980).

32. These numbers are based on the present author's reading of the *Handbook* tables, and excluded certain studies (qualitative, review) and counted studies with mixed findings (i.e., some positive and some negative) as among the positive category. Others, including Koenig, might come up with slightly different counts.

33. Jeffrey S. Levin, "Religion and Health: Is There an Association, Is It Valid, and Is It Causal?," *Social Science and Medicine* 38 (1994): 1475–82.

34. Measures included religious attendance, belief in afterlife, strength of religiosity, subjective religiosity, frequency of prayer, spiritual support, church-based support, importance of religion, belief in God or the devil, church participation, holding church office, public religiousness, private religiousness, self-rated commitment, marital religious conflict, strength of religious affiliation, supernatural fears, experiencing divine healing, intrinsic religiosity, extrinsic religiosity, religious social activity, existential certainty, religious knowledge, transcendental aspirations, belief in divine intervention, and mystical experience. From Jeffrey S. Levin, "Religious Research in Gerontology, 1980–1994: A Systematic Review," *Journal of Religious Gerontology* 10, no. 3 (1997): 3–31.

35. Jeff Levin, Linda M. Chatters, and Robert Joseph Taylor, "Theory in Religion, Aging, and Health: An Overview," *Journal of Religion and Health* 50 (2011): 389–406, quotation on p. 392.

36. Jeffrey S. Levin, "Religious Factors in Aging, Adjustment, and Health: A Theoretical Overview," in *Religion, Aging, and Health: A Global Perspective*, ed. William M. Clements, compiled by the World Health Organization (New York: Haworth Press, 1989), 133–46.

37. Neal Krause, *Aging in the Church: How Social Relationships Affect Health* (West Conshohocken, PA: Templeton Press, 2008).

38. Neal Krause, "Church-Based Social Support and Health in Old Age: Exploring Variations by Race," *Journal of Gerontology: Social Sciences* 57B (2002): S332–S347.

39. Jarvis and Northcott, "Religious Differences in Morbidity and Mortality."

40. This model appears in Harold G. Koenig, comp., *Research on Religion and Aging: An Annotated Bibliography* (Westport, CT: Greenwood Press, 1995), 154.
41. Kenneth Vaux, "Religion and Health," *Preventive Medicine* 5 (1976): 522–36.
42. The best known of these are by Ellen Idler, "Religious Involvement and the Health of the Elderly: Some Hypotheses and an Initial Test," *Social Forces* 66 (1987): 226–38; and various papers featuring Linda George and/or Christopher Ellison, such as Linda K. George, Christopher G. Ellison, and David B. Larson, "Explaining the Relationships between Religious Involvement and Health," *Psychological Inquiry* 13 (2002): 190–200. A rarely cited but outstanding early paper is by Berton H. Kaplan, "A Note on Religious Beliefs and Coronary Artery Disease," *Journal of the South Carolina Medical Association* 15, no. 5, suppl. (1976): 60–64.
43. The earliest comprehensive example addressing physical health is Daniel McIntosh and Bernard Spilka, "Religion and Physical Health: The Role of Personal Faith and Control Beliefs," *Research on the Social Scientific Study of Religion* 2 (1990): 167–94. A couple of more recent reviews focusing on mental health are Crystal L. Park, "Religiousness/Spirituality and Health: A Meaning Systems Perspective," *Journal of Behavioral Medicine* 30 (2007): 319–28; and Michael E. McCullough and Brian L.B. Willoughby, "Religion, Self-Regulation, and Self-Control: Associations, Explanations, and Implications," *Psychological Bulletin* 135 (2009): 69–93.
44. His most comprehensive list is found in the chapter entitled, "Psychological, Social, and Behavioral Pathways," in Koenig et al., *Handbook of Religion and Health*, 2nd ed., 579–99.
45. Several versions of this model have appeared in print. The earliest version is Levin and Vanderpool, "Is Religion Therapeutically Significant for Hypertension?" The most fleshed-out version is Jeffrey S. Levin, "How Religion Influences Morbidity and Health: Reflections on Natural History, Salutogenesis and Host Resistance," *Social Science and Medicine* 43 (1996): 849–64.
46. Jeff Levin and Linda M. Chatters, "Religion, Aging, and Health: Historical Perspectives, Current Trends, and Future Directions," *Journal of Religion, Spirituality and Aging* 20, no. 1–2 (2008): 153–72.
47. This issue has been commented on more times than can be counted and has received at least partial validation. The earliest warning within the epidemiologic literature was in Comstock and Tonascia, "Education and Mortality in Washington County, Maryland," 57.
48. Peter C. Hill and Ralph W. Hood, Jr., eds., *Measures of Religiosity* (Birmingham, AL: Religious Education Press, 1999).

49. The normative sociological tradition of religious assessment has its origins in the multidimensional approach pioneered in Charles Y. Glock and Rodney Stark's *Religion and Society in Tension* (Chicago: Rand McNally, 1965). The psychological tradition, which focuses instead on religious motivation, derives from Gordon W. Allport's distinction between "institutionalized" and "interiorized" religion, described in *The Nature of Prejudice* (New York: Anchor Books, 1958). This work led in turn to the dominant "intrinsic" versus "extrinsic" approach to religiosity among contemporary psychologists of religion.

50. *Multidimensional Measurement of Religiousness/Spirituality for Use in Health Research* (Kalamazoo, MI: The John Fetzer Institute, 1999).

51. See Levin, "How Religion Influences Morbidity and Health," 858–59.

52. See Harold G. Koenig and Harvey Jay Cohen, eds., *The Link between Religion and Health: Psychoneuroimmunology and the Faith Factor* (New York: Oxford University Press, 2002); and Jeff Levin, "How Faith Heals: A Theoretical Model," *EXPLORE: The Journal of Science and Healing* 5 (2009): 77–96, especially pp. 87–89.

53. The clearest example of this is the team of Robert Taylor and Linda Chatters at the University of Michigan, who have been publishing research on religion and health among African Americans since the mid 1980s, and since the early 1990s in ongoing partnership with the present author. See the chapters entitled, "Impact of Religion on Physical Health" and "Impact of Religion on Mental Health and Well-Being," eds. Robert Joseph Taylor, Linda M. Chatters, and Jeff Levin, *Religion in the Lives of African Americans: Social, Psychological, and Health Perspectives* (Thousand Oaks, CA: Sage Publications, 2004), 185–226.

54. See Jeff Levin, "Population Research on Judaism, Health, and Well-Being," in *Judaism and Health: A Handbook of Practical, Professional and Scholarly Resources*, eds. Jeff Levin and Michele F. Prince (Woodstock, VT: Jewish Lights Publishing, 2013), 282–97, 382–87; and Harold G. Koenig and Saad Al Shohaib, *Health and Well-Being in Islamic Societies: Background, Research, and Applications* (New York: Springer, 2014).

55. See Levin, "Population Research on Judaism, Health, and Well-Being"; see also a new study using data from Jewish community surveys in the United States: Jeff Levin, "Religious Differences in Self-Rated Health Among US Jews: Findings from Five Urban Population Surveys," *Journal of Religion and Health* 54 (2015): 765–82.

56. A detailed discussion parsing the distinctions between different types of religion and health studies is found in Jeff Levin, "'And Let Us Make Us a Name': Reflections on the Future of the Religion and Health Field," *Journal of Religion and Health* 48 (2009): 125–45.

57. An extended discussion of this point, including proposal of a "natural history of health," is found in Jeff Levin, "Integrating Positive Psychology into Epidemiologic Theory: Reflections on Love, Salutogenesis, and Determinants of Population Health," in *Altruism and Health: Perspectives from Empirical Research*, ed. Stephen G. Post (New York: Oxford University Press, 2007), 189–218.

SUGGESTED READINGS

Two books providing general overviews of research in this field, one academic and one popular:

Koenig, Harold G., Dana E. King, and Verna B. Carson, eds. *Handbook of Religion and Health*, 2nd ed. New York: Oxford University Press, 2012. The second, expanded edition of a bibliographic resource considered the "bible" of the religion and health field. An indispensable resource, it contains a table of over 350 pages with results and other details on the thousands of published studies that have appeared since 2000.

Levin, Jeff. *God, Faith, and Health: Exploring the Spirituality-Healing Connection.* New York: John Wiley & Sons, 2001. A popular book summarizing the scope of findings in this field. It identifies the "active ingredients" in public and private religious expression and spirituality that account for or make sense of a positive impact on physical and mental health.

Three of the earliest comprehensive literature reviews of published research:

Jarvis, George K., and Herbert C. Northcott. "Religious Differences in Morbidity and Mortality." *Social Science and Medicine* 25 (1987): 813–24. The first review to summarize findings from epidemiologic studies by categories of religious identity, with a special emphasis on Christian sects. Appeared simultaneously with the Levin and Schiller review (see below).

Larson, David B., E. Mansell Pattison, Dan G. Blazer, Abdul R. Omran, and Berton H. Kaplan. "Systematic Analysis of Research on Religious Variables in Four Major Psychiatric Journals, 1978–1982." *American Journal of Psychiatry* 143 (1986): 329–34. The earliest of Larson's renowned series of systematic reviews of studies of religion within the psychiatric literature. Essential reading for anyone interested in the history of research on religion and mental health.

Levin, Jeffrey S., and Preston L. Schiller. "Is There a Religious Factor in Health?" *Journal of Religion and Health* 26 (1987): 9–36. The first comprehensive review of those nonpsychiatric epidemiologic and biomedical studies that included analyses of religious variables. In contrast to the

Jarvis and Northcott review, findings are categorized by disease categories (e.g., heart disease, cancer, hypertension), and referenced studies go back to the nineteenth century.

Two specialized epidemiologic reviews by the present author:

Levin, Jeffrey S. "Religion and Health: Is There an Association, Is It Valid, and Is It Causal?" *Social Science and Medicine* 38 (1994): 1475–82. Takes the epidemiologic literature on religion through a series of evaluations, including regarding issues of validity (i.e., chance, bias, confounding) and causation. For the latter, the literature is evaluated in terms of Austin Bradford Hill's famous characteristics of a causal association.

Levin, Jeffrey S., and Harold Y. Vanderpool. "Is Frequent Religious Attendance *Really* Conducive to Better Health?: Toward an Epidemiology of Religion." *Social Science and Medicine* 24 (1987): 589–600. The first complete review of the literature on religious attendance and health. Focuses on epistemological, methodological, analytical, and measurement issues that arise in researching this topic, and includes a primer on investigating religion for epidemiologists.

Five important articles that summarize how thinking has evolved over the past forty years on "mechanisms," or explanations for significant religion–health associations:

George, Linda K., Christopher G. Ellison, and David B. Larson. "Explaining the Relationships between Religious Involvement and Health." *Psychological Inquiry* 13 (2002): 190–200. A sociological take on this issue, emphasizing social and behavioral explanations. Includes thoughtful discussions of psychosocial constructs, including sense of coherence, meaning, self-esteem, and self-efficacy, and of conceptual and methodological issues related to understanding how mediators function.

Idler, Ellen L. "Religious Involvement and the Health of the Elderly: Some Hypotheses and an Initial Test." *Social Forces* 66 (1987): 226–38. The first substantial effort by a sociologist to propose possible explanations for significant religion–health associations. Idler carefully outlines behavioral, social, and cognitive hypotheses and presents new empirical findings.

Levin, Jeffrey S. "How Religion Influences Morbidity and Health: Reflections on Natural History, Salutogenesis and Host Resistance." *Social Science and Medicine* 43 (1996): 849–64. An elaboration of a theoretical model first presented in a 1989 review of hypertension research. Its centerpiece is a detailed discussion linking respective religious dimensions, pathways to health (via particular religious functions or expressions), biobehavioral and psychosocial mediating factors, and salutogenic processes.

McCullough, Michael E., and Brian L. B. Willoughby. "Religion, Self-Regulation, and Self-Control: Associations, Explanations, and Implications." *Psychological Bulletin* 135 (2009): 69–93. A superb systematic, comprehensive, and up-to-date review of theory and research bearing on psychological explanations for religion's observed influence on physical and mental health. Emphasizes self-control and self-regulation, and features discussions of personality traits, self-transcendence, and prosocial behavior.

Vaux, Kenneth. "Religion and Health." *Preventive Medicine* 5 (1976): 522–36. Classic essay by a noted religious ethicist; the earliest effort to broach this topic comprehensively. Outlines three dozen "health activities" related to or grounded in religious beliefs and behaviors; these in turn may help to account for why religion has been observed to have an impact on health and disease indices.

ABOUT THE CONTRIBUTORS

Jeff Levin, PhD, MPH (Editor), is university professor of epidemiology and population health, professor of medical humanities, and director of the Program on Religion and Population Health, Institute for Studies of Religion, Baylor University, Waco, Texas.

Julie J. Exline, PhD, is professor and director of clinical training, Department of Psychological Science, Case Western Reserve University, Cleveland, Ohio.

Linda K. George, PhD, is professor, Department of Sociology and Department of Psychiatry and Behavioral Sciences, and associate director of the Center for the Study of Aging and Human Development, Duke University, Durham, North Carolina.

Anthony J. Gill, PhD, is professor, Department of Political Science, University of Washington, Seattle, Washington.

Barry G. Hankins, PhD, is professor and chair, Department of History, Baylor University, Waco, Texas.

William E. Jeynes, PhD, is professor, College of Education, California State University at Long Beach, Long Beach, California.

Byron R. Johnson, PhD, is distinguished professor of the social sciences and director of the Institute for Studies of Religion, Baylor University, Waco, Texas.

Annette Mahoney, PhD, is professor, Department of Psychology, Bowling Green State University, Bowling Green, Ohio.

Charles M. North, PhD, is associate professor and chair, Department of Economics, Baylor University, Waco, Texas.

Kenneth I. Pargament, PhD, is professor, Department of Psychology, Bowling Green State University, Bowling Green, Ohio.

INDEX

Page references followed *f* and *t* indicate material in figures and tables.

Baathist religion, 51
Baca, Janet, 24, 24nn46, 47
Bader, Christopher D., 186n14, 196n40
Bahr, Stephen J., 146n10
Baier, Colin J., 183, 183n7, 185n11
Bainbridge, William Sims, 5, 6n31, 44n14, 54n58
Baird, Robert, 111
Bakken, Nicholas W., 198n51
Baptists through the Centuries (Bebbington), 131n66
Barber, Benjamin R., 52, 52n39
Barber, Rebecca, 240n44
Barkan, Steven E., 222n38
Barro, Robert J., 90, 90n62, 91, 91n65, 94, 94nn75, 76, 77
Barth, Karl, 113
Bartkowski, John P., 148, 167nn83, 87
Barton, David, 238n30
BBC News, 241nn49, 50; 248n82
Beach, Steven R. H., 26–27, 26n63, 27n64, 148, 155n25, 164, 164nn68, 69, 70
Bebbington, David, 123n37, 131, 131n66
Beck, Allen, 188n28
Becker, Carl, 123, 124n38
Becker, Caroline, 264n25
Becker, Gary S., 54, 79n21
Becker, Sascha O., 97, 97n92, 98, 98n96
Beckford, James A., 6n27, 29
Beeghley, Leonard, 244n65
behavioral revolution, 49
Beit-Hallahmi, Benjamin, 6, 6n33
Belgium, 56
Bellah, Robert N., 5, 5nn20, 21; 43, 43n12
Beneke, Chris, 49, 49n26
Benjamins, Maureen R., 219n24
Berger, Peter L., 5, 5n17, 88n48, 132
Berkman, Lisa F., 213n12, 220, 220n30

Berman, Eli, 58, 58n79, 82, 83n31, 84, 84nn37, 38; 85, 85n39
Berman, Harold J., 99n100
Between Faith and Criticism (Noll), 123, 123n37
Beyond Belief (Bellah), 5n21
Beyond Toleration (Beneke), 49n26
Bible as literature, 245–46, 245n74
Bible Believers (Ammerman), 125n45
Billings, John Shaw, 261–62
biological correlates of religious expressions, 28
biomarkers and biological function, 220
Birren, James E., 264n20
The Birth of the Living God (Rizzuto), 21n22
Black, Kathy, 222n42
Black Religion and Black Radicalism (Wilmore), 117, 117n24
Black Youth Employment Crisis (Freeman & Holzer), 187n20
The Black Muslims in America (Lincoln), 5, 5n15
Blackwell, Debra L., 157n31
Blanchard, Troy C., 197n46
Blazer, Dan G., 187n23, 212n8, 219n24, 220, 220nn26, 29; 264n24
Bloom, Allan, 239n40
blue laws, 81–82
Blum, Edward J., 129, 129n58
Bock, E. Wilbur, 244n65
Bolce, Louis, 50n28
Boles, John, 112n9
Boniwell, Ilona, 22n28
Born to Believe (Newberg & Waldman), 21n21
Bowden, Henry Warner, 112nn8, 10
Bowlby's attachment theory, 25–26
Bradley, Don E., 187n23
Braithwaite, John, 197, 197n45
Braithwaite, Scott R., 26–27, 26n63, 164n68

Farr, Thomas F., 53n52
Faulkner Joseph E., 5n24
Feldman, Saul D., 54n58
Ferraro, Kenneth, xi, 264
Fetzer, Joel S., 53, 53n49
Fincham, Frank D., 26–27, 26n63,
    27n64, 148, 155n25,
    164nn68, 69, 70
Finke, Roger
    Acts of Faith, 55, 55n59,
        88n48
    economics of religion, 89, 89n53,
        90, 90n64, 91
    political science and religion,
        55nn61, 71; 56, 57, 60,
        60n88, 60n90
Finney, Charles, 248
Fish, Stanley, 133, 133n73
Fishbach, Ayelet, 19n13
Fisher, G. P., 111n5
Fitchett, George, 23, 23n35,
    219nn24, 25
Flannelly, Kevin J., 18n4
Folkman, Susan, 26, 26n57
Forbidden Fruit (Regnerus),
    160nn54, 55
Foreign Affairs, 51
forgiveness and prayer, 27
*The Forgotten Founders on Religion
    and Public Life* (Dreisbach
    et al.), 49n24
Forman, Tyrone A., 185n13
Fowler, James, 17
Fowler, Robert Booth, 49n27,
    50n28
Fox, Jonathan, 60, 60n89, 90,
    90n63, 91, 91n66
Frana, John F., 197n44, 197nn48, 49
France, 53, 56
Frankl, Viktor, 17
Franklin, Kameron J., 164n70
Frazier, E. Franklin, 116, 117n24
Frazier, Patricia A., 26n62
free riding, 85
Freeman, Richard B., 187n20
French, E. Geoffrey, 93n73

Freud, Sigmund, 17, 19, 19nn8, 11;
    41, 249, 250
Friedman, Ronald S., 19n13
Fritjers, Jan, 224n47
Froese, Paul, 44n13
Fromm, Erich, 17
*The Frontier Spirit in American
    Christianity* (Turner &
    Mode), 112
Frutchey, Robin, 22n29
Fuller, Graham E., 52n43
functional limitations, 219
fundamentalism, 118–19
*Fundamentalism and American
    Culture* (Marsden), 118n26,
    119, 119n31, 120, 121, 123,
    124, 127
fundamentalism and political
    violence, 51
Fundamentalism Project, 121
Fundamentalisms and Society
    (Marty & Appleby), 121n35
Fundamentalisms and the State
    (Marty & Appleby), 51n33,
    121n35
Fundamentalisms Comprehended
    (Marty & Appleby), 121n35
Fundamentalisms Observed
    (Marty & Appleby), 121n35
On Further Examination (Wirtz),
    238n23
future research, 274–77
The Future of an Illusion (Freud),
    19nn8, 11

Gall, Terry L., 26n59
Gallagher, Sally K., 148, 157n32
Gallego, Francisco A., 98n95
Garcia, Crystal, 184n9, 185n10
Garcia, David R., 240n44
Gardner, John W., 263n18
Garrido, Melissa M., 223n43
Gatto, John Taylor, 236nn9, 10
Gaustad, Edwin Scott, 115–16, 122
Gaza, 85
General Social Survey, 5

Scott, Eric, 147n11
Seawell, Asani H., 221n34
Second Great Awakening, 116
secular consumption options, 80–82
secularism, 53
Secularism and State Policies toward Religion (Kuru), 53n50
secularization theory, 54
Seeber, James J., 264n20
Seeing Things Their Way (Chapman et al.), 131n70
Seeking the Promised Land (Campbell et al.), 50n30
Seeman, Teresa, 220, 220n30
Seffrin, Patrick M., 197n45, 198
Seligman, Martin E. P., 18, 18n1, 187n22
sense of calling, 237
September 11, 2001, terrorist attacks, 42, 51
Sethi, Sheena, 187n22
Seventh-day Adventists, 82, 263, 267
Sewell, Jr., William H., 117n25
Shafranske, Edward P., 18, 18n6, 28n74, 143n1
Shah, Rebecca, 61n91
Shah, Timothy Samuel, 53n53, 61n91
Shakespeare, 245
Sharp, Shane, 222n42
Sheets, Virgil, 29n77
Sheldon, H. C., 111n5
Shema, Sarah J., 264, 264n21
Sherman, Roger, 49
Shields, Alexandra E., 264n23
Shils, Edward, 4n6
Al Shohaib, Saad, 276n54
The Shooting Game (Lieberman), 239n40
A Shopkeepers Millennium (Johnson), 127n51
Simpson, George, 262n10
Simpson, Zachary, 3n2
Skarupski, Kimberly A., 219n24
Skinner, B. F., 17
Skinner, Quentin, 132
Skocpol, Theda, 50, 51n31

Slattery, Martha L., 263n18
Slave Religion (Raboteau), 117, 117n24
Smidt, Corwin E., 50n28
Smith, Adam, 55, 55n62
Smith, Al, 119
Smith, Michael T., 23n36
Smith, Timothy B., 218n20, 219n21
Smith, Timothy L., 116, 116n23, 132, 248nn84, 87; 261n6
Snell, Tracy L., 188n28
Snyder, C. R., 151n23
Snyder, Thomas D., 237n18
Social Determinants of Health (Marmot & Wilkinson), 260n4
social epidemiology, 260
social foundations of well-being in late life, 212–14
Social Gospel, 116
Social Science and Medicine (Jarvis & Northcott), 262
The Social Sources of Denominationalism (Niebuhr), 4, 4n8, 114, 114n13
The Social Teaching of the Christian Churches (Troeltsch), 4, 4n7
Society for the Scientific Study of Religion, 5n26
Sociological Theory (Wallace), 4n6
sociology and religion, overview, 4–6
Sociology of Religion, 5n26
sociology of religion, history of, 5
Sociology of Religion (Wach), 4, 5n9
The Sociology of Religion (Weber), 4n5
Soenke, Melissa, 19n9
Solomon, Sheldon, 19n10, 212n9
Soper, J. Christopher, 53, 53nn48, 49
Sorenson, Ann Marie, 167n87
Sorokin, Pitirim A., 4, 5, 5n10
Southward, Penny, 29n78
Spalding, John A., 262n10
Spector, 242n55